STUDIES IN HISTORY, ECONOMICS AND PUBLIC LAW

EDITED BY THE FACULTY OF POLITICAL SCIENCE
OF COLUMBIA UNIVERSITY

Volume LVII]   [Number 1

Whole Number 139

THE CIVIL SERVICE OF GREAT BRITAIN

BY

ROBERT MOSES

AMS Press, Inc.

New York

1966

98196

AMS Press, Inc.
New York, N.Y. 10003
1966

INTRODUCTION

THIS essay is not an exhaustive history of the civil service of England. Its object is to present the steps in the reform of the English civil service with particular emphasis upon the success of competitive examinations and of the brilliant and farsighted plan to attract the most intelligent and capable young men in universities into the government service—a plan first introduced by Macaulay in the civil service of India and later adopted in the Home service. It may be said, then, that in this study the emphasis has been upon examinations, personnel, and prospects, rather than upon organization, economy, and conduct of business. In writing this monograph the author has had constantly in mind the influence of the reformed English civil service upon the civil service of the United States.

This influence begins with the early American reformers, especially with the American author of the only existing complete history of the English civil service, Dorman B. Eaton, our first United States Civil Service Commissioner. Mr. Eaton was sent by President Hayes to study the English service, with a view to reforming the American "spoils" system, and embodied his researches in *Civil Service in Great Britain*. This book was a leading contribution to the reform movement which resulted, after Garfield's murder by an office seeker, in the Pendleton Act [1] for open competition in 1883. Mr. Eaton began his volume with the Norman Conquest. As an historical work it leaves much to be

---

[1] Mr. Eaton drew up the Pendleton bill.

desired; but as a campaign document there is something very fine and effective in the fiery denunciation of old abuses, patronage and graft which shows more clearly than exact scholarship could do it, how greatly Mr. Eaton was affected by the question of American reform.

In truth, Mr. Eaton's honest Americanism rather blinded him to the true inwardness of English civil service democracy. Mr. Eaton was able to carry home with him ideas of open competition and of fair promotion which were of enormous and lasting benefit to the American civil service; but the essential feature of an upper, highly-educated division and a lower, more mechanical, second division—marking the definite appeal of the British service to the best scholars of British universities—seems to have made no real impression on Mr. Eaton,[1] and to have borne no fruit in

[1] " So democratic or republican an innovation as that of opening the whole civil service to the free competition of all classes, very naturally, not a little alarmed the more aristocratic officials; and they were strong enough in 1870 to enforce a division of the new clerks into two classes, known as Class I. and Class II., the attainments . . . of the former to be of a higher order. . . . We shall find that this aristocratic distinction *has been disapproved and substantially abolished by that same just and liberal sentiment which demanded open competition,* though *not before it had produced both jealousies and expensive complications."*

" The principle of free, open competition is repugnant to that distinction [the division into two classes]. The division was also as objectionable by reason of its effect upon economy, convenience, and good feeling . . . as it was on the score of justice and principle. Those of the first class had higher salaries, performed higher work, and they claimed social precedence; though they might be morally and intellectually inferior to those of the second class. . . . In accordance with the scheme of the report of 1874, the line of demarcation between the two classes has been substantially opened to merit, *and the division itself must soon, I think, cease to exist."* Eaton, *Civil Service in Great Britain,* pp. 235, 246.

This was an unfortunate forecast of the development of the civil service which led to the establishment of the present Home and Indian

the early reforms which he helped to institute in the United
States. Thus we have still in Washington a civil service
which offers little attraction to the educated young university graduate.

As a civil service reformer Mr. Eaton's work deserves
the highest praise. It is something to have set up an honest,
competitive civil service, though its standard be the truly
democratic one of uniform mediocrity; but such democracy
is false democracy, and until we have a service which attracts the élite of our young men, trained for intellectual
work and on a higher level than mechanical clerks, we shall
have no civil service worthy of the name.

On the question of universal open competition also Mr.
Eaton was mistaken. No one in England dreams of re-
verting to patronage now. Competition is the general rule;
but time has shown that open competition is not feasible
in some departments, for example, for lower situations
where merely physical qualifications are necessary or for
higher positions where proved technical skill or business
experience are requisites. As Graham Wallas shrewdly ob-
serves:

The invention of a competitive Civil Service, when it had
once been made and adopted, dropped from the region of
severe and difficult thought in which it originated, and took
its place in our habitual political psychology. We now half-
consciously conceive of the Civil Service as an unchanging
fact whose good and bad points are to be taken or left as a
whole. Open competition has by the same process become a
" principle," conceived of as applying to those cases to which

civil service examinations and of a university-bred class of clerks to
do the intellectual work of the civil service. It is strange that Mr.
Eaton could have studied the later reports so painstakingly and honestly, and have amassed material for the latter two hundred pages of
his book without discovering the essential feature of a division of
clerkships.

it has been in fact applied, and to no others. What is . . . for the moment most needed, if we are to think fruitfully on the subject, is that we should in our minds break up this fact and return to the world of infinite possible variations. We must think of the expedient of competition itself as varying in a thousand different directions, and shading by imperceptible gradations into other methods of appointment; and of the posts offered for competition as different each from all the rest, as overlapping those posts for which competition in some form is suitable, though it has not yet been tried, and as touching at the marginal point on their curve those posts for which competition is unsuitable. . . . We must meanwhile cease to treat the existing system of competition by the hasty writing of answers to unexpected examination questions as an unchangeable entity." [1]

Mr. Wallas probably does not want to be taken too literally. England is not so advanced in political morality and her statesmen are not so far above all suggestion of either partiality or error, that she can afford in other than exceptional cases to give up open competition or written examinations. Open competition and written examinations have their obvious limitations; but they are looked upon everywhere as the fairest and least capricious of all the competitions of life. Even if limited competition or nomination is more likely to secure the best man, open competition is almost always preferred because its resulting distinctions are mathematical and palpable. Reject a capable man on the score of written examinations, and he will grumble; discriminate however justly without open competition, and you make bitter enemies and public agitators.

Competition there always will be of one kind or another, and open competition where it is possible. The burden of proof that a new office should not be recruited by open

[1] *Human Nature in Politics*, pp. 255-256, 259.

competition rests heavily on the man who thinks that the necessary qualifications can be best ascertained otherwise. The division of the upper civil service into two classes, the one university-bred and academically educated to do the intellectual work, and the other possessing only a common-school education to do the more mechanical work, has been modified, like the " principle " of open competition, but has withstood all the assaults of those mistaken democrats who would abolish the first class and wait, as they have vainly waited in the United States, for the second class to develop the requisite first class administrative ability. We shall see that there are not merely two classes now; in some departments there is an intermediate division and there are new classes of the civil service with new standards of their own. The many admirers of professional, specialized training in law, economics and political science, and of such practical apprenticeship as is required in the German civil services, have made a determined assault on the academic and unprofessional requirements of Macaulay; but in England, as well as in India, Macaulay's plan remains substantially in force.

The thanks of the author are due to Mr. Graham Wallas of London University, a member of the present Royal Commission on the Civil Service, for assistance in studying at the British Museum; to the Rt. Hon. Sir William Anson, Bart, M.P., Warden of All Souls' College, Oxford, formerly Parliamentary Secretary to the Board of Education; to Mr. Stanley Leathes, C.B., First Civil Service Commissioner of Great Britain, and to many other members of the English [1] civil service; to Mr. Elliot Goodwin,

---

[1] In accordance with common usage the term " civil service of Great Britain " or " English civil service " is used in the following pages in reference to the employees of the home departments of the central government of the United Kingdom, excluding local civil services under county councils, etc., the Metropolitan police, ecclesiastical officers, law officers, and the army and navy.

former secretary of the National Civil Service Reform Association of the United States, and to Professors Goodnow and Powell of Columbia University, for information, suggestions and criticism; and, finally, to Miss Elsie Simpson, for invaluable assistance in preparing the manuscript.

ROBERT MOSES.

NEW YORK, 1913.

TABLE OF CONTENTS

PAGE

CHAPTER II

Macaulay and the Indian Civil Service

CHAPTER III

The Beginning of Reform

CHAPTER IV

Examination Introduced

CHAPTER V

John Bright and Others Investigate, 1860. Open Competition Introduced, 1870

CHAPTER VI

FURTHER INVESTIGATIONS—THE REACTION—THE DECADE OF SCEPTICISM

CHAPTER VII

THE RIDLEY INVESTIGATION, 1888–1890

CHAPTER VIII

The Civil Service To-Day—The Present Royal Commission—The Question of Intellectual Aristocracy

Purpose and personnel of the Commission—Scientific and sympathetic inquiry—Influence of the new sociology and democracy—Developments and changes in the civil service since the Ridley report—First division examinations, numbers, extension—Creation of the intermediate division, its extension—The Hobhouse report on the amalgamation of the Customs and Excise Departments—Employment of women and girls and objections to extension — Blind-alley employment of boy clerks; educational classes—The writer class—Proportion of positions filled by open competition, limited competition and nomination—New methods of appointment to the Labor Exchanges and to the National Health Insurance Commission—Methods of promotion—The present backdoors into the civil service; the case of Sir Matthew Nathan—Influence and patronage; the "private secretary scandal"—Expansion of the Post Office—Rights and powers of civil servants as against the state—Strikes and civil unionism—Political pressure—The postal and telegraph employees in France and in England—Threat of English postal and telegraph employees to strike—Future of these agitations—The question of division of the clerical service into distinct classes on the basis of superior education—Existing opportunities for second division clerks—Memorial presented to the Commission by these clerks—Opposition to patronage and barriers—Claim of second division that

CHAPTER IX

English Experience and the United States

CHAPTER I

THE ENGLISH CIVIL SERVICE IN 1853

" When you made your request to me, you should have considered, Madam, what you were asking. You ask me to solicit
a great man, to whom I never spoke, for a young person whom
I had never seen, upon a supposition which I had no means
of knowing to be true."—Dr. Johnson, to a lady who solicited
him to obtain patronage for her son.

THE history of the modern English civil service, with
its accepted implications of open examinations, merit as
the basis of appointment and promotion, permanent tenure,
and complete aloofness from all political bias and subservience, begins in 1853. That year is the Independence
Year of the English civil service, and its Declaration is
the famous Report of 1853 of Sir Stafford Northcote and
Sir Charles Trevelyan. It is the purpose of this opening
chapter to review the laws and to describe briefly the condition of the civil service in the period between the Reform Act of 1832 and the Report of 1853. From this
report itself and from the immense amount of correspondence which it invited and the discussion which it aroused,
we may get a fairly accurate conception of the status of
the civil service in the preceding decades.

The right of nomination to civil service posts, once
the most powerful prerogative of the crown, had passed
gradually, with the development of the cabinet system of
government under the Hanoverians, into the hands of the
ministry, and consequently into the hands of the majority
in Parliament. Thus drawn into the arena of party poli-

tics, the civil service, with its enormous patronage, gave a powerful stimulus to the political corruption which, beginning with the cabinet and spreading downward through the House of Commons to the individual voter, poisoned the whole political life of the nation. The harm which such a partisan system did to the civil service itself was insignificant compared to the demoralization of the House of Commons and the electorate:

Let anyone who has had experience, reflect on the operation of patronage on Electors, Parliament and the Government. Over each it exercises an evil influence. In the Elections it interferes with the honest exercise of the franchise; in Parliament it encourages subservience to the administration; it impedes the free action of a Government desirous of pursuing an honest and economical course, and it occasions the employment of persons without regard to their peculiar fitness. It is a more pernicious system than the mere giving of money to Electors or members of Parliament to secure their votes. It is bribery in its worst form.[1]

Parliament and the civil service itself had been protected from the worst excesses of political corruption by a series of statutes widely separated in point of time, yet all aimed at withdrawing the civil service from the political arena. After the Revolution the danger that the king would purchase the support of Parliament by direct gifts of civil offices and pensions was clearly seen. An Act of 1694, for a new revenue board for stamp duties, had provided that its members should not have seats in Parliament, and this, says Hallam, is the first exclusion from membership of that body on account of employment.[2]   A

[1] Evidence submitted to the Commission on Civil Service. *Parliamentary Reports,* 1854-5, vol. xx, p. 302; hereinafter referred to as *Civil Service Papers,* 1854-5.

[2] Eaton, *Civil Service in Great Britain* (New York, 1880), p. 72.

law of 1699 extended the exclusion to various other excise offices.

Then came the sweeping provision of the Act of Settlement. Besides its famous clause insuring tenure of good behaviour to judges, the Act provided that "no person who has an office or place of profit under the king, or receives a pension from the Crown shall be capable of serving as a member of the House of Commons." [1]

But this measure was obviously too sweeping for the cautious reformers of the day, and it had the awkward effect of excluding the great secretaries of state from parliamentary control and responsibility. The members of Parliament of the day freed themselves [2] from the awkward effects of the new law and saddled it on their successors by the simple device of applying the exclusion from Parliament only to a few existing offices and to all *new* offices created after October 25, 1705.[3] This was a fair beginning of a great reform. Subsequently when new offices of importance were created special statutes had to be passed to give holders the right to sit in Parliament, and as regards the mass of old officials not excluded by the new law, these were excluded by the thousands as opportunities arose.[4] And we have the beginning of the salutary principle that the public officers consist of a small number of temporary political chiefs who sit in Parliament and represent the majority, and the army of permanent officials who cannot sit in Parliament.[5]

---

[1] 12 & 13 William III, c. 2.

[2] 4 Anne, c. 8. *Cf.* W. R. Anson, *Law and Custom of the Constitution* (Oxford, 1893), pt. i, p. 75.

[3] 6 Anne, c. 7, sec. 24.

[4] For a complete list of official disqualifications created by statute, see Anson, *op. cit.*, p. 85 *et seq.*

[5] "The distinction between the offices which are and those which are

Such expedients as these, however, were powerless to prevent the mass of subordinate servants from being forced to play a partisan rôle at elections in the interest of those members and other politicians to whom they owed their appointments. By an Act of Anne,[1] postal servants were forbidden on pain of fine and dismissal to take any part in elections, but the majority of lower officials still retained the franchise. The question became more acute and, all protests and warnings having failed, the disfranchisement of all these minor officers was resorted to as a desperate remedy. Burke's famous Act of 1782 [2] provided that " no commissioner, collector, supervisor, gauger or other officer or person, whatsoever, concerned in the charging, collecting, levying or managing the duties of the excise . . . or concerned in the charging, collecting, levying, or managing the customs or any of the duties on stamped parchment and paper . . . or duties on salt . . . windows or houses, nor any postmaster, postmaster general, nor any person employed under him . . . shall vote for members of parliament." This restriction was maintained until the modern reformed civil service was well established in 1868,[3] and we shall see that since then the pres-

not compatible with a seat in the House of Commons, is made complete by the regulations of the service itself. These cannot render void an election to the House which is not invalid by statute. They cannot make the holding of office a disqualification for Parliament, but they can make a seat in Parliament a reason for the loss of office. They can and do provide that if any civil servant intends to be a candidate he must resign his office when he first issues his address to the electors." A. Lawrence Lowell, *Government of England* (New York, 1912), vol. i, p. 146.

[1] 9 Anne, c. 10.

[2] 22 George III, c. 41. This was opposed by Lord Mansfield, with that jealous intolerance of reform for which the Bench had long been famous, on the ground that the bill " tended to a dangerous depression of the regal authority ".

[3] 31 & 32 Victoria, c. 73, and 37 & 38 Victoria, c. 22.

sure which dock workers, revenue and postal employees, and other dissatisfied civilians have brought to bear on Parliament through their representatives, has again aroused demands for disfranchisement.[1] By an Act of 1809,[2] far more difficult to enforce, the brokerage of offices, and all promises of and consent to appointments for anything of value, and all negotiations relating to vacancies, exchanges, nominations, removals, and transfers, were made misdemeanors.[3] This last restriction, at any rate, was not very effective, and there is no evidence that the law was enforced in any conspicuous case. It is true that, once in the service, the great majority of lower officers could play no partisan rôle in parliamentary elections and bring no partisan pressure to bear on members of Parliament, but their original appointment was strictly partisan, and no amount of legislation against brokerage of office could prevent this.

The Reform Bill of 1832 which Carlyle had so valiantly hailed as the beginning of a golden age in English politics left patronage and the civil service undisturbed. It was succeeded by a period of controversy as bitter as it was barren of results; and in 1840, the Whigs, who had ushered in the auspicious era of reform, had sunk into little more than a patronage bureau. Carlyle, in his wrath and disappointment, could see in Parliament nothing more than " hungry Greek throttling down hungry Greek on the floor of St. Stephen until the loser cried, ' Hold! the place is thine '." And in 1845, Macaulay, as nearly non-partisan as a staunch Whig could be, was asking: "Are we to go on as Lord Melbourne's Ministry did—unable to carry our own

[1] Lowell, *op. cit.*, vol. i, pp. 149, 150. *Cf.* also *infra*, pp. 202-203 *et seq.*
[2] 49 George III, c. 118.
[3] *Cf.* also 49 George III, 118; 7 & 8 George IV, 37; all consolidated by 17 & 18 Victoria, 102.

bills, and content with holding the executive functions, and distributing the loaves and fishes? " [1]

The English civil service of this period was, at any rate, singularly free from one extreme form of political control which had worked havoc in the United States. No system of rotation and " spoils " plunged the service into periodical electioneering fights for its very existence, and made an orderly routine and quiet uninterrupted labor impossible. On the other hand the partisan, or at any rate political appointee, who was utterly inefficient or hopelessly lazy, enjoyed the protection of a permanent tenure, which only death or voluntary resignation could interrupt.

Why was there no system of rotation in the English civil service? The original appointments were partisan, and political pressure was brought to bear on promotions. In America these conditions resulted in a complete upheaval of the whole service at each election involving a change of party, the discharge of all employees of the supplanted political faith, and the introduction of a new and inexperienced horde of orthodox successors. It has been said that the traditions of the English constitution and the advanced political morality [2] of the English (as compared with the Americans of the same period) effectually precluded such a development. There is enough evidence in the succeeding pages to prove that the political morality of the time was not very high; and we need not speculate about the traditions of an unwritten constitution to find an explanation of this problem. President Lowell shrewdly

[1] Sir G. O. Trevelyan, *Life and Letters of Lord Macaulay* (New York, 1909), p. 455.

[2] The presence of ardent and upright reformers in the cabinet did not preclude rotation in England. Those who think that men like Gladstone and Sidney Herbert would not have tolerated rotation, should remember that Lincoln and Charles Sumner did not tolerate it in the United States. It went on just the same.

suggests that a respect for vested rights prevented rotation in office in England. But whence came this respect? President Lowell seems to refer it to some rooted and inexplicable political category of the English mind or to some human sympathy peculiar to the English people. It is much more probable that this respect for vested rights arose through the most elementary political expediency.

In the first place there was not in England, as in many of the United States, a reasoned principle of rotation. In the United States the fear of the entrenched and arbitrary authority of permanent office holders, inherited from colonial days, had led a number of states to make express provision for short official terms and rotation.[1] In spite of the opposition of the first two presidents, this principle, like so many other state principles, was passed on to the national government. Without such a philosophical background, it is doubtful whether rotation in office would have become so firmly entrenched at Washington. Perhaps the absence of such a philosophical justification was a safeguard against rotation in England; but the real safeguard is nearer at hand. The fact is that under the cabinet form of government, rotation in office would have resulted in complete chaos in Parliament and in the civil service, and could not conceivably have benefited anyone concerned. Where, in the United States in 1854, rotation in office hindered sound and stable government, in England it would have stopped government altogether. We have only to remember that the party in power in England must always be ready to resign on an adverse vote in the House of Commons to appreciate what rotation would have meant. With a tenure of at least four years, and probably at least four more, the United States

---

[1] Cf. Woodrow Wilson, The State (Boston, 1895), p. 498.

could survive rotation though the troubles of appointment might kill the president; but no English cabinet could maintain itself in office a single year supported at Whitehall by an untrained rabble without certain tenure and opposed in Parliament at every turn by an embittered and rapacious minority. Who would form a cabinet under such circumstances? Who would care to enter the civil service with so hazardous a tenure? Who would want to be a government clerk for six months, or even an undersecretary? Obviously the simplest solution of the whole patronage question in Great Britain was a compromise—permanent tenure on reasonably good behavior guaranteed to everyone in the service no matter whether the Government or the Opposition made the original appointment.

England escaped the principle of rotation, but the party in power still had a goodly patronage existing in the natural course of deaths, resignations, dismissals and the creation of new offices. Of the character of nominees at this time we have a wealth of contemporary evidence. Lord Morley quotes from a memorandum of an early reformer, found amongst Gladstone's papers.

"*The old established political families habitually batten on the public patronage*—their sons legitimate and illegitimate, their relatives and dependents of every degree, are provided for by the score. Besides the adventuring disreputable class of members of parliament, who make God knows what use of the patronage, a large number of borough members are mainly dependent upon it for their seats. What, for instance, are the members to do who have been sent down by the patronage secretary to contest boroughs in the interest of the government, and who are pledged twenty deep to their constituents." [1]

Mr. Lowe, Chancellor of the Exchequer under Glad-

[1] Morley, *Life of Gladstone* (London, 1908), vol. i, p. 379.

stone, in his examination before a committee on civil service,[1] made the sweeping statement that "under the former system there never was such a thing known as a man being appointed because he was supposed to be fit for the place." [2]   But then, we must remember that Lowe's conception of his own reforms in the civil service gave him a poor idea of conditions preceding them.

Mr. Chadwick, head of the Poor Law Board, in a remarkable letter contributed on the 1853 report, writes of the personnel of the civil service before that time:

[The larger proportion of appointments by patronage has been given not only to persons of lower condition, but to persons of education and qualifications greatly below the average of their class. . . . Out of 80 clerks supplied by the Patronage Secretary of the Treasury to one department, not more than twelve were worth their salt.] . . A faithful portrait of the parties who have procured appointment in the public offices might

---

[1] *Parliamentary Papers,* 1873, vii.

[2] Lowe was an interesting type of unsuccessful reformer. He was an Albino and was known to the civil service as the Whitehead Torpedo.   His physical peculiarity had brought about the not unusual result of making him retiring, terribly sensitive, pedantic and exacting.   Toward his subordinates in the Treasury and in the Home Office, he was intolerant of human failings, and in his official demands ruthless and inhuman. He was a sincere reformer, but his lack of sympathy prevented an appreciation of his services and caused him to make at least one gigantic blunder. Within the service he was exceedingly unpopular. When he conceded anything to the agitations, often quite justified, of the lower divisions of the civil service for increased pay or better conditions of time or promotion, it was with a cold, analytical and reluctant justification which made the beneficiaries feel that they had wrung a small concession from a tyrant. Lowe became so unpopular and so dangerous as a political ally, that Gladstone had to resort to kicking him up into the House of Lords as Viscount Sherbrooke. *Cf.* James Bryce, *Studies in Contemporary Biography;* Hogan, J. F., *Robert Lowe, Viscount Sherbrooke; The Civilian,* 1869-1872.

well be considered as a scandalous misrepresentation. Many instances could be given of young men, the sons of respectable parents, who were found unable to read or write. Two brothers, one almost imbecile, the other much below the average of intelligence, long retained appointments, though never equal to higher work than the lowest description of copying. Another young man was found unable to number the pages of a volume of official papers beyond 10. The head of the department knows from old experience that a representation of this fact to higher quarters would merely draw down ill-will on himself; the first official duty with which the young man is charged is, therefore, to take a month's leave of absence that he may endeavor to learn to write. Beside the imbecile who is below work and the coxcomb who is above it, there are other kinds of unprofitable officers, including a large class who have ability enough if they would apply it. The Public Offices have been a resource for many an idle, dissipated youth with whom other occupations have been tried in vain. Such a person can be made of little use whatever his abilities, because he cannot be trusted. No one can tell to-day where he will be to-morrow. The ice is in fine condition and he skates for a couple of days; a review tempts him; a water party cannot be resisted; and after dancing all night he is not seen at the office in the morning. In fact, causes of absence are endless. Incessant altercations take place with his superiors, with little effect, for he knows they cannot degrade or dismiss him, as a merchant or a banker would do, and he is proof against fines and minor punishments. At last he is given up as utterly incorrigible. Instances also occur of good abilities and dispositions rendered powerless by unconquerable indolence." [1]

Major Graham, Register General from 1836 to 1854, has a similar grievance against a system which crippled his department:

[1] *Civil Service Papers*, 1854-5, p. 181.

One person had been an insolvent debtor. Another man I sent
with some money to the Bank of England, but he did not pay it
in, and tried to impute the blame to one of the clerks in the Bank
of England. . . . there was one man whom I was forced to keep
in a room by himself, as he was in such a state of health that
he could not associate with the other clerks. . . . There was another clerk of whom complaints were made . . . that he was so
offensive that the other clerks could not be with him. I asked
that person how he got his appointment. He was a very old
man; and he told me he had been a student in law in early
life, and he then happened to be intimate with a legal friend
who attained a very high position in this country afterwards,
and, upon getting into difficulties, without having seen or heard
anything of that gentleman for 30 years, he went to him,
and told him he had not a shilling. This high legal gentleman
sent his name to the Treasury, and he was immediately appointed to my office. The great legal gentleman only saw his
poverty, and he procured him the appointment. . . . There
was a Deputy Register-General; he was not in attendance;
he was ill; and I got a letter from him, asking if he might be
allowed to remain absent, which I consented to, because I
really did not know what to do with him. . . . At the end of 15
months (I did not want to be in a hurry) I reported to the
Lords of the Treasury that the appointment was unnecessary,
and their Lordships removed him, and did away with the office.[1]

Sir James Stephen, Permanent Under Secretary of State
for the Colonies and later professor of modern history
at Cambridge, a civil servant of whose character as an administrator we shall have something more to say later,
after thirty years' experience of civil servants divided them
into three classes.[2] The first class was difficult to describe
without exaggeration. Its members were characterized by

---

[1] Report on Civil Service, *Parliamentary Papers*, 1860, vol. ix, pp.
176-177.

[2] *Civil Service Papers*, 1854-5, p. 72.

large capacity of mind, literary powers, scholarship, energy, and experience of public affairs. These, of course, were appointed from outside the service for merit after being well educated. The second class consisted of the diligent and faithful average servants, appointed through patronage, but after considerable education. The third class—and this consisted of the great majority of members of the Colonial Department in Stephen's time—possessed a low, and some of them an incredibly low, degree of intelligence and industry. They had enjoyed only a very incomplete school education, and had never improved themselves afterward. Stephen himself confessed that he was guilty of nepotism in appointing a son and a nephew to clerkships in his department, but he pleaded in his behalf that he dismissed his son after three months on finding him unqualified! The number of such clerks was constantly increased. As a result the burden of work on the higher officials became at times almost intolerable. Serious mistakes and oversights were inevitable.

Another high official [1] commented caustically on the inequalities of the service: One person did one-third of his work, another more than his own share; one part of an office was busy, another idle; every functionary had his function after the plan of the Hindoo household, a bookkeeper for each book, etc. Time was generally unaccounted for—on a question of an outlay of £40 an unnecessary delay of three weeks, eventually caused the public a total loss of £4,000 a week. An enormous amount of time was wasted by disconnected offices and departments, duplication of machinery and every other conceivable lack of coördination. It was said that there were few instances where the actual cost of business was considered. Hundreds of pages of

---

[1] *Civil Service, Papers,* 1854-5, p. 194. Letter, Chadwick.

further evidence might be adduced to elaborate the deficiencies of the civil service at the time of the first official report of 1853.

But, lest anyone should be deceived by the apparent simplicity of the moral question at issue, into the misapprehension that there could be only one right-minded opinion about the old, unreformed civil service, it is well to remember that men of undoubted integrity, insight, and courage, the leading officials of great offices, stubbornly insisted that the civil service was in no great need of reform and defended its existing personnel with vigor and effect. Such a man was the Rt. Hon. Sir Thomas Fremantle, chairman of the Board of Customs, who categorically denied the accuracy of the above evidence and stated that in his experience as regards the faithfulness, diligence and competency of clerks and higher officers, the smooth dispatch of business and the general efficiency of departments, the civil service did not suffer by comparison with the army, the navy, or with any public companies or large establishments under the management of private individuals.[1] A former under secretary in the Foreign Office wrote in the same strain—though it is well to bear in mind that the peculiar nature and requirements of the Foreign Office demanded and probably always will demand, considerable departures from the methods of appointment which prevail elsewhere:

[1] *Civil Service Papers,* 1854-5, p. 319. Sir Thomas was neither blind nor bigoted. He made the mistake of generalizing from the Revenue departments. These were in advance of other offices. As early as 1820 Lord Melbourne had instituted in the Customs and Excise offices high qualifying examinations, filling of higher offices by existing members of the service, a qualified system of promotion by merit, including the opening of certain superior appointments to the lowest ranks. The unqualified success of these provisions had anticipated the course of reform.

I fully admit the existence of partial blots in several of the Government Departments, and I have no reason to doubt that even in the best offices there is room for amendment; but having myself been for twelve years personally connected with the Foreign Office, and having seen day after day an incredible amount of work done in that Office with a degree of dispatch and accuracy not easily to be surpassed; having also witnessed in the same office a demeanour and a spirit of which it would be difficult to speak too highly, it is impossible for me to conceive that a system of Civil Service can be flagrantly and fundamentally bad under which such an office has grown up and such working power is daily exhibited. For in the organization of the Foreign Office there is no peculiar feature to distinguish it from the other Offices of State of the higher class. The clerks have always been appointed by the Head of the Department; there has been no examination, " competing " or simple, either prior to admission or to subsequent promotion; neither has there been any fixed period of probation. . . . Every clerk has . . . entered as a mere copying clerk, and has worked his way upwards, *improving and educating himself as he went from one stage to another;* and the result is an office of unsurpassed, if not unequalled, working power and good conduct. . . . I conscientiously believe, that by applying a very moderate amount of correction here and there to departments *in which defects are found to exist,* at least as much good work may be obtained under the present system from those employed in the Civil Service—I speak of the higher departments, —as from any Civil Servants in the world; and, moreover, as much as can justly be expected by the Government or public from its Civil Servants.[1]

In a pamphlet [2] to which we shall have occasion to refer

---

[1] *Civil Service Papers,* 1854-5, pp. 348-349.

[2] *Observations upon the Report by Sir C. E. Trevelyan and Sir S. H. Northcote on the Organization of the Permanent Civil Service,* 1854.

later on, there are quotations from various newspapers of 1854, loud in their denunciation of commissioners who had weighed the civil servants and found them wanting. The permanent head of the Home Office, the Auditor of the Civil List and Comptroller of the National Debt Office were among the prominent civil servants who expressed the keenest resentment at what they called the unjust and unfounded imputations on the character of the civil service.

The truth would seem to be that there was a great divergence in different departments. All sweeping generalities about the personnel and efficiency of the civil service of the decade before 1854 were in a sense false, for there were departments presided over by such men as Fremantle and Addington which set up a high standard of entrance examination and an admirable organization and conduct of business, while there were other departments more under the baneful influence of the Patronage Secretary or of a compliant minister, which perpetuated some of the worst abuses of eighteenth century maladministration.

In studying civil service patronage in the United States we can get a reasonably clear idea of conditions at any period by studying the attitude and acts of the president. In England not only the prime minister, but the Chancellor of the Exchequer, and the parliamentary and permanent heads of other departments had each his own policy or standard. If there was patronage in one department under Jackson there was patronage in all—but in 1853 in England there were as many policies as there were ministers. Chadwick, the head of the Poor Law Commission, was able to abolish patronage in local government positions after encountering powerful opposition, with resulting benefits which read like a fairy tale. The same results were similarly attained in the Education Department and the

Board of Public Works.[1]   Again the trouble involved in
managing the 70 clerks which the Law Stationer supplied
to the Poor Law Commission increased so much that
Chadwick decided to have all the work done as piece work
by mere copyists.   The result was that the work was done
by 35 instead of 70 clerks, and that these 35 increased their
pay from £60 and £70 to £80, £90 and £100.   Another
department was prevented from introducing this system
by the Parliamentary Secretary of the Treasury who needed
patronage.

Perhaps we cannot get a more vivid idea of the differences in departments than from Anthony Trollope's description of the entrance into the civil service of two of the
heroes of *The Three Clerks*:

It is generally admitted that the Weights and Measures is
a well-conducted office; indeed . . . it may be said to stand
quite alone as a high model for all other public offices whatever.   It is exactly antipodistic to the Circumlocution Office,[2]
and as such is always referred to in the House of Commons
by the gentleman representing the Government when any attack
on the Civil Service generally is being made. . . . The esoteric
crowd of the Civil Service, that is, the great body of clerks
attached to other offices, regard their brethren of the Weights
as prigs and pedants, and look on them much as a master's
favourite is apt to be regarded by other boys at school.

Henry Norman was educated at public school, and thence
sent to Oxford; but before he had finished his first year at
Brasenose his father was obliged to withdraw him from it,
finding himself unable to bear the expense of a university education for his two sons. . . .

Whether Harry Norman gained or lost most by the change
we need not now consider, but at the age of nineteen he left

[1] *Civil Service Papers,* 1854-5, pp. 142-150.
[2] *Cf.* Dickens, *Little Dorrit.*

Oxford and entered on his new duties. It must not, however, be supposed that this was a step which he took without difficulty and without pause. It is true that the grand modern scheme for competitive examinations had not as yet been composed. Had this been done, and had it been carried out, how awful must have been the cramming necessary to get a lad into the Weights and Measures! But, even as things were then, it was no easy matter for a young man to convince the chief clerk [1] that he had all the requirements necessary for the high position to which he aspired.

Indeed, that chief clerk was insatiable, and generally succeeded in making every candidate conceive the very lowest opinion of himself and his own capacities before the examination was over. Some, of course, were sent away at once with ignominy as evidently incapable. Many retired in the middle of it with the conviction that they must seek their fortunes at the bar, or in medical pursuits, or some other comparatively easy walk of life. Others were rejected on the fifth or sixth day as being deficient in conic sections, or ignorant of the exact principles of hydraulic pressure. And even those who were retained were so retained, as it were, by an act of grace. The Weights and Measures was, and indeed is, like heaven; no man can deserve it. No candidate can claim as his right to be admitted to the fruition of the appointment which has been given him. Henry Norman was found at the close of his examination to be the least undeserving of the young men then under notice and was duly installed in his clerkship.

It need hardly be explained that to secure so high a level of information as that required at the Weights and Measures, a scale of salaries equally exalted has been found necessary. Young men consequently enter at £100 a year. We are speaking, of course, of that more respectable branch of the establishment called the Secretary's Department. At none other

---

[1] Sir Gregory Hardlines is drawn from real life, and represents Sir C. E. Trevelyan, the famous civil service reformer and exponent of competitive examinations. See third chapter.

of our public offices do men commence with more than £90 except, of course, at those in which political confidence is required. Political confidence is indeed as expensive as hydraulic pressure, though generally found to be less difficult of attainment.

Quite different was the experience of Charley Tudor, another clerk, on entering the Internal Navigation office.

The men of the Internal Navigation are known to be fast, nay, almost furious, in their pace of living; not that they are extravagant in any degree, a fault which their scale of salaries very generally forbids, but they are one and all addicted to Coal Holes and Cider Cellars; they dive at midnight hours into Shades, and know all the back parlours of all the public houses in the neighbourhood of the Strand. Here they leave messages for one another, and call the girl at the bar by her Christian name. They are a set of men endowed with sallow complexions, and they wear loud clothing, and spend more money in gin and in water than in gloves.

The establishment is not unusually denominated the " Infernal Navigation," and the gentlemen employed are not altogether displeased at having it so called. . . .

The spirit who guards the entrance into this elysium is by no means so difficult to deal with as Mr. Hardlines. And it is well that it was so some years since for young Charley Tudor—for Charley would never have passed muster at the Weights and Measures. Charles Tudor . . . is the son of a clergyman, who has a moderate living on the Welsh border, in Shropshire. Had he known to what sort of work he was sending his son, he might have hesitated before he accepted for him a situation at the Internal Navigation Office. He was, however, too happy in getting it to make many inquiries as to its nature. . . . Exactly at 10 in the morning Charley walked into the lobby of his future workshop, and found no one yet there but two aged, seedy messengers. He was shown into a waiting-room, and there he remained for a couple of hours, during which every clerk in the establishment came to have a look at him. At last he was ushered into the Secretary's room. "Ah!" said the Secretary, " your name is Tudor, isn't it?"

Charley confessed to the fact. " Yes," said the Secretary, " I have heard about you from Sir Gilbert de Salop . . . and you wish to serve the Queen?" said the Secretary.

Charley, not quite knowing whether this was a joke or not, said he did. " Quite right—it is a fair ambition," continued the great official functionary, " quite right—but, mind you, Mr. Tudor, if you come to us you must come to work. I hope you like hard work. You should do so if you intend to remain with us. . . . The Internal Navigation requires great steadiness, good natural abilities, considerable education, and—and—and no end of application."

With these preliminaries Charley was put through an examination which consisted of copying a leading article from a newspaper. He misspelled several words and then dropped a blot on the paper. The Secretary then sent him home to do some more copying at leisure, and the next day Charley came back with his carefully prepared manuscript, only to find that his examination was already passed and that he had been appointed an "Infernal Navvy." He soon found out that the assurance made to him by Mr. Secretary Oldschole, that the Internal Navigation was a place of herculean labours, was a matter of the most delightful ridicule. He was one of six young men who habitually spent about five hours a day in the same room, and whose chief employment was to render the life of the wretched chief clerk, Mr. Snape, as unendurable as possible. " There were copies, and entries to be made, and books to be indexed. But these things were generally done by some extra hand, as to the necessity of whose attendance for such purpose Mr. Snape was forced to testify."

Lest anyone should think this account and the subsequent

description of Charley's shortcomings and debts highly colored, it may be well to mention that Charley is Trollope himself and that such an examination and such conditions actually existed in the Post Office when Trollope, who later became a high official, was a clerk there from 1834-1841.[1]

Post Office memoirs of the next decade are carried on by Edmund Yates, the author and playwright. Yates had an even keener sense of humor than Trollope, and the Post Office afforded plenty of stimulation. On his promotion by Sir Rowland Hill, the famous postal reformer, Yates writes:

In my new position I saw, for the first time, the virtual head of my office, the Secretary, Colonel Maberly, and was frequently brought into communication with him so long as he remained with us. . . . He used to arrive about eleven o'clock, and announce his arrival by tearing at the bell for his breakfast. This bell brought the head messenger, whose services he arrogated to himself, who, being a venerable-looking and eminently respectable personage, probably well-to-do in the world, was disgusted at having to kneel at the Colonel's feet, and receive the Colonel's dirty boots into his arms with the short adjuration, " Now, Francis, my straps!" He wrote a most extraordinary illegible hand, and perhaps for that reason scarcely any holograph beyond his signature is to be found in the official records. The custom was for certain clerks of recognized status, who had a distinct portion of the official work

[1] " I was taken, therefore, to the assistant secretary, and by him I was examined as to my fitness. The story of that examination is given accurately in one of the opening chapters of a novel written by me, called *The Three Clerks*. If any reader of this memoir would refer to that chapter and see how Charley Tudor was supposed to have been admitted into the Internal Navigation Office, that reader will learn how Anthony Trollope was actually admitted into the Secretary's office of the General Post Office in 1834." *An Autobiography* by Anthony Trollope (London, 1883), p. 47.

in their charge, to submit the reports which had been received from the postmasters or district surveyors, on complaints or suggestions of the public, to the Secretary, and receive his instructions as to the course to be pursued, or the style of reply to be sent. This performance we used to call " taking in papers to the Colonel," and a very curious performance it was. The Colonel, a big, heavily-built, elderly man, would sit in a big chair, with his handkerchief over his knees and two or three private letters before him. Into a closely neighbouring seat the clerk would drop, placing his array of official documents on the table. Greetings exchanged, the Colonel, reading his private letters, would dig his elbow into the clerk's ribs, saying, " Well, my good fellow, what have you got there—very important papers, eh?" " I don't know, sir; some of them are, perhaps—" " Yes, yes, my good fellow; no doubt *you* think they're very important: *I* call them damned twopenny-ha'penny! Now read, my good fellow, read!" Thus adjured, the clerk would commence reading aloud one of his documents. The Colonel, still half engaged with his private correspondence, would hear enough to make him keep up a running commentary of disparaging grunts, " Pooh! stuff! upon my soul!" &c. Then the clerk, having come to the end of the manuscript, would stop, waiting for orders; and there would ensue a dead silence, broken by the Colonel, who, having finished his private letters, would look up and say, " Well, my good fellow, well?" " That's all, sir." "And quite enough too. Go on to the next!" " But what shall I say to this applicant, sir?" " Say to him? Tell him to go and be damned, my good fellow!" and on our own reading of those instructions we had very frequently to act. With all this, Colonel Maberly was a clear-headed man of business; old-fashioned, inclined to let matters run in their ordinary groove, detesting all projects of reform, and having an abiding horror of Rowland Hill.[1]

[1] *Edmund Yates, His Recollections and Experiences* (London, 1884), vol. i, pp. 96-99.

So much for the permanent head of the Post Office. Yates' experience with the Postmaster General, Lord Stanley, was even more astonishing. It was absolutely necessary that his lordship's signature be attached to a certain warrant before midnight, or the whole warrant would have lapsed as informal. Lord Stanley was supposed to be at the Newmarket races; and Yates was selected for the disagreeable job of bearding him there. He went to Lord Stanley's residence and found that he had just returned from Newmarket. This is his story:

I gave the man Sir Rowland's letter of introduction, and in a few minutes was bidden to follow him. I can see that room and the scene which occurred perfectly, plainly, at the present moment. Standing on the hearthrug, with his back to the fireplace, and facing me as I entered, was a thickset elderly man of middle height. On a table close by him was a yellow paper-covered French novel . . . and on a further table were three or four of the heavy leather pouches in which official documents were forwarded to the Postmaster General. As the butler closed the door behind me, I made the gentleman a bow, of which he took not the smallest notice. He did not offer me a seat, so I remained standing . . . " What do you want?" was his gracious query. " I have come about the reduction of the registration-fee, my lord. I thought Sir Rowland Hill had explained in his letter. It is necessary that your lordship's signature—." " Yes, yes, I know all about that," he interrupted. " I have signed the damned thing!" going to one of the official pouches and rummaging in it. " It's here somewhere— no, that's not it. I can't find it; but I know I've signed it. Look here, have you got a cab outside?" " Yes, my lord." " Then," pointing to them, " just take these pouches back to the Office; you'll find it when you get there." It was just too much. I am of a hot temper and I boiled over. " What!" I cried, in a tone which made my friend jump again. "What! do you expect me to carry those bags to the cab? If you want that done, ring the bell and tell your servant to do it. I'm not your servant, and I won't carry bags for you or any man in London!" He looked petrified; but he rang the bell. "What's your name, sir?" he asked. "My name is Yates, my lord," I replied. "I don't like your manner, sir," said he. "And I don't like yours, my lord," I rattled out.... "You shall hear more of this, sir!" "Whenever you please, my lord; I shall be quite ready!" and off I went. . . . I did not hear any more of it in the way I anticipated. But the story got wind, and another was speedily improvised to the effect that Lord Stanley had been so frightened by my display of independence that the next time one of the messengers was sent to him with some official papers, he rushed at the astonished man, seized him warmly by the hand, and insisted on his stopping to luncheon.[1]

Even in the departments where the efficiency of the chief officials and of the clerks was highest, there flourished not infrequently a bureaucratic formalism which was the more dangerous because the powers of the under secretary and his chief clerks were in many cases almost unlimited. Such cases arose through the necessary absorption of the minister at the head of the office in political business and ambitions. Sir Henry Taylor, an Under Secretary of the Colonial Office who wielded an enormous power, explained the position of the minister in his somewhat Machiavellian essay on *The Statesman.*[2]

The far greater proportion of the duties which are performed in the office of a minister, are and must be performed under no effective responsibility. Where politics and parties are not affected by the matter in question, and so long as there is no flagrant neglect or glaring injustice which a party can take hold of, the responsibility to Parliament is merely nom-

---

[1] *Ibid.*, vol. i, p. 106.

[2] London, 1836. *Cf.* Chapter on Reform of the Executive, p. 155.

inal, or falls otherwise only through casualty, caprice, and a misemployment of the time due from Parliament to legislative affairs. Thus the business of the office may be reduced within a very manageable compass, without creating public scandal, By evading decisions wherever they can be evaded, by shifting them on other departments and authorities wherever they can be shifted, by giving decisions on superficial examinations,— categorically, so as not to expose the superficiality in expounding the reasons; by deferring questions till, as Lord Bacon says, " they resolve of themselves;" by undertaking nothing for the public good, which the public voice does not call for; by conciliating loud and energetic individuals at the expense of such public interests as are dumb or do not attract attention; by sacrificing everywhere what is feeble and obscure to what is influential and cognizable; by such means and shifts as these, the single functionary granted by the theory, may reduce his business within his powers, and perhaps obtain for himself the most valuable of all reputations in this line of life, that of a " safe man."

Under these conditions the actual control of the office falls more and more to the under secretary and the chief clerks, especially if they be old, experienced civil servants of strong character. Such dependence of the ministry on the permanent officials is to some extent inevitable and will always exist; but in the first half of the nineteenth century, especially in the Colonial Office, the domination of the permanent officials was so complete and its effects so irritating and harmful to the colonies that the strongest protests were made against it. Charles Buller's *Responsible Government for Colonies* contains a bitter character sketch of Rogers, who was then the leading permanent official in the Colonial Office, whom he calls " Mr. Mothercountry ". Mr. Mothercountry is thoroughly efficient, absolutely methodical and rules the colonies after long es-

tablished precedents, from which he departs only under
the inspiration of certain merchants and politicians whose
influence greatly outweighs that of the colonists themselves. The actual needs of the colonists Mr. Mothercountry is by temperament unwilling, and by training unable, to consider. Successive ministers find that they must
consult Mr. Mothercountry or blunder and lose their reputations as " safe " men. Thus by dint of unremitting toil
and of mastery of a routine which no one else can understand, Mr. Mothercountry, the sober, starched, middle-class
English clerk with a large family in the suburbs, becomes
the *de facto* ruler of the British colonies. The patronage
which Mr. Mothercountry uses to conciliate the various
juntos and interests " is the prey of every hungry department of the government. Jobs which Parliamentary rapa-
city would blush to ask from the Treasury are perpetuated
with impunity in the silent realm of Mr. Mothercountry."
Sir James Stephen who, as legal adviser and later as Under Secretary, was virtually the Colonial Office for many
years, had many of the bureaucratic characteristics of Mr.
Mothercountry, and was better fitted to be a professor of
modern history at Cambridge than a maker of modern
history at Whitehall.[1] The masterly report of Lord Dur-
ham on *The Affairs of British North America* complained
boldly that the acute state of civil strife was in no small
measure due to the fact that the real management of the
colonies fell into the hands of " the permanent, but utterly
irresponsible members of the Office."

[1] Sir James' more famous son, Sir James Fitzjames Stephen, seems apparently to have thought his father's authority in the Colonial Office un-
duly restricted: " The difficulty of the transaction of all this business
was aggravated by the fact that though great weight was attached to
Sir James Stephen's opinions and advice by his official superiors, and
though he held strong opinions of his own upon the subjects which
came before him, *he had no real authority whatever*." Introduction
to *Essays on Ecclesiastical Biography* by Sir James Stephen.

The result of this bureaucratic misrule from the point of view of disgruntled colonists is well summarized by Carlyle:

Every colony, every agent for a matter colonial, has his tragic tale to tell you of his sad experiences in the Colonial Office; what blind obstructions, fatal indolences, pedantries, stupidities, on the right and on the left, he had to do battle with; what a world-wide jungle of redtape, inhabited by doleful creatures, deaf or nearly so to human reason or entreaty, he had entered on; and how he paused in amazement, almost in despair; passionately appealed now to this doleful creature, now to that, and to the dead redtape jungle, and to the living Universe itself, and to the Voices and to the Silences;—and, on the whole, found that it was an adventure, in sorrowful fact, equal to the fabulous ones by old knights-errant against dragons and wizards in enchanted wildernesses and waste howling solitudes; not achievable except by nearly superhuman exercise of all the four cardinal virtues, and unexpected favour of the special blessing of Heaven. . . . Such is his report of the Colonial Office; and if we oftener hear such a report of that than we do of the Home Office, . . . or the rest,—the reason probably is, that Colonies excite more attention at present than any of our other interests.[1]

It was indeed high time that the whole question of civil service organization and personnel was honestly investigated. The patronage system had become more and more intolerable as public opinion became more educated. Members of Parliament and the Treasury ministers themselves were growing weary of the incessant demands of office seekers, and of the contemptible meanness and petty irritations attendant on a distribution of favors which in the end left everyone dissatisfied. The reform

[1] *Latter Day Pamphlets,* "Downing Street" (London, 1885), pp. 77, 78.

movement had already begun in certain departments under the more enlightened and courageous officials; but there was no uniform system or standard of examination at admission, of probation, of division of labor according to intellectual or mechanical requirements, of promotion, of office routine, of salaries. The discipline and efficiency of different parts of the service varied enormously, and almost all of them were overstaffed, and in the conduct of business archaic, unpractical, and wasteful. What was needed was a renovation of each office according to its peculiar requirements and a complete reorganization of the civil service personnel. Such a reform could not have come from the House of Commons. As a prominent civilian of the day put it:

Notwithstanding the constant interference of the House of Commons in matters relating to the Civil Service, the reform of the Civil Service remains just where it was. Their single panacea for all the evils they supposed to exist in it is, was, and ever will be, retrenchment, the abolition and consolidation of offices, and the diminution of salaries. The mode of making the service *efficient* seems never to have entered their minds; and the real reform of the Civil Service is still left for the Civil Service itself to accomplish.[1]

Evidently, then, this was a task which the Treasury was best qualified to undertake. The Treasury supervises the revenue departments with their enormous roll of minor employees, and it controls the expenditure, therefore the organization, of all departments. As a matter of fact, for some five years before 1853,[2] Sir Charles Trevelyan (who,

---

[1] *Civil Service Papers,* 1854-5, p. 272.

[1] "The revolutionary period" (1848), which, says Sir Charles Trevelyan, "gave us a shake and created a disposition to put our house in order". *Parliamentary Papers,* 1875, xxiii, *Second Report of Commission of Inquiry into the Civil Service,* Appendix.

it is significant to remember, was Macaulay's brother-in-law), assisted by Sir Stafford Northcote and others, had been investigating various public offices.

The investigation began modestly enough with the Treasury establishment itself. It was then extended to other departments. These inquiries were undertaken with practical objects. The commissioners found many defects and suggested specific remedies as they went along. On pursuing their inquiries through various offices, the same deficiencies were found to exist, with varieties in the particular circumstances. Sameness of evils suggested uniformity of remedies, and out of the separate inquiries the idea of a general reorganization sprang up naturally.[1]

The real general reorganization of the civil service is sketched in a report of Sir Stafford Northcote and Sir Charles Trevelyan, some twenty pages long, which aroused a discussion which fills a large volume and extends far beyond the limits of official criticism and blue books. The great problem which the two commissioners undertook to solve was that of combating all patronage, of reorganizing the personnel of the service, of raising the standard of clerkships and attracting the best talent among young men to do the intellectual work of the offices. Let no one, in the light of modern experience, think this problem was an easy one. The solution which seems to most of us so natural and simple today, was fraught with gravest dangers in the eyes of the most enlightened half a century ago, and was realized only after a long and arduous struggle, though by no means universally accepted or enforced. It was easy

[1] *Cf. Spectator*, March 4, 1854, and Sir Charles Trevelyan's substantiation in *Second Report Civil Service Inquiry Commission*, 1875, Appendix.

enough for Carlyle [1] to thunder forth with that excremental eloquence of which he was a master, demands that the ten or more most heroic statesmen of the day be forthwith sought out and placed at the head of the government offices to clean out these Augean stables and the " obscene owl-droppings " of generations of stupid, hooting officialism. The commissioners had a sterner task before them than to plan an heroic civil service for Heaven or Valhalla —and yet it was just this ideal of Carlyle's of the civil servant of luminous intelligence which was to appear in the Report of 1853 and to constitute its most startling feature.

But it was hardly to Carlyle that the commissioners owed this or the other new ideas in their report.   It is very doubtful whether they could have invented them themselves, without impulse or precedent.   The new plan sprang from the genius of Macaulay, who had created a new civil service for India which produced all the features of the Report of 1853.   Though in the nature of things no less controversial than that of his brother-in-law, Macaulay's plan had been put into effect immediately and almost without dissent.   Before we consider the Report of 1853, we must pause and review briefly the history of the East India civil service up to that date.

[1] *Latter Day Pamphlets*, " Downing Street " and " The New Downing Street."

CHAPTER II

Macaulay and The Indian Civil Service

"The creation of this [the Home] service was the one great political invention in nineteenth-century England, and like all other inventions, it was worked out under the pressure of an urgent, practical problem—the problem of the Indian Civil Service."—Graham Wallas, *Human Nature in Politics*.

A NOT overscrupulous trading company, guided by a wise expediency, gradually extended its dominion over Madras, Bombay, and Bengal, and over millions of Indian people elsewhere, and accomplished without much bloodshed and with comparatively little injustice to the natives, results which the crown could probably not have accomplished at all. There are many reasons why a chartered company is the most successful of all conquerors and colonizers. Not the least of them is that the company has at first no ulterior motives and rules only that it may trade.. A chartered company is constrained by expediency to try to govern well. It may be unscrupulous and at times corrupt, but here the merchant restrains himself far better than the early proconsul under a distant and irresponsible executive; its patronage may be showered on its friends, but its servants are capable, even if they are not the men whom an open competition would enlist. But the position of a trading company turned into a government is inevitably a false one.

In 1784 Pitt's India Act put an end to the anomolous civil and military control of the East India Company, but left its trading monopoly and its vast patronage untouched. Pitt attempted also to enforce regulations as to the qualifications and promotion of the company's servants, but these seem to have been tacitly ignored.

Even at this time of unregulated patronage the company's servants were by no means an inefficient or corrupt body. Certainly there were numbers of young men who went to India to shake the pagoda tree, but the directors were too shrewd and too cautious to endanger their privileges at home and abroad by a shameless misuse of their powers. It is said that Clive interrupted the fortune-hunting idlers who came with appointments from the directors, asked them how much they wanted, paid the amount, and shipped them back on the first vessel for England. It is not improbable, in view of Fox's famous India Act, which was only defeated through the personal intervention of the king and the threat of royal displeasure, that it was safer at this time to entrust the patronage, as distinguished from the military and civil power, to a company of directors than to leave it in the hands of a ministry. The Roman politicians and Tammany Hall might have found an equal in England if every member of the party in power had been allowed a hand in the spoils of India. Certainly Burke's speech against Warren Hastings, and on the Nabob of Arcot's debts, and Pitt's motion for parliamentary reform in 1782, would go to show that this danger was by no means visionary, and that there was a time when India, like the rich colonies of Rome, bade fair to wreak a terrible vengeance on the conquering nation by corrupting her politics with luxury and patronage.[1] Those who are prepared to criticize Pitt's scheme of dual Indian control, would do well to study the reactionary gov-

[1] J. R. Seeley, *Expansion of England* (London, 1901), p. 289.

ernment of this period, its unscrupulous use of every in-
strument to reward its followers and to exclude reformers
from power.

As the importance of the civil administration gradually
overshadowed the commercial, Lord Wellesley conceived a
brilliant and somewhat visionary idea of a training college
for civil servants at Calcutta, which should include all the
writers, the name under which the civil servants were then
known, for the three great presidencies of Madras, Bombay,
and Bengal, and should embrace both liberal and Oriental
studies.   In practice this ambitious scheme was limited to
Bengal writers and confined to law and Oriental languages.[1]   After a preliminary examination in England,
six months to four years were to be spent at Fort William
College.   With this limited sphere Fort William survived
until open competition was introduced in 1853.

In 1806 the directors of the company decided to found
a college in England, partly as a substitute for Lord
Wellesley's college, partly as ancillary.[2]   This became the
regular door to the service, and by a statute of 1813[3] no
writer was allowed to proceed to India unless he had
spent four terms at Haileybury.   The college was a success from the start, and its standards soon rose as high as
that of the great universities, though its discipline was
much closer to that of an English Public School.   The age
limit at admission was fixed at 21, and at 23 for appointment to India.   The appointments to the college were, of
course, by patronage plus a qualifying entrance examination, and the nominees of the time were members of old
Anglo-Indian families, acquainted by tradition with the
life of India and destined from the cradle for the com-

[1] A. Lawrence Lowell, *Colonial Civil Service* (New York, 1900),
passim.

[2] *Ibid.*   [3] George IV, c. 55, sec. 46.

pany's service. In 1833 when the company's charter
was renewed it was provided that there should be four
times as many candidates as there were vacancies at Haileybury, but this early attempt to introduce limited competition
was soon suspended. Naturally enough the college suffered from the presence of a number of black sheep, who
were protected from dismissal by the directors. The
directors, however, spared no pains in attracting a distinguished group of teachers, and among the faculty at
Haileybury we find such names as Malthus, the economist,
Sir James MacIntosh, Sir James Stephen, and Sir Monier
Monier-Williams, the Sanskrit scholar, later a professor at
Oxford. The latter, in the *Memorials of Old Haileybury*
says:

> According to my own individual experience as a student,
> the mental training at ... old Haileybury was so varied and ex-
> cellent that nothing at all equal to it—at any rate in the diver-
> sity of subjects which it embraced—was to be had either at
> the Universities or elsewhere. . . . I soon discovered that if
> I wished to rise above the level of the average student, I should
> have a task before me compared to which my previous work
> at Oxford could only be regarded as child's play.[1]

Many of the best men from the Public Schools were attracted and we need only compare the intellectual life of
Old Haileybury, as evidenced by the *Haileybury Chronicle*
and by the reminiscences of graduates, to the intellectual life
of a training college like West Point, in order to appreciate
the directors' nominees. On the other hand we must not
overestimate them. The best men were those who, like
Professor Monier-Williams, had previously enjoyed a
classical education. The average man did not measure up
to the highest standards of the universities.

[1] *Memorials of Old Haileybury*, p. 75.

The college did not fill all the positions in India. The patronage of the directors included lower positions which did not fall under the Haileybury regulations. It was to such positions as these that Sir George Trevelyan probably referred when he said:

In the year 1820 all the towns north of the Tweed together contained fewer voters than are now on the rolls of the single burgh of Hawick, and all the counties together contained fewer voters than are now on the register of Roxburghshire. So small a band of electors was easily manipulated by a party leader who had the patronage of India at his command. The three Presidencies were flooded with the sons and nephews of men who were lucky enough to have a seat in a Town Council, or a superiority in a rural district.[1]

In 1833 the company lost its exclusive privilege of trade, and from this time it existed only as a patronage bureau. The old Indian officials bought stock for the sake of gaining patronage for their families, and gradually the corporation became closed to all but these Anglo-Indian families. In 1837 Macaulay succeeded in getting a reform bill for competitive examination through Parliament, but he was defeated with the aid of influential members of both houses, who had been made directors. As Sir George Trevelyan aptly puts it,

they were not going to resign, without a struggle, the most valuable patronage since the days when the Roman senate sent proconsuls and propraetors to Syria, Sicily, and Egypt. Backstairs influence in Leadenhall Street contrived that the clauses embodying Macaulay's plan lay dormant in a pigeonhole at the Board of Control, and backstairs influence in Parliament at length found an opportunity to procure their repeal.[2]

[1] *Life and Letters of Lord Macaulay* (London, 1909), p. 113.
[2] *Ibid.*, p. 587.

Certainly in the Indian civil service it could be argued with much more plausibility than at home, that the kind of qualities in demand were those which no open competition could insure, and that the son of an Anglo-Indian family, conversant from his youth with Indian problems and taught to look forward to the life of an Indian official, though unable to pass a difficult competitive examination, was a man who would probably be far more useful in India than a cloistered Oxford scholar, mechanically proficient perhaps in the classics, but totally unprepared to become a governor or judge over several millions of strange people in a strange country.

In 1853 the charter came up again for revision, and Parliament abolished the directors' right of nomination and upheld Macaulay's plan for open competition. Macaulay's speech on this occasion was, as his nephew justly says, the most masterly vindication of the principles of competition ever left unanswered. There had been talk of giving the Governor General unlimited power of appointing whom he chose.

There is something plausible in the proposition that you should allow him to take able men wherever he finds them. But my firm opinion is, that the day on which the Civil Service of India ceases to be a closed service will be the beginning of an age of jobbing,—the most monstrous, the most extensive, and the most perilous system of abuse in the distribution of patronage that we have ever witnessed. Every Governor-General would take out with him, or would soon be followed by, a crowd of nephews, first and second cousins, friends, sons of friends, and political hangers-on; while every steamer arriving from the Red Sea would carry to India some adventurer bearing with him testimonials from people of influence in England. The Governor-General would have it in his power to distribute Residences, Seats at the Council Board, Seats at the

Revenue Board, places of from 4,000*l.* to 6,000*l.* a year, upon men without the least acquaintance with the character or habits of the natives, and with only such knowledge of the language as would enable them to call for another bottle of pale ale, or desire their attendant to pull the punkah faster. In what way could you put a check on such proceedings? Would you, the House of Commons, control them? Have you been so successful in extirpating nepotism at your own door, and in excluding all abuses from Whitehall and Somerset House, that you should fancy that you could establish purity in countries the situation of which you do not know, and the names of which you cannot pronounce? I believe most fully that, instead of purity resulting from that arrangement to India, England itself would soon be tainted; and that before long, when a son or brother of some active member of this House went out to Calcutta, carrying with him a letter of recommendation from the Prime Minister to the Governor-General, that letter would really be a Bill of Exchange, drawn on the revenues of India for value received in Parliamentary support in this House.

We are not without experience on this point. We have only to look back to those shameful and lamentable years which followed the first establishment of our power in Bengal. If you turn to any poet, satirist, or essayist of those times, you may see in what manner that system of appointment operated.[1]

Macaulay then referred to Sir Charles Wood's proposal that admissions to the civil service of India should be distributed according to the result of an open competitive examination. He expressed his satisfaction at the support which that proposal had received from the present Earl of Derby, and the surprise and disappointment which had been aroused in his mind by the nature of Lord Ellenborough's opposition to it.

[1] *Life and Letters of Lord Macaulay*, pp. 588-590.

If I understand the opinions imputed to that noble Lord, he thinks that the proficiency of a young man in those pursuits which constitute a liberal education is not only no indication that he is likely to make a figure in after life, but that it positively raises a presumption that he will be passed by those whom he overcame in these early contests. I understand that the noble Lord holds that young men who gain distinction in such pursuits are likely to turn out dullards, utterly unfit for an active career; and I am not sure that the noble Lord did not say that it would be wiser to make boxing or cricket a test of fitness than a liberal education. It seems to me that there never was a fact proved by a larger mass of evidence, or a more unvaried experience than this;—that men, who distinguish themselves in their youth above their contemporaries, almost always keep to the end of their lives the start which they have gained. This experience is so vast that I should as soon expect to hear any one question it, as to hear it denied that arsenic is poison or that brandy is intoxicating. Take down in any library the Cambridge Calendar. There you have the list of honours for a hundred years. Look at the list of wranglers and of junior optimes; and I will venture to say that, for one man who has in after life distinguished himself among the junior optimes, you will find twenty among the wranglers. Take the Oxford Calendar, and compare the list of first-class men with an equal number of men in the third class. Is not our history full of instances which prove this fact? Look at the Church, or the Bar. Look at Parliament, from the time that Parliamentary government began in this country;—from the days of Montague and St. John to those of Canning and Peel. Look to India. The ablest man who ever governed India was Warren Hastings, and was he not in the first rank at Westminster? The ablest civil servant I ever knew in India was Sir Charles Metcalfe, and was he not of the first standing at Eton? The most eminent member of the aristocracy who ever governed India was Lord Wellesley. What was his Eton reputation? What was his Oxford reputation?

A commission was appointed, of which Macaulay, Jowett, the master of Balliol, and J. G. Shaw Lefevre, later a civil service commissioner, were the most prominent members. The report was evidently written by Macaulay.

It is difficult, [says the report] to estimate the effect which the prospective prizes so numerous and so attractive will produce. . . . At Trinity College, . . . Cambridge, about four fellowships are given annually by competition. These fellowships can be held only on condition of celibacy, and the income . . . is a very moderate one for a single man. It is notorious that the examinations for Trinity fellowships have, directly or indirectly, done much to give a direction to the studies of Cambridge and of all the numerous schools which are the feeders of Cambridge. What, then, is likely to be the effect of a competition for prizes which will be ten times as numerous as the Trinity fellowships, and of which each will be more valuable than a Trinity fellowship? We are inclined to think that the examination . . . will produce an effect which will be felt in every seat of learning throughout the realm . . . The number of candidates will doubtless be much greater than the number of vacancies. It will not surprise us if the ordinary number examined should be three or four hundred. The great majority, and among them many young men of excellent abilities and laudable industry, must be unsuccessful. If, therefore, branches of knowledge specially Oriental should be among the subjects of examination, it is probable that a considerable number of the most hopeful youths in the country will be induced to waste much time, at that period of life at which time is most precious, in studies which will never, in any conceivable case be of the smallest use to them. We think it most desirable that the examination should be of such a nature that no candidate who may fail shall, to whatever calling he may betake himself, have any reason to regret the time and labour which he spent in preparing himself to be examined. . . . We believe that men who have been engaged, up to one or two and twenty, in studies which have no immediate connexion with the business of any profession, and of which the effect is merely to open, to invigorate, and to enrich the mind, will generally be found, in the business of every profession, superior to men who have, at eighteen or nineteen, devoted themselves to the special studies of their calling. . . . Indeed, early superiority in literature and science generally indicates the existence of some qualities which are securities against vice — industry, self-denial, a taste for pleasures not sensual, a laudable desire of honorable distinction, a still more laudable desire to obtain the approbation of friends and relations. We, therefore, think that the intellectual test about to be established will be found in practice to be also the best moral test that can be devised.[1]

Macaulay's plan was briefly this: The probationers for the Indian civil service were to be selected by open competition in liberal studies of the character and standard of studies at British universities. As many as possible should be men who had taken their B.A. at Oxford or Cambridge. The minimum age was fixed at 18, but Macaulay hoped that the difficulty of the tests would keep out almost every candidate below 21. The examinations should include classics, mathematics, French, German, Italian, natural sciences, moral sciences and the literary languages of India, Sanskrit and Persian. It was not expected that any one would take all these subjects, but the exigencies of competition would compel a candidate to take as many as possible. On the other hand, Macaulay laid emphasis on the precaution that smattering and superficial knowledge of a number of subjects should have no consideration at all, as against intimate and thorough knowledge of a few subjects. Macaulay suggested a tentative scheme of marks, which is very noteworthy, because it has become the model for all higher civil service examinations in England:[2]

[1] Lowell, *Colonial Civil Service*, pp. 80-82.   [2] *Ibid.*, p. 87.

Required.

English Language and Literature—

Composition	500
History	500
General Literature	500
	1500

Optional.

Greek	750
Latin	750
French	375
German	375
Italian	375
Mathematics—Pure and Mixed	1000
Natural Sciences	500
Moral Sciences	500
Sanskrit	375
Arabic	375
	6875

Macaulay expressed the opinion that no candidate would attain more than half of the total number of points. The ablest scholars available should be employed to mark the papers.

The successful candidates, a number determined by the needs of the service, were then to become probationers, for a period not exceeding two years. During their term of probation their studies should be peculiarly Indian— namely history, geography and government of India, jurisprudence, finance and political economy, and the vernacular language of the province to which they had been appointed by lot. Attendance at the courts in London was urged. The final examinations in all these subjects could be taken at the end of one or two years as the candidate preferred, and the ranking in the final examinations should determine seniority in the service.

Macaulay evidently did not care to keep up Haileybury. His plan swept away its undergraduate instruction. He would have preferred to do away with the college entirely; but, as it seemed that the college was to be retained, Macaulay recommended that it should exist as a graduate school in Indian subjects for probationers, with a more eminent faculty and no undergraduate discipline.   The closing sentence of the report is significant: " We must leave it to the Board of Control to discover whether any plan can be devised by which such a training can be made compatible with residence at Haileybury."

The case for open competition and liberal education had been fairly stated, but it is by no means to be presumed that these were the factors which terminated the patronage of the directors and closed the doors of Old Haileybury. The fact was that the directors' patronage was very unpopular.   An exclusive few were interested in the spoils of India, not the varying and powerful multitude who, we shall see, were bitterly opposed to introducing the principles of open competition at home, though they were perfectly willing to see them applied to India.   Haileybury College had been so closely associated in the minds of the public with the directors' patronage that the two fell together.[1]

Mr. Lowell seems to think that it never occurred to Macaulay that open competition might have been introduced for entrance to Haileybury, and that the undergraduate college which had trained the men who ruled India for fifty years might thus have been maintained.   Judging by Macaulay's speeches and by the report, there seems little reason to believe that Macaulay was guilty of such stupidity.   Suppose open competition had been introduced for entrance to Haileybury—it would have been competition amongst boys of 16 or 18.   And in what subjects?   Cer-

[1] Lowell, *Colonial Civil Service*, p. 14.

tainly judging by the report, technical or Indian subjects would not have been favored. Therefore, in academic subjects. Now what test does an academic education, based on the Public School curriculum, afford that you will get not the best but even average boys at the beginning? A competition amongst schoolboys, in schoolboy subjects, would afford little proof of real ability and character or of adaptability to Indian official life and, once at Haileybury, the difficulty of getting rid of an unsuitable candidate would be enormous. What could such a boy do if he failed in the final examinations or were refused by the government after several years at Haileybury? No doubt there are military schools recruited by open competition and producing excellent officers; but military officials can hardly be trained otherwise. There is no reason to doubt that Macaulay weighed the Haileybury idea and found it wanting. There would have been little sense in picking boys at 16 or 18, with small ground for choice and by no real competition, giving them an academic education at Haileybury which they could better obtain at the universities and an oriental education in Indian languages, laws, and government which the universities could supply with the assistance of a small annual grant from the India Office, and sending them to India as a clique without the experience of life and broadness of mind which they might have obtained at Oxford or Cambridge.

Discussion as to the comparative efficiency of the Old Haileyburians and their open competition successors, known as the "Competition Wallahs," raged for years after the fall of Haileybury. Macaulay's nephew and biographer [1] contributed to it a series of articles criticizing the Competition Wallah. No doubt the Haileyburians had

---

[1] Trevelyan, *The Competition Wallah* (London, 1866), *passim*.

much more in their favor than Macaulay saw; but as the
problems of governing India have become more refined
if less acute, demanding on the part of civil servants the
subtlest mental adjustments, the superior mental equipment
and experience of the Competition Wallahs must compensate for the absence of *esprit de corps* which characterized the Anglo-Indians who had the common bond of education at Haileybury.

Macaulay was sincere enough in his championship of
high intellectual attainments as a qualification for ruling
in India. He knew that a university career was well calculated to prepare a young collector for the ceaseless
dilemma, the paradoxes and the restless mental question-
ings and compromises which are part of the white man's
burden in India. Macaulay knew the public to whom he
was opening the examinations; he knew perfectly well that
open competition did not involve attracting the ill-bred and
ill-balanced middle class into the Indian service. Macaulay meant to open the competition to undergraduates of the
great universities, and he expected that in an open competition with a high standard based on the Oxford and
Cambridge honor schools, Oxford and Cambridge would
more than hold their own. The scheme was not quite as
democratic as it looked. Like the English cabinet and the
English aristocracy, the Indian civil service was to be
opened to gentlemen who had inherited breeding and culture, and to those of the middle class who had made themselves gentlemen by acquiring the same breeding and
culture.

Macaulay's logic was borne out by the events. Instead
of following his plan, the maximum age of entrance into
the Indian civil service was lowered to 22 and then to 21.
Led by Sir Henry Maine, the famous legal theorist and
Indian official, the disciples of specialization, who believed

that candidates should be caught young and then trained in studies peculiarly suited to the Indian service, succeeded in forcing Lord Salisbury to lower the maximum age to 19. We can see how shrewd was Macaulay's fear of specialized or technical examinations for the Indian civil service if we consider the modern German and Prussian civil services. Had Macaulay introduced oriental languages or any specialized Indian studies into the first and all-important competition, those who failed would have been in a desperate condition, and the only alternative to casting them on the world, unfit for any profession, would have been to lower the examination standard so that few could fail, and thus lose all the benefits of competition. This alternative has been conspicuous in the Prussian civil service where the *Staats* or *Regierungsreferendar,* who had undergone a peculiar practical and theoretical training in *Staatswissenchaft* and *Staatsökonomie,* must be conspicuously incapable to fail in the ultimate examinations when family and political pressure are added to the scruples of the examiners against turning a man of 28 loose in the world without a vocation.

As a result of thus lowering the age of entrance into the Indian civil service, the efficiency, if not the personnel of the service, fell noticeably. Finally Macaulay's proposed age limit was reinstated, and the regulations of a general university education were restored. The question of admitting natives to the covenanted service comes up now and again, but it can hardly be said to be acute. Even with the present age limit, few care to prepare themselves for examination and make the trip to England. The simple and natural expedient of holding examinations simultaneously in India and England, which has fortunately been voted down thus far, has come before a commission this year, along with other Indian civil service problems. It seems palpable, however, that natives are not wanted in the covenanted Indian service.   There are as many places open to them now as they are reasonably capable of filling without endangering the British rule or prestige.

Macaulay's wisdom has thus been affirmed.   The recent history of the Indian civil service proves that the best men are those who have had the highest general academic education which England can afford, and that training in special subjects is not of the first importance and may be acquired by probationers in a year with comparative ease.   Recently some of the subjects of examination were changed, and the standard was raised.   Oxford standards were followed for classics and philosophy, Cambridge standards for mathematics and the natural sciences.   In 1895 the highest clerkships in the Home civil service and in 1896 the cadetships in the Far East were consolidated with the Indian civil service for purposes of examination.   A more detailed description of this consolidated examination must be reserved for a later chapter.[1]   How far in practice this examination may be said to be open and public is hard to say.   In the 1911 competition Oxford provided 51 and Cambridge 26 of the 93 successful candidates for the three services.   Undoubtedly these results are not due entirely to the superior education at the two great universities. We must remember that the examinations are based on the Oxford and Cambridge " Schools ", that these are the recognized avenues into the services, that the newer universities give a practical rather than an academic education.   When the question of democracy comes before the present Royal Commission, we shall probably read many startling denunciations and all the threats of radical changes—and in the end, when the report has been submitted to Parliament, the great reorganization will dwindle

[1] *Cf.* Appendix C.

to a few comparatively small changes, and the personnel will remain much as before. If at some time in the future the University of London should provide fifty successful candidates, ambitious and capable young men of the lower classes, who might well be unsuited to rule in India, the present system of open competition would probably be re-modeled to suit the " changing needs of the service," and we should have a new kind of open competition calculated to attract the " right class of young men ".   Even at present the scheme is not undemocratic.   The majority of undergraduates at Oxford and Cambridge are drawn from the *bourgeoisie*; moreover, most of the successful candidates are " scholars "—that is, men of small means who have won scholarships at the universities; and the aristocrats in point of wealth or social position are not likely to choose the rigors of an Indian life in preference to a comfortable career at home.

However the choice may be safeguarded, it remains an extraordinary fact that the twelve hundred men who are employed in the civil government of some 230 million people and in the partial government of some 80 million more,[1] whose peculiar fitness for Indian life we should suppose would be subjected to the minutest scrutiny, are selected simply for their proficiency in a certain number of general academic studies, and their special knowledge of Greek philosophy, chemistry, or quaternions.[2]

[1] *Gazetteer of India,* vol. iv, p. 42.

[2] There is indeed one severe physical test imposed—a riding test, which has unseated not a few of the highest probationers.

For a succinct and lucid description of the Indian civil service of to-day, written for Canadians, see Professor W. L. Grant's article, on " British Experience with Tropical Colonization," in the *Queen's Quarterly Magazine,* 1912.

CHAPTER III

The Beginning of Reform

" The proposal to select candidates for the Civil Service by a competitive examination appears to me to be one of those great public improvements the adoption of which would form an era in history."—John Stuart Mill.

" Most of his [Trevelyan's] correspondents thought that the idea was hopelessly impracticable. It seemed like the intrusion into the world of politics of a scheme of cause and effect derived from another universe—as if one should propose to the Stock Exchange that the day's prices should be fixed by prayer and casting of lots."—Wallas, *Human Nature in Politics*.

In 1853 the report of the select committee appeared. Gladstone had been bold in his choice of Sir Charles Trevelyan and Sir Stafford Northcote. Trevelyan was a graduate of Haileybury and, once in India, his rise in the company's service had been remarkable. He returned to England to become Assistant Secretary of the Treasury. Sir Stafford Northcote was a distinguished young Oxonian, formerly private secretary to Gladstone and Vice-President of the Board of Trade. Later he became a Conservative, but accepted Gladstone's invitation to report on the civil service. Both members of the committee were ardent reformers.[1] Trevelyan had been an enthusiastic supporter

---

[1] Trollope has represented Trevelyan as a pharisaical, jealous and conceited bureaucrat, who had become a reformer by accident. "Great changes had been going on at the Weights and Measures, or rather it might be more proper to say that great changes were now in progress. From that moment in which it had been hinted to Mr. Hardlines that

of open competition in the Indian civil service, and had
looked over Macaulay's shoulder as the latter wrote his
famous plea for academic distinction as a test of fitness

he must relax the rigor of his examinations, he had pondered deeply
over the matter. Hitherto he had confined his efforts to his own
office, and so far from feeling personally anxious for the amelioration
of the civil service generally, had derived no inconsiderable share of
his happiness from the knowledge that there were such sinks of in-
iquity as the Internal Navigation. To be widely different from others,
was Mr. Hardlines' glory. He was perhaps something of a civil service Pharisee, and wore on his forehead a broad phylactery, stamped
with the mark of Crown property. He thanked God that he was not
like those publicans at Somerset House, and took glory to himself in
paying tithes of official cumin. But now he was driven to a wider
range. Those higher Pharisees who were above him in his own pharisaical establishment, had interfered with the austerity of his worship.
He could not turn against them there, on their own ground.

" He, of all men, could not be disobedient to official orders. But if
he could promote a movement beyond the walls of the Weights and
Measures; if he could make Pharisees of those benighted publicans in
the Strand; if he could introduce conic sections into the Custom
House, and political economy into the Post Office; if, by any effort of
his, the Foreign Office clerks could be forced to attend punctually at
ten; and that wretched saunterer, whom five days a week he saw
lounging into the Council Office—if he could be made to mend his
pace, what a wide field for his ambition would Mr. Hardlines then
have found.

"Great ideas opened themselves to his mind as he walked to and from
his office daily. What if he could become the parent of a totally different order of things! What if the Civil Service, through his instru-
mentality, should become the nucleus of the best intellectual diligence
in the country, instead of being a byword for sloth and ignorance!
Mr. Hardlines meditated deeply on this, and, as he did so, it became
observed on all sides that he was an altered man as regarded his
solicitude for the Weights and Measures. One or two lads crept in,
by no means conspicuous for their attainments in abstract science;
young men, too, were observed to leave not much after four o'clock,
without calling down on themselves Mr. Hardlines' usual sarcasm.
Some said he was growing old, others that he was broken-hearted.
But Mr. Hardlines was not old, nor broken in heart or body. He was
thinking of higher things than the Weights and Measures, and at last
he published a pamphlet."

to serve the government.   Northcote was a typical product
of Eton and of Balliol College, firmly convinced of the
superiority of such an education to any other as a preparation for Parliament or the public services.   He was,
like Gladstone, shrewdly aware that in an examination
based on the Oxford and Cambridge schools, the upper
class would more than hold its own; but like Macaulay, he
seems to have had the idea that a man who was distinguished in the humaner letters would probably be capable
and a gentleman, no matter what his antecedents or who
his sponsors.   Unlike the usual reports which follow and
are based upon numberless pages of tedious and often conflicting testimony, this report preceded official testimony
and discussion and thus avoided a compromise without
any strong principle.

   The committee complained that the civil service did not
attract the ablest men.

   It would be natural to expect that so important a profession would attract into its ranks the ablest and most ambitious
of the youth of the country; that the keenest emulation would
prevail among those who had entered it; and that such as were
endowed with superior qualifications would rapidly rise to distinction and public eminence.   Such, however, is by no means
the case.   Admission into the Civil Service is indeed eagerly
sought after, but it is for the unambitious, and the indolent or
incapable, that it is chiefly desired.   Those whose abilities do
not warrant an expectation that they will succeed in the open
professions, where they must encounter the competition of
their contemporaries, and those whom indolence of temperament or physical infirmities unfit for active exertions, are placed
in the Civil Service, where they may obtain an honourable live-
lihood with little labor, and with no risk; where their success
depends upon their simply avoiding any flagrant misconduct,
and attending with moderate regularity to their routine duties;

and in which they are secured against the ordinary consequences of old age, or failing health, by an arrangement which
provides them with means of supporting themselves after they
have become incapacitated.[1]

The committee went on to discuss the difficulties in
the way of attracting able young men into the service,
and mentioned a number of obstacles, some more theoretical than practical, and some quite inevitable—the youth of
entrants, the absence or ineffectiveness of qualifying examination, routine work which deadens ambition and usefulness, promotion by seniority and the feeling of security
engendered by the certainty that all will rise together, the
fact that strangers from outside the service are often
necessarily appointed to higher posts, thus adding to the
grievances of the really ambitious clerks, the fragmentary
character of the service which restricts promotions to the
one department which the aspirant first entered.   To meet
these difficulties Northcote and Trevelyan laid down some
general principles for attracting the best men.   *They would
attract the ablest men by a competitive examination open
to all classes, conducted by an independent central board.*[2]
They favored training young men rather than appointing
old ones from other professions, that is, training them
so that they might be eligible for higher administrative
positions.   *For the superior situations endeavors should
be made to secure the services of the most promising young*

---

[1] *Parliamentary Papers,* 1854-5, vol. xx, p. 450; hereinafter referred
to as *Civil Service Papers,* 1854-5.

[2] " In the examinations which we have recommended, we consider
that the right of competing should be open to all persons of a given
age."   " These examinations cannot be conducted in an effective and
consistent manner throughout the Service while it is left to each department to determine the nature of the examination and to examine
the candidates."   *Cf. Civil Service Papers,* 1854-5, pp. 409-13.

men of the day by a competing examination on a level with
the highest description of education in the country. It
would be impossible, the committee thought, to impose
upon each candidate for a clerkship the necessity of passing an examination equal to that of the first class men of
universities; but if on the occurrence of a vacancy a number of candidates presented themselves, of whom some
could pass such an examination, there was no reason why
the public should not have the benefit of such a man's services, in preference to those of a person of inferior merit.

Two essential features are distinguishable in this report
—open competition and an academic examination of university standard, wherever there are a sufficient number
of candidates of university education to warrant it. Obviously the committee had in mind something more than
a vague idea of waiting for B.A's. to apply for clerkships.
The civil service posts should be graded like the Indian
civil service; there should be two distinct divisions of
clerks—the higher division to consist of university men to
do the intellectual work of the office and destined for its
highest posts, the lower to consist of clerks of ordinary
education to do the lower and more mechanical work, and
to rise only in exceptional instances above clerical work.
Great emphasis was laid on this distinction between intellectual and mechanical labor. Examinations for the higher
positions should be held at London, but for the lower appointments, in several different localities so as to exclude no
one. The age of admission to superior appointments
should be 19 to 25; to inferior posts, 17 to 21.

The committee also recommended examinations so as to
secure special attainments for particular branches, and
periodical competition rather than competition for specific
appointments. Successful candidates could be distributed
among the various offices by the choice of heads or on

recommendation of examiners.   Probation should be made
universal.   In the extensive range of examination subjects
recommended—history, jurisprudence, political economy,
modern languages, besides classics and mathematics—we
see again the influence of Macaulay's Indian civil service
plan and of the university idea.   The committee recommended a proper system of transfer within offices,
so that a clerk might be made master of the whole routine;
also the grading of all offices, so as to break down the
barriers between different departments and encourage the
free flow of promotion throughout the whole civil service.[1]
Promotion should be by merit, three or four names to be
submitted by the immediate superior to the secretary and
by the secretary to the head of an office.   A book of promotion record should be kept for reference.   They recommended an annual increment and a consistent pension
system.

As an appendix to the report, the committee published
a letter from Benjamin Jowett in which the famous master
of Balliol College sketched his ideal of a civil service
based on university education.   The indispensable requirements for all clerks must be arithmetic, bookkeeping, English composition and writing.   For the higher class of
clerks the requirements should include the best elements
of English education, classics, philosophy, law, physical
sciences, foreign languages, etc.   No theory of education
should be enforced, "but a test should be made of what
a man knows, not of what we think he ought to know,"
i. e., the examiners should allow men to compete in the
subjects in which they had specialized at the universities.
Four "schools" were to be founded to test special require-

---

[1] This was, as we shall see, the most visionary of the committee's
proposals, and the least workable.

ments, wider groups than the Oxford "School," or the Cambridge "Tripos", but based on them—(1) classics; (2) mathematics and natural sciences; (3) political economy, law, and moral philosophy; (4) modern languages, history, and international law. English composition should be a large element in all examinations. Each candidate for the higher clerkships should be required to take two of the Jowett "schools," the third being required from candidates for the Board of Trade and Treasury, the fourth from aspirants to the Foreign Office. A certain number of appointments should be announced beforehand as appropriated for each examination, and the choice of these appointments should be given to candidates in order of merit. The examinations should be held at London, Edinburgh, and Dublin, and there should be eight examiners. Evidently the master of Balliol had a very clear idea of what he wanted, and it is astonishing to find how closely the present first division examinations follow his scheme. For the lower grade of clerkships, Jowett recommended examinations in reading, writing with dictation, geography, a general paper of useful knowledge, and a general *viva voce* examination to test intelligence.

Jowett, Northcote, and Trevelyan were sure that with such a standard examination and the promise of a highly honorable and not ill-remunerated career, the government service would attract, as Macaulay expected that the Indian civil service would attract, some of the ablest men in the universities. They recognized also how much such a competition would quicken and stimulate the life of universities, and intensify the competition for their highest scholastic honors. We have only to consider the effect on American universities if the United States Government should set up an academic examination of high standard for lucrative positions at Washington. The committee was also confident that the examinations for the lower grade of clerk-ships would stimulate and standardize the education of the lower classes.

When the report appeared, shouts of disapproval and scorn arose on all sides. The plan which Macaulay had introduced in India without any great opposition, when proposed for England by his son-in-law, appeared as un-familiar as it was startling, and Northcote and Trevelyan quickly learned how much easier it is to introduce reforms in a dependency than at home. In the first chapter we have described the conditions existing in London offices. In 1854, in a return to an order of the House of Commons demanding the list of subjects of examination in various offices, it appeared that in the Board of Trade, Board of Woods, Poor Law, County Council, Home, Colonial, and Foreign offices, even in the Exchequer, which was otherwise a model department, there were no examinations at all; [1] and that in the Treasury, Register General's office, Audit, Customs, Irish Poor Law and Ordinance departments and in the office of the Chief Secretary for Ireland, the examin-ations consisted of simple arithmetic and an abstract of documents. In the Excise, War, and Post Office depart-ments, bookkeeping, geography, and history of England were further requirements, and only the Admiralty had any thing like a real qualifying examination. We have seen how diverse were the opinions of various officials as to the need of reform, how different the practices of dif-ferent offices, how flourishing was the system of patronage which led to the selection of the " properly qualified per-sons." It was no small thing to sweep away this patron-age and the traditions, good or bad, which had developed in various offices, with which the leading officials and the

[1] The clerks in the Board of Works were all recruited from other departments.

governing classes had grown up, and which they had come to consider permanent and indispensable.

The opponents of the plan poured a torrent of eloquent abuse upon its authors. " Early supporters," says Trevelyan himself,[1] " *might have been counted upon the fingers,* and if the matter had been put to the vote in London society, or the clubs, or even in Parliament itself *by secret voting* [*i. e.*, without pressure from constituents], the new system would have been rejected by an overwhelming majority." Macaulay had hopes that the example of the Indian Government would be followed in the offices in Whitehall.

" There is good public news," he writes in January, 1854. " The plan for appointing public servants by competition is to be adopted on a large scale, and is mentioned in the Queen's Speech..." "...I had a long talk about the projected examination with Trevelyan. I am afraid he will pay the examiners too high, and turn the whole thing into a job. . . . If the thing succeeds it will be of immense benefit to the country . . . "

But it soon became evident,

adds the biographer, Macaulay's nephew and Trevelyan's son,

that very few of our leading politicians had their hearts in the matter. It was one thing to deprive the East India Directors of their patronage, and quite another to surrender their own. The outcry of the dispensers and expectants of public employment was loud and fierce, and the advocates of the new system were forced to admit that its hour had not yet come. " I went to Brooks's," says Macaulay ... " and found everybody open-mouthed, I am sorry to say, against Trevel-

[1] Eaton, *Civil Service in Great Britain*, p. 430. Letter of Sir Charles Trevelyan to Mr. Eaton.

yan's plans about the Civil Service. He has been too sanguine. The pear is not ripe. I always thought so. The time will come, but it has not come yet. I am afraid that he will be much mortified."

Trevelyan's career, [says his son] was seriously threatened by the hostility of some of the most powerful men of the day ... Accustomed, according to the frequent fate of permanent officials, to be pushed to the front in the moment of jeopardy, and thrust into the rear in the moment of triumph, he had weathered more formidable storms than that which was now growling and blustering through all the clubs and board-rooms of Piccadilly and Parliament Street. Macaulay, who lived sufficiently behind the scenes to discount the full gravity of the situation, was extremely uneasy on his brother-in-law's account. [Later on Macaulay wrote:] " The news is worse. There is a set made at him by men who will not scruple to do their utmost." During the next few weeks Macaulay was never so depressed as when he had been spending part of his afternoon at Brooks's.[1]

Sarcasm, ridicule, and gloomy prophecies of evil assailed Trevelyan and Northcote. Forceful and weighty expressions of conservative opinion, bigoted intolerance of change, and stupid pride in the existing service were powerfully represented. We are told by one critic that the proposed system is Chinese,[2] by another that it is Utopian,[3] by a third

[1] Trevelyan, *Life and Letters of Lord Macaulay*, pp. 611-612.

[2] "About China the critics know nothing except that the Chinese consume large quantities of opium, that their ladies have small feet, and that there are public examinations to test the fitness of candidates for the government service." *The Times*, March 17, 1854.

[3] *The Spectator* was conspicuous in bringing this charge. Like all Conservative organs, when it was unable to call the authors of a new plan scoundrels, demagogues, or iconoclasts, it fell back on the time-worn expedient of branding them as dreamers, and took comfort in the thought that after all their dreams had no official sanction and would not be realized.

that it is Prussian. One prophesied a bureaucracy and another predicted the ruin of the existing *esprit de corps*. One group of critics was sure that the plan would attract only academic prigs; another group foresaw the clever but ill-bred middle class youth [1] parading his Cockney smartness at Whitehall; a third group was sure that open competition would not attract any really able men at all. The report was assailed because it would deprive the service of its aristocratic [2] character and because it would give unjust preference to aristocratic education; because it would deprive the government of necessary patronage although the patronage was directed with sole regard to merit; because examinations are no test of merit at all and because they test only qualities which are not essential to the service. It was argued that the projected examining board would be too expensive, that it would become a patronage bureau, and that it would take responsibility and authoritative influence away from the heads of offices.[3] One wiseacre said that no one had ever suggested such a reform in the church where patronage was even more flourishing; others asked triumphantly what would have

---

[1] This contingency was guarded against in a letter to Trevelyan and Northcote from the Reverend W. H. Thompson, Regius Professor of Greek at Cambridge, almost funny in its solemn priggishness. He wrote from Trinity endorsing Jowett's plan, and advised that classics or mathematics should be compulsory in order that there would not be admitted into the higher branches of the civil service " persons whose birth and training may not have been favorable to the development of those sentiments which characterize the class of gentleman." The reverend gentleman advocated a Latin essay on some subject of ancient history, literature, or philosophy.

[2] *The Times*, April 20, 1854.

[3] See quotations from the *Morning Post, Daily News, Morning Herald*, and *Morning Chronicle* of 1854, quoted in a pamphlet *Observations upon the Report by Sir C. E. Trevelyan and Sir S. H. Northcote*, etc., by a Civil Subaltern.

become of Wellington and Clive if there had been competitive examinations.

The fact is that, with the exception of *The Times,* which was from the beginning a staunch supporter of civil service reform, current literature contained much abuse and vituperation, but little intelligent criticism.

The really intelligent and forceful criticisms of the report came from the civil service itself. The official criticisms from heads of offices and from prominent professors and schoolmasters, which appeared as an appendix to the report, are among the most illuminating documents ever published by the government printers. All the questions of civil service reform were argued in this appendix and subsequent years have added nothing to their scope and force. But we must not expect to find these officials in agreement. Victorian narrowness, class pride, and the innate conservatism of the old-school official clashed with the alert and ingenious individualism of a new era. But it is certain that in no other country at this time could the chief permanent officials of state departments have written opinions on their organizations so logical, complete, and illuminating, manifesting at once the highest literary education and the most profound experience. Even where an official was arguing against higher education as a test of fitness for office, the temper, the form, and the lucidity of his arguments often constituted an effectual rebuttal of his conclusion. For example, Mr. Chadwick of the Poor Law Board quoted the following arguments against the test of higher education:

" Many persons expect great improvements to the Civil Service from university examinations, or from examinations conducted in a similar manner and on similar subjects; and some persons desire to restrict all responsible public offices to persons who have taken a degree, by way of securing respectability and capacity. There would be force in this notion if university graduates were invariably, or usually found to be in office superior to other men of their class. But this is not the case in official life. . . . Certainly many first-rate public men have been brought up at public schools and universities, because the majority of the classes from which they are taken are educated at these places, but many equally able officers have not been so educated; and it is well known to all minutely acquainted with public offices, that the universities furnish many of the most worthless. The first requisites of a young man entering life, public or private, are good handwriting, a familiarity with common arithmetic, and common forms of business and accounts, and the power of writing correctly his own language. Now, it is notorious that young men from the universities usually enter public offices very deficient in these qualifications, and that they commence and often remain very bad men of business." No merchant or banker would require his clerk to undergo an initiatory examination in the Antigone of Sophocles or in De Morgan's Differential and Integral Calculus, nor would he think that such qualifications, however interesting in themselves, would be of more use in his business than the power of copying a painting of Turner's or a statue of Canova's—very interesting things in their way also, and which in truth did formerly serve the purpose of tests, when Rubens was made an ambassador. . . . The merchant hires what he wants, and not qualifications that are no use to him, . . . for which he would have to pay extra; yet the qualifications he requires are quite as high as those of a Government clerk. Many an awkward-looking fellow of no great attainments is found to distance his more elegant and university-educated competitors in the long run, because he has steadiness and self-command; it is found that whatever he can do, he can be trusted to do: he is punctual, regular, industrious and pains-taking; acquires soon a knowledge of official details and a power of carrying them out; knows all that is going on, and can always be referred to with reliance. In time he cannot be done without, and will and must be promoted. Had it been a question of acquired knowledge, he would have stood no chance with a university examiner, because he has not a smattering of the calculus, and does not make Latin verses. He understands accounts, however, which are of much greater importance, though the examiner himself in all probability, neither knows nor values them. He is not above hard work, or below it, or afraid of it.[1]

Sir James Stephen gave several "unanswerable objections" to the report. The prizes are not worthy the pursuit of the university honors' man. Money is the only attraction. He labors in an obscurity as profound as it is unavoidable. His official character is absorbed in his superior's. He must listen silently to praises for others which his pen has won for them. No man of real mental power, to whom the truth was known beforehand, would subject himself to an arduous examination, in order to win a post so ill-paid, so obscure, and so subordinate. " Of the six ablest men in the Colonial Office in my time, three left altogether, two by luckily serving in Canada were promoted, and one has found solace and atonement in his literary reputation." [2] The successful candidates in the higher examinations would not be the men wanted. They might have the courage, resource, and intelligence to succeed in open competition, but these are gifts ill-suited to one who is to be entombed for life at Downing Street. The promotion of brilliant men over superiors would merely insure bitter jealousies and enduring quarrels and would render all cordial coöperation impossible. The depressed and disappointed majority would fall back on passive re-

---

[1] *Civil Service Papers,* 1854-5, pp. 161-162.

[2] *Ibid.,* p. 75, *et seq.*

sistance impossible to combat. " *Detur digniori* " has only been the rule in Utopia, not in commerce nor in the legal and medical professions. If there were competitive examinations, the crown would surrender an undoubted right and the ministers their just patronage.

On the other hand, another critic agreed with Macaulay that almost without exception those who have taken high honors in university examinations, have been distinguished for good conduct as well as for learning and ability. " Without steady application a longe course of study cannot be mastered, and habitual diligence brings other virtues in its train—temperance, self-control, punctuality, accuracy," etc. Another critic answered Sir James Stephen's contention that Oxford and Cambridge men would think themselves underpaid: " But surely a moderate salary at starting, a prospect of increase, comparatively light work, a good social position, and the hope of advance in public life, would more than counterbalance the attractions of law and medicine, with their expensive and often uninteresting special training, and their long years of poverty and obscurity."

Fremantle, head of the Customs Board, emphasized the uselessness of highly trained men for routine work:

The highest posts in these offices [Revenue and Customs] are few, and those few by no means highly rewarded; and it is manifest—the total number of Clerks being very considerable—that the proportion who can hope to attain these posts is exceedingly small. The majority are left to pass through the respective classes of their various branches without special notice or distinction, and conclude a laborious official life without having been required to exhibit any qualities beyond those of industry and integrity. Surely there can be no advantage in seeking to fill such clerkships . . . with young men of talents and ambition, or of superior literary attainments, nor in inviting them, by competition, to come into a service which can neither reward them for success nor compensate them for the chances of failure. The performance of routine duties, after the lapse of one or two years, could not fail to " exercise a depressing influence upon them;" the work " would become distasteful;" the clerks discontented and seeking to obtain promotion or removal to better situations, and on failure of such promotion (there being, in fact, no offices to which they could be removed), they would be finally induced to retire from the public service with mortification and disappointment.[1]

On the other hand, Spottiswood, head of the Government Printing Office, wrote that even among the inferior clerks general information and education are of great use.

Sir George Cornwall Lewis, statesman and essayist, wrote to Trevelyan the most brilliant summary and criticism of the report. Lewis's arguments against a single, interchangeable civil service personnel, transferable from office to office, are probably unanswerable. His arguments against open competition and for promotion by merit are less cogent.

The permanent officers of a department are the depositories of the official traditions, . . . and knowledge . . . acquired in one department would be useless in another. The special experience . . . which the chief clerk of the criminal department of the Home Office has acquired there is useless in the Foreign Office or Admiralty. Where a general superintendence is required, and assistance can be obtained from subordinates, and where the chief qualifications are judgment, sagacity, and enlightened political opinions, such a change of offices is possible; but as you descend lower in the official scale, the specialty of functions increases—the duties must be performed in person, with little or no assistance, and there is consequently a necessity for special knowledge and experience.

[1] *Civil Service Papers*, 1854-5, p. 329.

Hence, the same person may be successively, at the head of the Home Office, the Foreign Office, the Colonial Office, and the Admiralty; but to transfer an experienced clerk from one office to another would be . . . like transferring a skilful naval officer to the army, or appointing a military engineer officer to command a ship; [in practical life] an architect may direct the execution of different classes of buildings . . . but the subordinate workmen . . . retain their separate functions unchanged—a carpenter does not become a mason, a painter or glazier . . . an ironmonger or plasterer.[1] [Thus a single Civil Service, including all clerks advanced without regard to departmental divisions, is impossible.]

One of the ablest administrators in England, Addington, the Under Secretary for Foreign Affairs, corroborated the evidence of Lewis as to transfers, and like Fremantle, emphasized the commonplace routine of government offices and the danger of raising civil service requirements too high. The civil service is heterogeneous.

The Foreign Office and Excise Office . . . are equally component parts of the Civil Service; and yet they are so totally dissimilar in all essential points that the same rules touching qualifications, and consequently touching examinations, cannot possibly apply to both. I am therefore quite at a loss to conceive how the various and heterogeneous classes of the Civil Service can well be included in one general category and scheme of treatment; and it seems consequently to me that at the very outset the reasoning and observations employed in the Report are, in this essential point, based in error, since, according to my conception, the term " Civil Service " is but a term popularly used for general convenience, but that it represents a thing heterogeneous in its nature, and, as such, requiring in its practical treatment the application of separate rules and principles suitable to its separate parts.[2]

[1] *Civil Service Papers*, 1854-5, pp. 110-111.   [2] *Ibid.*, pp. 347-348.

As to genius and the service, Addington had this to say:

It appears to me that the scale of intellectual cultivation and power which is assumed in the Report as needed in the Civil Service is greatly overrated, and also that by overestimating the requirements of the Civil Service we shall be liable to contract unnecessarily and injuriously the circle of candidates. However paradoxical, or perhaps even grovelling, such an opinion may appear, I apprehend that, except in the Heads, or the highest officers, of departments, no transcendant degree of talent, or of literary or scientific cultivation, will be found necessary to fit a man for performing properly the duties assigned to him. . . . A good Departmental Clerk is, in fact, mainly an aggregation of cumulative daily experience and tradition, combined with that readiness of mind and pen which practice gives, and which enables a man to come to the assistance of his superiors at the right moment and in the right manner. But it is the dry and hard discipline and drudgery of the desk which, however wearisome they may have been, have mainly contributed to lay the foundations of those qualities which in after years shine forth so eminently in the accomplished Departmental Clerk, and which render him one of the most useful and valuable members of the body politic.[1]

Addington's conclusion, like Sir James Stephen's, was pessimistic.

I fear that the tendency to favouritism, and what is vulgarly termed " jobbing," must be looked upon as inherent in every system of Government. . . . " Jobbing " is a part, though an ugly part, of the price which a free people pay for their constitutional liberty.[2]

The question of promotion by merit which the report had advocated, is one which every nation has found difficult to realize. The claims of seniority are potent everywhere. Promotion by merit could not be introduced into the civil

---

[1] *Civil Service Papers*, 1854-5, pp. 350-351.   [2] *Ibid.*, p. 356.

service at one stroke of the official pen. The secretary of the Board of Control was a leading opponent of this proposal.

In the promotions, therefore, through the classes of junior clerks, I think the principle of seniority must be allowed to prevail in some degree, and I should myself be more disposed to act on the principle of rejecting an inefficient rather than of rewarding the most efficient clerk, when the difficulty of really determining who is the most efficient is so great. I am aware that many of the old Civil Servants regard these views unfavourably, and see in this proposal, not a security for merit being duly rewarded, but rather an opportunity for the exercise of favoritism; while and with truth it is urged that the long services of unpretending but hardworking public servants may be unfairly dealt by, when preference is given to less modest merit.[1]

We have seen that the report was received by press and public with anger and contempt. We have seen that the genuine critics were civil servants and schoolmasters whose views were published with the report, who favored reform but were unprepared for such radical action. We must now see what was the decisive attitude of the Queen, the Cabinet and Parliament.

As regards Parliament, those who had profited by the patronage system and those who were too conservative to tolerate a change, were united against the report. The supercilious attitude of the House of Lords was aptly expressed by Lord Brougham, who " did not think it necessary to enter at any length into the subject, first, because he was not exactly aware what was the plan which the government had in contemplation and secondly, because he had an impression on his mind that their lordships were not likely to hear much more about it (a laugh)." [2]

[1] Civil Service Papers, 1854-5, pp. 232-233.
[2] Hansard, H. L., March 13, 1854.

Lord Brougham was quite justified in his first remark but he was grievously mistaken in the second. Nobody knew what was the plan of the Government. Thus far the report was merely a report to the Treasury, and did not represent any settled policy of government. In fact the Cabinet was far from united on this subject. Within the Cabinet Gladstone found his most uncompromising opponent in Lord John Russell. Gladstone's defense of the new plan in a letter to Russell is noteworthy.

May we not get, I will not say more ease and certainty for the leader of the House, but more real and more honourable strength with the better and, in the long run, the ruling part of the community, by a signal proof of cordial desire that the processes by which government is carried on should not in elections only, but elsewhere too be honourable and pure? I speak with diffidence; but remembering that at the revolution we passed over from prerogative to patronage, and that since the revolution we have also passed from bribery to influence, I cannot think the process is to end here; and after all we have seen of the good sense and good feeling of the community, though it may be too sanguine, I cherish the hope that the day is now near at hand, or actually come, when in pursuit not of visionary notions, but of a great practical and economical improvement, we may safely give yet one more new and striking sign of rational confidence in the intelligence and character of the people.[1]

Lord John wrote him curtly in reply: " I hope no change will be made, and I certainly must protest against it." [2] In reply to even a second assault he remained quite unconvinced. "At present," he said, " the Queen appointed the ministers, and the ministers the subordinates; in future

---

[1] Morley, *Life of Gladstone*, vol. ii, appendix, p. 608.
[2] *Ibid.*, vol. i, p. 380.

the board of examiners would be in the place of the Queen. Our institutions would be as nearly republican as possible, and the new spirit of the public offices would not be loyalty but republicanism!"[1] As one of Lord John's kindred spirits declared, "The more the civil service is recruited from the lower classes, the less will it be sought after by the higher, until at last the aristocracy will be altogether dissociated from the permanent civil service of the country."[1] Gladstone returned the attack in a letter to Graham (January 3, 1854). "I do not want any pledges as to details; what I seek is your countenance and favor in an endeavour to introduce to the cabinet a proposal that we should give our sanction to the principle that in every case where a satisfactory test of a defined and palpable nature can be furnished, the public service shall be laid open to personal merit . . . This is *my* contribution to parliamentary reform."[2] After a long discussion the Cabinet acquiesced.

It was not only in the clubs in Fleet Street and amongst the politicians and members of Parliament that the plan was unpopular. Mr. Gladstone as its sponsor met with cold approval at the hands of the Sovereign, whose wishes he always affected to consider with the utmost conscientious scrutiny and usually ultimately disregarded. The Queen wrote to Mr. Gladstone begging him to be sure of the Victorian respectability of appointees.

Buckingham Palace, *17th February*, 1854. The Queen has received Mr Gladstone's letter and memorandum, and has heard from the Prince the further explanation of the grounds upon which he, Mr Gladstone, thinks the new regulations respecting the Civil Service necessary. The Queen, although

[1] Morley, *Life of Gladstone*, vol. i, p. 380.

[2] *Ibid.*, vol. i, p. 381.

not without considerable misgivings, sanctions the proposed plan, trusting that Mr Gladstone will do what he can, in the arrangements of the details of it, to guard against the dangers, which she has pointed out in her former letter and through the Prince when he saw Mr Gladstone. A check, for instance, would be necessary upon the admission of candidates to compete for employment, securing that they should be otherwise eligible, besides the display of knowledge which they may exhibit under examination. Without this a young man might be very ineligible, and still after having been proclaimed to the world as first in ability, it would require very strong evidence of misconduct to justify his exclusion by the Government.[1]

Gladstone's reply was characteristic. He explained his attitude patiently, but hardly with the subtle flattery by which Lord Beaconsfield governed with the consent of his Sovereign.

Downing Street, *17th February*, 1854. The Chancellor of the Exchequer presents his humble duty to your Majesty, and has the honour to acknowledge your Majesty's gracious letter. He takes blame to himself for having caused your Majesty trouble by omitting to include in his short memorandum an explanation of the phrase " qualified persons." Experience at the universities and public schools of this country has shown that in a large majority of cases the test of open examination is also an effectual test of character ; as, except in the very remarkable cases, the previous industry and self-denial, which proficiency evinces, are rarely separated from general habits of virtue. But he humbly assures your Majesty that the utmost pains will be taken to provide not only for the majority but for all cases, by the strictest enquiries which the case will admit ; and he has the most confident belief that the securities for character under the system, although they cannot be un-

---

[1] *Letters of Queen Victoria* (New York, 1907), vol. iii, pp. 12-13.

erring, will be stronger and more trustworthy than any of which the present method of appointment is susceptible.[1]

Gladstone achieved a merely nominal victory over his colleagues. In the Speech from the Throne in 1854 there was a paragraph clearly implying the intention of the Government to propose a bill embodying the principles of the Trevelyan-Northcote report. Somehow the reform was arrested. The Treasury adopted several recommendations of the report in the departments under its supervision, but attempted no general reorganization. The promised bill was never laid on the table, partly owing to the Crimean War which was to afford a startling proof of the administrative incompetence, partly because the Ministry had never really been convinced and was only too glad of an excuse for postponing action.

In November Gladstone wrote to Trevelyan:

My own opinions are more and more in favour of the plan of competition. I do not mean that they can be more in its favour as a principle, than they were when I invited you and Northcote to write the report which has lit up the flame; but more and more do the incident evils seem curable and the difficulties removable.[2]

The Times voiced the.irritation of honest reformers in an effective editorial, openly accusing the Ministry of bad faith.

The existence of a measure has been solemnly announced by Royal Order; its advent has been foretold with pomp and ceremony; but as to the nature of the change intended, we are left most provokingly in ignorance. It is true that an inquiry has been instituted—that a report has appeared; but the

---

[1] *Letters of Queen Victoria* (New York, 1907), vol. iii, pp. 13-14.

[2] Morley, *op. cit.*, p. 381.

Ministers have taken the greatest precautions to divest this report of any small official sanction it might be supposed to possess. If the scheme proposed is that adopted by the government, why is it scouted and ridiculed by their organs? If it is not, why is the public to be tantalized with the prospect of a reform that is never intended to be realized?[1]

The reformers were sincere, but they were bewildered by the eloquent abuse of their adversaries, and their generous enthusiasm was a trifle chilled by the just censure of those who knew even better than they the temper of Whitehall. The report was too broad and sweeping. Such gigantic schemes must be tested and evolved gradually in practice. The civil service was not prepared for so great a revolution, and public opinion had to be educated up to it. Great obstacles arose as the plan was developed in detail. Political expediency dictated compromises. Time and chance came to modify Gladstone's proposition. Fifteen years passed before open competition was finally established, and thirty before the other essential features of the Report of 1853 were adopted.

[1] *The Times*, April 20, 1854.

CHAPTER IV

EXAMINATION INTRODUCED

"The moment favoritism ceased to be powerful, it became contemptible."—Eaton, *Civil Service in Great Britain.*

THE Aberdeen Ministry went out after the War. Palmerston, who succeeded, understood the civil service situation. Parliament did not favor open competition. A statute dealing with limited competition would have been too narrow to have been really effective, and too rigid to have gained more than reluctant obedience from the department heads. It was better to leave the tentative reforms to the Treasury, than to drag the civil service into Parliament, where the majority was either hostile or apathetic. The Treasury is the heart of the civil service. The two most important cabinet officials are usually at its head; its permanent officials are the ablest in the service; it directly controls the great revenue departments and, through finance, exercises an indirect control over all the other departments of state. Almost no change in the civil service of any office can be made without touching finance, and when finance is affected the Treasury decides on the general merits of the question. The Parliamentary Secretary of the Treasury is Patronage Secretary, and through him the chief appointments are made. The Treasury officers and clerks are accustomed to deal with all the other departments of state. They understand the problems and personnel of the various departments, the relations of the departments among themselves and to the other organs of the state.

It is important to fix our eyes on the Treasury as the source of civil service reform. With the exception of pensions, legislation affecting the civil service has come through Orders in Council emanating from the Treasury.

The Order in Council of May, 1855, was the first step after the storm following the Report of 1853 had subsided. It established a central board of examiners independent of the departments—the Civil Service Commission—and it appointed as commissioners three distinguished men—Sir Edward Ryan, a close friend of Macaulay, formerly Chief Justice of Bengal, recently a prominent officer of the Exchequer, Sir J. G. Shaw Lefevre, Clerk Assistant to the House of Lords, and Edward Romilly, a distinguished civil servant, the chairman of the Board of Audit. This board was to examine all candidates for the civil service—but the standard of examination in each department was left to be fixed by agreement with the head of the department, and it was expressly stated that no change was to be made in the existing method of nomination and appointment. The examinations were not made competitive, but it was obvious that limited competition was expected. A six months' probation was established in every case. An important loophole was left by a provision for the appointment of men of mature age and special qualifications without certificates. The duty of the commissioners in the case of each aspirant was to ascertain and certify that the candidate was (1) within the limits of age prescribed by the department in question; (2) free from physical defect or disease; (3) of good character; and (4) of the requisite knowledge and ability for the discharge of his duties.

Not long after the commission was appointed, the question of open competition was brought up in Parliament. There was a limited attendance. Some members evidently had no convictions; others lacked the courage to put themselves on record before their constituents, and gracefully avoided the issue by absenting themselves. Sir Stafford Northcote made his maiden speech to a hostile audience. The vote was 140-125 against open competition.

The commission had a delicate task to perform. The press, the rank and file of the service, many members of Parliament, and the relatives and friends of nominees were openly hostile; leading officials disapproved of the commission, but it must be owned that they put no obstacles in the way of the commissioners and were quick to recognize their judicial status. The commissioners showed great tact and firmness. They provoked no antagonism. They were wise in making their standards moderate and rejecting only for conspicuous incompetence.[1] They published their first annual report in 1856, before the year was up in order to correct misapprehensions and answer unfounded charges. All kinds of allegations were made about the difficulty of the examination. It was said that candidates who would previously have been appointed were dismissed, by means of fantastic tests and nightmares of pedantry.[1] The commissioners pointed out that the number of vacancies was about the same, and that more candidates were bound to fail because more were nominated for each vacancy. They showed that the majority of failures was due, not to deficiency in abstruse sciences, but to gross and discreditable ignorance of spelling and arithmetic, and inability to write legibly.[2] The critics had some reason

---

[1] *Cf. First Report of the Civil Service Commissioners, Parliamentary Papers,* 1856, xxii, and the *Guide to Government Appointments,* by James Hurst (London, 1856).

[2] To remove the impression that the standards were too high, some

to quarrel with the first history examination. The first question would test the inventive faculties of the average intelligent collegian. " Give the dates, adopting common chronology, of the following events—The Deluge, Exodus, Building of Rome, Peloponnesian War, The Hegira, Coronation of Charlemagne, Invention of Printing, The Revolution, Separation of Crowns of Great Britain and Hanover." No doubt the commissioners were liberal and accepted approximate answers, say within a few hundred years, as correct. In spelling, furthermore, the failures were not in technical words or in those of rare occurrence, but in those of every-day use.

The commission had arranged the standards with the heads of various offices and the examinations were held separately for each office. Some standards were higher than others. The indispensable requirements were almost everywhere the same — dictation, English composition, arithmetic, bookkeeping, and précis. The optional subjects, which were certified by the commission only when the

of the history answers were published by the Civil Service Commission (*Second Report, Parliamentary Papers,* 1857 [sess. i] vol. iii). *E. G.:* " The Star Chamber consisted of twelve members, whose business it was to invent torments for the prisoners whom they thought was against the safety of the country." " Trial of ordeal were employed in the trial of Warren Hastings, and were legally prohibited in the reign of George I." " George II is the sovereign to whom the name of the English Justinian has been sometimes applied." " Marlborough fought against the Spanish Armada and completely destroyed it in Elizabeth's reign." " William the Conqueror was a king who introduced many good laws into England; learning and all sorts of science flourished under him." Also that William the Conqueror was " a passionate man, rather inclined to tyranny, much beloved, however, by his subjects, a kind father, and a faithful husband." " The Roman Walls were built to keep the Tartars from invading the country, and were so thick that two carriages could be driven abreast." " Henry VIII divorced Catherine of Arragon in order to marry Lady Jane Grey," etc.

indispensable examinations had been passed, varied. Almost every office included Latin or one foreign language. and English history as optional subjects.

The Colonial Office set the example of real limited competition. Mr. Labouchere arranged an examination with the Civil Service Commission, divided into two parts, the first qualifying and consisting of handwriting, spelling, arithmetic, geography, and translation from German, Latin, French, or some other language, and précis. The second and competitive part consisted of three of the following subjects—languages and literature of Greece and Rome, languages and literature of France, Germany, and Italy (required for the home Colonial Office), geology, chemistry, and English (required for Ceylon writers).

The Civil Service Commission Office and Admiralty were not far behind the Colonial Office in offering optional subjects, which soon became, by reason of competition, requisites. The majority of offices, however, had the lower standards first mentioned. The Customs Department especially was obdurate. Here the Civil Service Commission showed their tact and finally succeeded in getting the standard raised to that of the Internal Revenue.

The fears which had been entertained that no highly educated men would apply were from the first dispelled. In the War Office, where there were a number of men competing for a single vacancy, two Cambridge men, one a Wrangler, were adjudged equal. As special subjects, one offered Latin and mathematics, the other bookkeeping, Spanish, German, Italian, Latin, and Greek. They were both appointed and, following the policy of emphasizing the requisite subjects, the man who stood highest in arithmetic was given the priority of rank.[1]

[1] The Civil Service Commission opened four Junior clerkships, three beginning with £100 and the fourth with £200 a year, to competition.

The Civil Service Commission set about quietly to standardize age limits, and rules as to physical condition and character. The age limits varied from 17 to 45. The commission set up 18 to 25 as a future standard.

This report, and the subsequent reports of the commission, silenced criticism. It was seen that the new scheme was a vast improvement over the old. But the reformers had as yet made little headway. The existing examinations furnished a method of excluding the incompetent. There was no open competition anywhere. Only five offices made a point of nominating over three members for a vacancy, and many of the nominees were proved utterly ignorant of the first principles of spelling and writing. Of 1,078 applicants mentioned in the first report, 676 passed, and 309 were rejected mostly for conspicuous ignorance of the three R's. Intellectual qualifications were tested ony when candidates subjected themselves to voluntary examination in special subjects. For the majority of vacancies there were still absolute nominations. The Civil Service Commission said: " Many inferior appointments are made, without personal knowledge of the fitness of the party, on the recommendation of some other person, who is desirous not of supplying the public with a useful official, but of making a competent provision for a friend."

In 1856 the reformers, emboldened by their first success,

The competition was known only to a few heads of schools and to others to whom it had been casually mentioned. Forty-four candidates appeared, the sons of professional men and "independent gentlemen." Twenty-five were graduates of universities, and sixteen came from large public schools. Four passed good examinations in four languages, twenty-seven in more than one foreign language, and this proficiency in higher subjects was generally combined with a competent knowledge of elementary practical subjects. Evidently there was no dearth of candidates of respectable family and sound education, who were ready to come forward and compete if patronage did not bar the way. *Second Report of Civil Service Commission.*

again brought up the subject of open competition in the House of Commons.[1] Viscount Goderich was spokesman and his motion was seconded by Sir Stafford Northcote. The motion was: " If Her Majesty shall see fit to make trial in the Civil Service of the method of open competition as a condition of entrance, this House will cheerfully provide for any charges which the adoption of that system may entail."

This was opposed by the Chancellor of the Exchequer, Sir G. C. Lewis, who urged that individual responsibility of various heads of departments would be lost.

If you remove all limitations to the competition for appointments, you will relieve all the members of the government from any responsibility with regard to appointments made in the respective departments of which we are at the head. The plan . . . of my noble friend would get rid of the important security of the individual responsibility of the head of each Department with regard to the character of the candidates.

It is hardly necessary to emphasize the fallacy of this argument. The fact was that the majority of nominees were people quite unknown to the minister or parliamentary secretary, whose individual responsibility was usually imaginary.[2]

One of the arguments emphasized in the debate was that an open civil service would constitute itself a dominating bureaucracy. Gladstone made an eloquent reply.[3]

[1] Hansard, April 24, 1856, pp. 1401, *et seq.*

[2] Sir George Lewis argued against the motion on another ground. He claimed that while the crown had the right to introduce limited competition, open competition was an entire innovation which could be properly carried only through an Act of Parliament. But Sir George knew that the motion was merely one of approval.

[3] *Ibid.*

In England we need not be afraid to make the Civil Service too powerful. In France and Germany they fear this; for in countries where you have not got free institutions in full vigor and unfettered action, it may be a question whether it is desirable to concentrate all administrative and political power in a single class; but if I am told that in such a country as ours there is a danger of making the Civil Service too strong for the safety of the State, my answer is that the Commons of England are strong enough to prevent the growth of any power that may be prejudicial to the safety and liberties of the people. As long as the House of Commons continues to possess the strength it has derived from its origin, its history, and its character, it is idle, pusilanimous and womanish to talk with terror about making the Civil Service so strong in skill and knowledge that it may be likely to interfere with the free action and institutions of the country. England happily occupies in this respect a different position from other countries. In certain continental States the experiment may be perilous, but in England you may make the Civil Service as strong as you please—confident that the stronger you make it the more competent will you render it for the satisfactory transaction of the public business. The invitation is merely to make further trial, the result of which, as introduced in a modified form, has been such as to encourage you to proceed.

Gladstone's eloquent plea helped to carry the motion, but Sir George Lewis took no action and simply ignored the vote. For a year nothing further was heard of open competition.

In 1857, nothing daunted, Viscount Goderich reintroduced his motion of 1856 and carried it.

Resolved, That, in the opinion of this House, the experience acquired since the issuing of the Order in Council of the 21st of May, 1855, is in favour of adoption of the principle of competition as a condition of entrance to the Civil Service, and that the application of that principle ought to be extended in conformity with the Resolution of the House, agreed to on 24th day of April, 1856.

Palmerston agreed—not to open competition, but to limited competition among a number of approved candidates. Goderich rather lamely accepted this interpretation and the debate ended with matters much as before.

It is a way an experienced minister has of silencing an eloquent and inexperienced opponent: After all we both mean the same thing, there is no real difference of principle, merely a difference of language and definition. We agree etc., etc. The Ministry will do everything in its power to further this excellent motion, etc., etc. The ambitious gentlemen of the Opposition, somewhat staggered, accepts the minister's apparent conversion with cordial enthusiasm. The motion is passed as interpreted by the minister—and half an hour later when the House is appropriately discussing the Sleeping Sickness in Uganda, the eager young man suddenly realizes that the bland support of the minister has really crippled his motion.

One important assistance Parliament did give to the cause of reform. In 1859 the existing arrangements regarding superannuation, which consisted of periodical deductions from already slender wages, were changed. The important feature of the new Superannuation Law was that its benefits were restricted to civil servants who had entered the service *with the certificate of the Civil Service Commission.* Thus another door was banged in the face of backstairs employees. But had there been no provision for certification save by examination, an important class of higher officials appointed from public life, would have lost their pensions. Thus Clause 4 of the Superannuation Act of 1859 enacted that such persons shall be eligible for pensions.[1]

[1] 22 Victoria, c. 26. Clause IV provided: Commissioners of the

Let us see now what actual progress competition had made between 1855 and 1860.[1] In 1858 there were 230 competitions with 647 candidates. Thus the number of competitors did not average three candidates for a vacancy. There were 962 places allotted without competition by a qualifying examination or without it. Of these 962 places, 335 were clerkships in the upper division of the civil service. Below the grade of clerkships there was no competition at all. The Excise officers—numerically an important part of the civil service, and discharging duties of a higher order—were appointed by patronage. Not only was the service cheated of the benefits of competition, but the anticipated effect on the education of the masses, was lost. It was only by applying the principle of competition to places for which the humbler people were can-

Treasury may decide that professional or other peculiar qualifications not to be acquired in the public service are required and for the interest of the public, persons over age at which public service begins may be appointed, and such a person on retirement may have added to his service a number of years not exceeding 20, and the period of service required to entitle him to superannuation may be fixed by order or warrant at less than 10, and superannuation may be granted even though he does not hold appointment directly from the Crown, or may not have entered with a certificate from the Civil Service Commission.

Clause XVII enacted that no *person shall be deemed to have been in the permanent civil service of the state unless he holds his appointment directly from the Crown or has been admitted to the civil service with a certificate from the Civil Service Commission.*

[1] From 1854-1859, 10,860 nominees were examined. Of these nominations 8,039 were of one candidate only, *i. e.*, qualifying non-competitive examination. The 2,821 competitors were competing for 732 appointments, *i. e.*, four to one. In 1859, 391 competed for nine clerkships in the India office—the only example of open competition. Certificates were granted to 5,705; 1,972 were rejected in examinations, all but 106 *for deficiency in arithmetic and spelling;* 507 were rejected for health, character, and age. The examinations were mostly of clerks, Excise officers, tidewaiters, and letter carriers. *Parliamentary Papers,* 1860, xxiv.

didates that any considerable effect upon popular education could be produced.[1]

The Civil Service Commission commented on the fact that the old system of patronage still flourished. They urged that there should be at least three candidates for each vacancy. They pointed with satisfaction to the action of Lord Stanley in throwing open clerkships in the London India Office to competition with the result that there were over 300 candidates for eight places.

Even where there was competition, it was often illusory. Thus under the system of examining for each office separately, it often happened that the winner achieved a nominal victory over hopelessly stupid rivals who were sometimes nominated merely to simulate a race, and then retire from the contest. Among the blind the one-eyed man is king. Thus a prominent civil servant tells how he entered the civil service:

It was towards the end of the year 1859 that, fresh from Marlborough, I distinguished myself by gaining first place in a competition held by the Civil Service Commission for a clerkship in the Privy Council Office. Frankness compels me to add that the two other nominees (required by the regulations to make up the prescribed number of three) may have been the special couple known as the " Treasury Idiots " who could not pass anything and were sent up to give a walkover to any minister's protégé able to reach the minimum qualifications. At

---

[1] See *National Association for Promotion of Social Sciences*, vol. 1859, pp. 274-286. Even so, the stimulus which examinations, especially the optional ones, gave to education was considerable, though it did not touch the masses. King's College, London, opened a department of Civil Service and Commerce, with courses in Latin, American history, mathematics, English literature, modern history, geography, French, German, law, etc., for prospective civil service candidates and for commercial aspirants. *Cf. London Times*, April 20, 1854.

any rate, they could hardly read and write, and so I found myself entitled to a desk at Downing Street.[1]

The most acute criticism of the existing service was that of John Stuart Mill, the economist and social reformer, who spent the better part of his life as a civil servant in the India House. He had intimate personal experience of the civil service; he was a philosopher whose view embraced all the theory and practice of political science. Thus beyond most of his contemporaries in and out of the service, he comprehended the subject of competitive examination in its threefold significance—to efficiency, to political honesty, and to popular education.

Being, as a rule, appointed at the commencement of manhood, not as having learnt, but in order that they may learn, their profession, the only thing by which the best candidates can be discriminated, is proficiency in the ordinary branches of liberal education: and this can be ascertained without difficulty, provided there be the requisite pains and the requisite impartiality in those who are appointed to inquire into it. Neither the one nor the other can reasonably be expected from a minister; who must rely wholly on recommendations, and however disinterested as to his personal wishes, never will be proof against the solicitations of persons who have the power of influencing his own election, or whose political adherence is important to the ministry to which he belongs. These considerations have introduced the practice of submitting all candidates for first appointments to a public examination, conducted by persons not engaged in politics, and of the same class and quality with the examiners for honours at the Universities. This would probably be the best plan under any system; and under our parliamentary government it is the only one which affords a chance, I do not say of honest appointment, but even of abstinence from such as are manifestly and flagrantly profligate.

[1] Herbert Preston-Thomas, *The Work and Play of a Government Inspector.*

It is also absolutely necessary that the examinations should be competitive, and the appointments given to those who are most successful. A mere passing examination never, in the long run, does more than exclude dunces. When the question, in the mind of the examiner, lies between blighting the prospects of an individual, and neglecting a duty to the public which, in the particular instance, seldom appears of first-rate importance, and when he is sure to be bitterly reproached for doing the first; ... while in general no one will either know or care whether he has done the latter; the balance, unless he is a man of very unusual stamp, inclines to the side of good nature. A relaxation in one instance establishes a claim to it in others, which every repetition of indulgence makes it more difficult to resist; each of these in succession becomes a precedent for more, until the standard of proficiency sinks gradually to something almost contemptible. . . . Where there is no inducement to exceed a certain minimum, the minimum comes to be the maximum: it becomes the general practice not to aim at more. . . . When, on the contrary, the appointments are given to those, among a great number of candidates, who must distinguish themselves, and where the successful competitors are classed in order of merit, not only each is stimulated to do his very utmost, but the influence is felt in every place of liberal education throughout the country. It becomes with every schoolmaster an object of ambition, and an avenue to success, to have furnished pupils who have gained a high place in these competitions; and there is hardly any other mode in which the State can do so much to raise the quality of educational institutions throughout the country. Though the principle of competitive examinations for public employment is of such recent introduction in this country, and is still so imperfectly carried out, the Indian service being as yet nearly the only case in which it exists in its completeness, a sensible effect has already begun to be produced on the places of middle-class education; notwithstanding the difficulties which the principle has encountered from the disgracefully low existing state of education in this country, which these very examinations have brought into strong light. So contemptible has the standard of acquirement been found to be, among the youths who obtain the nomination from the minister ... that the competition of such candidates produces almost a poorer result, than would be obtained from a mere pass examination; ... it is said that successive years show on the whole a decline of attainments, less effort being made, because the results of former examinations have proved that the exertions then used were greater than would have been sufficient to attain the object. ... we have it on the word of the Commissioners that nearly all who have been unsuccessful have owed their failure to ignorance not of the higher branches of instruction, but of its very humblest elements—spelling and arithmetic.

The outcries which continue to be made against these examinations, by some of the organs of opinion, are often, I regret to say, as little creditable to the good faith as to the good sense of the assailants. They proceed partly by misrepresentation of the kind of ignorance, which, as a matter of fact, actually leads to failure in the examinations. They quote with emphasis the most recondite questions which can be shown to have been ever asked, and make it appear as if unexceptionable answers to all these were made the *sine quâ non* of success. Yet it has been repeated to satiety, that such questions are not put because it is expected of every-one that he should answer them, but in order that whoever is able to do so may have the means of proving and availing himself of that portion of his knowledge. It is not as a ground of rejection, but as an additional means of success, that this opportunity is given. We are then asked whether the kind of knowledge supposed in this, that, or the other question, is calculated to be of any use to the candidate after he has attained his object. People differ greatly in opinion as to what knowledge is useful. ... About one thing the objectors seem to be unanimous, that general mental cultivation is not useful in these employments, whatever else may be so. If, however (as I presume to think), it is useful, or if any education at all is useful, it must be tested by the tests most likely to show whether the candidate possesses it or not. To ascertain whether he has been well educated, he must be interrogated in the things which he is likely to know if he has been well educated, even though not directly pertinent to the work to which he is to be appointed. Will those who object to his being questioned in classics and mathematics, in a country where the only things regularly taught are classics and mathematics, tell us what they would have him questioned in? There seems, however, to be equal objection to examining him in these, and to examining him in anything *but* these. . . . Nothing will satisfy the objectors but free admission of total ignorance.

We are triumphantly told, that neither Clive nor Wellington could have passed the test which is prescribed for an aspirant for an engineer cadetship. As if, because Clive and Wellington did not do what was not required of them, they could not have done it if it had been required. If it be only meant to inform us that it is possible to be a great general without these things, so it is without many other things which are very useful to great generals. . . . We are next informed that bookworms, a term which seems to be held applicable to whoever has the slightest tincture of book-knowledge, may not be good at bodily exercise, or have the habits of a gentleman. This is a very common line of remark with dunces of condition; but whatever the dunces may think, they have no monopoly of either gentlemanly habits or bodily activity. Wherever these are needed, let them be inquired into, and separately provided for, not to the exclusion of mental qualifications, but in addition.[1]

The time had come for a second investigation into the civil service to see what progress had been made under the new order of things. The Civil Service Commission had weeded out numerous dunces. Limited competition was a great improvement but few offices made any attempt to insure *honest* competition, and the majority of places, par-

[1] J. S. Mill, *Representative Government* (London, 1876), pp. 108, 109.

ticularly in the lower branches of the service, were filled by single nomination. The recommendations of North-cote and Trevelyan were still mere paper—there was no open competition with high standards, no division of the service according to intellectual and mechanical labor, no promotion by merit and no attempt to grade the service as a whole. Classification of the service was haphazard and ill-defined. Since the introduction of limited com-petition able and highly educated young men had been attracted into offices which made no special provision for their ability, assimilated them with mere clerks, and gave them no hope of promotion to responsible positions. The attempts which had been made to give the most mechanical work, mere copying to a pariah class of ill-paid human ma-chines, had provoked widespread discontent and criticism.

Still, reform had made great strides. The House of Commons had put itself on record as favoring the exten-sion of the principle of competition. If it had not been proved that the public should have the right to compete for the public services, it had at least been demonstrated that honest competition was better than patronage and that open competition, where it had been attempted, introduced the most efficient men. The question of reform which had been obscured by fierce controversies, was beginning to stand out in the clear cold light of reason, if not in the sunshine of common sense.

Horace Mann, secretary of the Civil Service Commis-sion, put the matter tersely:

The question now stands pretty clear of all the real and imputed extravagancies of its advocates and opponents. Few persons now really believe that the friends of competition rely upon it as an *infallible* test of official aptitude, or as any-thing more than the best available test; nor are there many persons who really believe that such infallible guarantee is

secured when the Secretary to the Treasury appoints an unknown youth, upon the mere recommendation of a political
friend to whom he is equally unknown. . . . The only question . . . now is as to the extent to which the plan, thus
generally appreciated, should be adopted, and the rate at
which we should proceed in the work.[1]

[1] *Transactions, National Association for the Promotion of Social
Science*, vol. iii, p. 279.

CHAPTER V

John Bright and Others Investigate, 1860—Open Competition Introduced, 1870

> " The opening of the civil and military services, in its influence upon national education, is equivalent to a hundred thousand scholarships and exhibitions of the most valuable kind—because unlike such rewards in general, they are for life —offered for the encouragement of youthful learning and good conduct in every class of the community."—Sir Charles Trevelyan. Letter to Mr. Eaton.

THE House of Commons awoke from the usual period of indifference to the existence of the civil service reform question.   It could not be said that the question was acute. The service was conscientious and fairly efficient, but the supporters of open competition were increasing and the opponents of patronage were beginning to arouse democratic opinion against it.   There were, in fact, two classes who favored open competition, differing in emphasis: those who favored open competition because they were sure that it would improve the service, and those in favor of it because they thought that the service should be open to the public.   The history of the English civil service is peculiarly valuable because it proves that these two ideals are identical, that the public service should be open to public competition, and that public competition recruits the most efficient civil service.

The Estimates Debate of 1860 gave the civil service reformers their annual opportunity to taunt the Ministry for inaction. A certain Mr. Hennessey moved for a committee to investigate the methods of attracting men into the service. He said that he had tried to get one of his constituents on the nominating list but, being an independent member, had failed. The Ministry opposed Mr. Hennessey. Even Sir Stafford Northcote said that the time was not ripe for inquiry. A Treasury Under Secretary again brought out the startling fact that competition had been attempted only in China, and Palmerston, probably caught unawares, said something about the danger of attracting all first class intelligence into the civil service to the permanent detriment of the independent private concerns.[1] Mr. Roebuck made short work of these objections.

Suppose A B, one of my constituents, comes to me and says, ' I have a son whom I want to compete for a situation in the Home Office. Do you think you can get his name put down for me?' I answer, ' I have no doubt of that. I shall be able to do so.' I go to the Home Office and, because I am an M.P. I get what I ask for. But that is not open competition. Suppose that man was not one of my constituents. Suppose he was a person of no importance in the borough or county in which he lived, and yet had a large family of children, one of whom wished to compete for a public appointment; if he did not know an M.P. or some one of influence, he would have no more chance of admission to this competition than I now have of competing for the seat of the Great Mogul. By a competitive system we have obtained first-rate men for India. And what harm can possibly arise from this inquiry? The honorable gentleman says this subject is not ripe for inquiry. What! is it not ripe for ascertaining what the present practice is? For, remember, that is the real question before us. We wish, in fact, to lay bare what you now

[1] Hansard, February 16, 1860.

do that the world may know what your system of competition is, which I denounce here as an absolute sham, covered up under a stale pretense.

The motion was agreed to and a committee of investigation, including Lord Stanley, Sir Stafford Northcote, Mr. Roebuck, Mr. Bright, Monckton Milnes, and Robert Low, was appointed to inquire into nominations and examinations only and to afford greater facility for the admission of properly qualified persons.[1]

At this point (1860) a table of persons employed in the civil service may not be uninteresting:

I Heads of Departments—political	34
Heads of Departments—non-political	156
II Sub-heads of Departments and heads of branches	1,489
Clerks—established	13,768
Clerks—temporary	389
III Professional officers—superior	1,922
Professional officers—inferior	1,921
IV Inferior officers—indoor	2,259
Inferior officers—outdoor	36,566
V Artisans and labourers	29,613
VI Persons not wholly employed—women, etc.	14,941
	103,058

The first and sixth classes did not fall under the cognizance of the committee; nor did the artisan and labourers; nor were professional examinations closely inquired into, except in so far as solicitors' departments were concerned, and here the committee thought that no system attracts men as well qualified as those obtained by appointment of persons of standing in their professions. The investigation dealt with clerks, higher and lower, and inferior officers such as excise officers, tidewaiters, letter carriers, etc.

[1] *Parliamentary Papers*, 1860, ix, referred to hereafter as *1860 Report*.

The committee began on the supposition that the higher clerks enter upon routine work but that they rise to influential positions in the offices of the Treasury and secretaries of state, but that the lower clerks are chiefly employed in the revenue departments where intellectual qualifications are highly desirable, but not the same " liberal education, knowledge of men, and general information as are essential in higher departments."

The committee went about its work very thoroughly, though the explicitness of questions and the restriction of the inquiry to leading members of the civil service, gave little opportunity to the rank and file, or to the educator and political theorist, to air grievances and paint official Utopias. Indeed there is in the inquiry none of the fight and rhetoric of the first discussion of 1854, nor of subsequent investigations.

The investigation of 1860 showed that limited competition was successful where it was fairly tried, that many of the opponents of open competition had been converted, but that there were still a considerable number of officials who feared open competition and laid the emphasis upon personal qualities which could not be tested by an academic education at all. There was a small number of reactionaries and malcontents who were constitutionally wedded to patronage. These had never given competition a fair trial in their departments, and grumbled about the new clerks who had not been under observation long enough to demonstrate their superiority.

A few quotations will suffice to show the diversity of opinions and to indicate the logical weakness of the reactionaries.

Romilly, chairman of the Board of Audit, granted that there had been a decided improvement in the clerks admitted since 1855; but he was strenuously opposed to the introduction of unlimited competition—there being no responsibility for appointment and no assurance of moral character in the case of open competition.   Mr. Romilly thought the certificates of character of no value.   As a matter of fact nominations to his department had been made *singly* by the Treasury, the examinations being merely qualifying.   But when Mr. Romilly himself was examined he showed the weakness of his philosophy of patronage.

Q. Would you give me some reason which would justify your belief that the Treasury are in any way competent to determine the moral qualities of a man, or his capacity for or his willingness to work in his department? . . .

A. He can know nothing of him in that respect.

Q. Therefore, what guarantee is there or any security for the moral qualifications of this man?

A. I do not think that there is any full security at all.

Q. Practically, is there any?

A. I think that you are more likely to get a man who will do his duty in the public office to which he is appointed in that way, than if you had open and public competition.[1]

Similarly, Bromley, the Accountant General of the Navy, did not believe in competition.   He believed in minimum standards and favored examinations graded according to the age of nominees.   Throughout his testimony he showed the bias of a man who had worked his way up from the bottom of the service.   He disliked the higher examinations which did not exist in his day.   Having hmself been frequently transferred or promoted from department to department, he believed in the fusion of all departments into one service and free transfer therein.[2]   Bromley

[1] *1860 Report*, p. 201.

[2] This proposal comes up frequently.   It was first suggested in 1854 by Northcote and Trevelyan.   Apart from the impossibility of putting

conceded that the new men were much superior, even in their devotion to the details of office work. At the same time he hoped that the link of patronage between the House of Commons and the civil service would never be severed, and foresaw bureaucracy as the result of competition.

I trust that the system will never be carried to open competition. . . . As an old public servant, I hope never to see that kindred feeling or tie which exists between Members of the House of Commons and the public service severed. My belief is, that if you carry the system forward to open competition, Members of the House of Commons will in time lose that interest in the civil service which they now in a great degree feel for it.[1]

Parliament and the civil service should not be separated, said Mr. Bromley. Let us see now how the patronage business was worked, and how members of Parliament themselves liked it. Mr. Fremantle, secretary to the Patronage Secretary of the Treasury, gave most arresting

it into practice on a large scale, it is radically against the theory of administrative and executive cabinet government. The temporary executive head of a department, the Minister, comes with his broad, general experience of policies from public life. He depends for his knowledge of the intimate workings and traditions of his department upon the permanent head of the office. If this permanent head is to be a gypsy head, transferred from one department to another, the Minister will have to depend in turn upon a still lower official who had been, through some oversight, permitted to remain in the department in question long enough to understand its economy and to represent its traditions. This is a dangerous practice. It is simply creating new strata of ministers. It is quite feasible, though by no means always desirable, to transfer younger clerks and even exceptionally higher officials, but to have a constantly shifting personnel in every office is unthinkable.

[1] *1860 Report*, p. 224.

testimony relative to petty local positions under the Treasury.

Q. Where a lower-class office is vacant, do you say that you generally place the appointment at the disposal of the sitting Member?

A. Yes.

Q. If that sitting Member did not happen to be a supporter of the Government, as a general practice, is it sent to him?

A. As a general practice, not . . .

Q. Is there any reason why all those [tidewaiter] persons in a particular port who are qualified to fill that office should not compete for it?

A. No, except that I should not consider it worth while, for the situation referred to, to test the relative qualifications of 20 or 30 candidates. . . .

Q. Have you very frequently heard complaints from Members of Parliament, that, although this was, as it were, a duty which they could not escape, yet it was one the performance of which was very irksome, and which did them, politically speaking, damage in their boroughs, because of the number of people whom it was necessary to disappoint, and of the very few who could be satisfied?

A. We have received many such complaints.

Q. Do you believe, generally, that Members of Parliament are at all anxious for this sort of patronage?

A. No.

Q. Do you believe that it is at all necessary that the Government, for any of those purposes of strengthening their party, or matters which you will thoroughly well understand, and which always have existed, and which do exist, and which have been looked upon as a sort of necessity, should have in their hands patronage of this kind, or, if they have it in their hands, should entrust it at all for any political purposes to Members of Parliament.

A. Certainly not, so far as any advantage to the Government is concerned.

Q. In your opinion this system, which is generally supposed to be one by which the Government of the day gratifies its supporters, and strengthens its own hands, answers neither the one purpose nor the other; that it does not gratify the supporters of the Government, and does not strengthen the hands of the Government.

A. No. I think this has even been more the case since the system of competitive examinations has been introduced.

Q. Are you aware that since the competitive examinations have been introduced, Members of Parliament or other gentlemen who have recommended to you candidates, have been exceedingly annoyed by complaints from unsuccessful candidates?

A. Yes.

Q. The system, according to your experience, is one full of inconvenience to the gentlemen who recommend, and is of no great value to the Government?

A. That is so. . . .

Q. Are you, then, of opinion that the Government ought to abandon that patronage?

A. Certainly not; it is the duty of the Government to find candidates for the appointments, and to make appointments to the public service.[1]

---

[1] *1860 Report*, pp. 59, 60, 62, 63. It seems that the Treasury had arrogated to itself the right of nominations in the Customs and Excise departments. For instance, formerly the commissioners of the Inland Revenue had all the indoor appointments in the Excise. In 1830 the Treasury took half; in 1858 the last commissioner who had patronage died, and the Treasury took all the patronage except 10 per cent of the outdoor offices which the commissioner was allowed to give to sons of employees. Thus, in the Excise Department at least, limited competition was very exceptional. There were mostly simple nominations on the recommendations of members of Parliament or of the cabinet, for which no one was accountable. In the Land Tax Department, the Land Tax Commissioners were appointed by parliamentary patronage, and these in turn appointed the assessors, who in turn appointed the collectors, who gave security for collecting the

Lingen, the secretary to the Committee of the Council on Education, favored the existing system of division into two distinct classes, the inspectors, who were mostly university men, who had taken high honors and who "must be persons of standing in society," and a second clerical division of three sections. Lingen saw no reason why there should not be open competition for the lower division, but quite irrationally he thought open competition inapplicable to the higher division. Strangely enough, this opinion prevails even now in this department and has staunch supporters in present and former secretaries.

On the other hand, the Under Secretary for the Colonies, Merivale, and the Under Secretary for the Home Office, Waddington, and the Registrar General, Graham, had modified their views since 1854. Waddington now thought open competition fairer to the public and had no fears on the score of moral character, but he thought the expense and difficulty of examining hordes of candidates would not be justified by the results. Merivale still opposed competition on principle, but he had had no inefficient men since 1854, and favored an extension of limited competition at any rate. Graham, whose office had formerly been a sad example of the effects of unregulated patronage,[1] gave eloquent testimony to the improvements

revenue. These last were often dishonest, and their bankruptcy left the government without a remedy:

Q. "And the subsequent consequence is that by reason of these collectors not being appointed by the government, but appointed by private commissioners, persons are re-taxed for the amount of the deficiencies incurred?" A. "Yes." (Evidence of Sargent, *1860 Report*.)

[1] His office, we remember, was one of the worst. Suddenly supplemented in 1836, when the registration of births, marriages, and deaths came into effect, this office was filled with incompetents, insolvent debtors, the diseased, the aged, and the crippled. In the course of time

effected by competition, and now declared himself in favor of open competition, with perhaps some restriction, so as to get dependable references.

The Under Secretary of State for War, Sir Benjamin Hawes, showed that the right to compete for his department was very freely granted to applicants even without any political influence. But the final choice rested with the Secretary of War, and Hawes conceded that there was little responsibility for it and that the moral qualities which competition could not test, were not assured in the existing scheme either. In Hawes' department the method of a appointment was peculiarly bad. All clerks were appointed as temporary clerks for one month. Then they went to the Civil Service Commission for a certificate and were allowed to compete for permanent, established clerkships. Sometimes as many as sixty competed for one place. This was real competition, but when we consider that clerks competed again and again for the establishment, and that those who did not succeed were still employed in the *same work* as the established clerk, we see the beginning of a state of affairs which was to cause much bitterness throughout this and other departments. As to the success of the public school and university men, whose adaptability and capacity for drudgery had been doubted, Hawes lent eloquent testimony.

Q. Have you the means of testing the effect of competitive examination different from those which most offices have?

A. I am bound to say that men who have obtained honours

Graham succeeded in getting many of them removed. After twenty-four years only the seventeen best were left, two deaf and dumb men among them whom Graham liked very much and who were said to be very competent.

at Cambridge or at Oxford, or at public schools, who have shown themselves superior scholars, and who have succeeded in obtaining appointments, have formed admirable clerks; I avoid mentioning names, but I could refer to instances of men who have not flinched from the official drudgery, and who have worked themselves into the office, and have given the greatest possible satisfaction.[1]

One of the real grievances brought out in the report was the tendency to make examination standards too high, and thus to attract a class of men too cultured and too ambitious for the positions and prospects open to them. This was especially true in the case of the supplementary clerkships. Naturally enough many reactionaries took advantage of this maladjustment in organization and examination to blame the unfavorable results on competition and to see an additional argument against its extension.

In answer to questions about usefulness of clerks, tidewaiters, etc., appointed since the Order in Council of May, 1855, a Customs officer said:

Having had several clerks under my supervision who have been admitted into the service since May, 1855, and also several who were appointed within the six years preceding the examinations by the Civil Service Commissioners, I am enabled to state that I have not found that the former display any greater energy or aptitude for business than the latter; and, although generally tractable, I have experienced, both personally and towards the public, a self-sufficiency and presumption, from an imagined superiority in having undergone such examination, and also a desire for literature in business, that I have been obliged to check.

The business of this office being of perfectly routine character, and in many branches almost mechanical, no superior mental acquirement is needed; and clerks possessing more in-

[1] *1860 Report*, p. 90.

tellectual capabilities than the duties demand become dissatisfied with its monotony, and are less valuable than clerks of sufficient though less attainment.[1]

He complained that the civil service tidewaiters and other manual laborers recently appointed were totally unfitted for the duties, and that those who failed were often thoroughly efficient men used to the sea from boyhood.

Anthony Trollope had the artist's love of *The Three Clerks* who dwelt in the lights and shades of the crazy shanties and back alleys of the old Post Office. He shuddered at the notion of tearing it all down, and constructing a new Post Office with a new race of over-educated prigs with no regard for the good old days. Trollope and Tilley, his brother-in-law, gave evidence for the Post Office. Their antagonism to open competition, even to extending limited competition, was quite unconcealed.[2] They said

[1] *1860 Report*, appendix, p. 339.

[2] The statistics of the Post Office show a deplorable confusion in classification, nomination and pay. There were three nominations for one vacancy and the pay ranged from £80 to £800. Examinations were conducted by the Civil Service Commission. Sorters and letter carriers were chosen by pure nomination and qualifying examinations. The Civil Service Commission urged a higher educational test, but the Post Office authorities steadily refused. The Civil Service Commission characterized the qualifications for sorters, letter carriers, etc., as:

(1) Writing their own names and addresses.

(2) Reading the addresses of letters.

(3) Adding a few figures together.

Postmasters in London and large towns were appointed by the Postmaster General; in smaller towns by the Treasury. No examinations were necessary.

Postmasters appointed for the first time (who had not been in the service before with the Civil Service Commission certificate) were not entitled to superannuation under the Superannuation Act of :859 (22 Victoria, ch. 26). Hence they got no superannuation benefits.

A number of auxiliary letter carriers were appointed, some of whom never went before the Civil Service Commission and thus remained at 9 shillings a week and did not qualify for superannuation.

Letter carriers worked 47 hours and got 18 shillings per week pay. (*1861 Reports*, vol. xix.)

that the new clerks were not more or less useful than before and came from the same class. Some who had passed higher examinations were less contented and less good clerks than others, some not as well trained. Knowledge beyond what was required for performance of duties was not advisable.

They had no objection to an open examination in which the physical qualities were emphasized—like the police examination—for lower positions, but not for clerkships. The reason given for this distinction was that qualities which make a good clerk are not discoverable by examination. They believed that open competition would introduce better educated but less efficient men. However, it might be that men of intelligence were needed.

Trollope and Tilley were no doubt right in saying that intellectual talents of a very high order were not necessary in the Post Office. But there were departments in which they *were* very necessary. For instance, in the department of the Solicitor to the Board of Inland Revenue. In this board there were five classes of clerks. A knowledge of law was necessary to achieve high position, and could not be easily learned and practiced by inexperienced minor clerks.

Here was a case in which there was need of higher requirements—either professional or academic. The solution of this question is interesting. How should the Solicitor's Office attract young men who would be capable of promotion to its highest positions? It was only very exceptionally that a junior clerk qualified himself for the higher clerkships without having entered with training in a solicitor's office. On the other hand, it was found that able young men with solicitor's training entering the lowest positions, were for some time forced to do mechanical work which any clerk could perform. Under such conditions it was becoming almost impossible to get young solicitors of ability and thus it was often necessary to appoint older men, usually solicitors of standing, directly to superior offices. This is one of the ever-recurring problems of civil service in every country—the greatest problem of the national civil service of the United States.

Evidently there are three ways of solving it—first, you may divide the office into two classes, the second to consist of ordinary clerks who do not expect to rise to the higher division, which consists of men with a legal and academic education and destined for the highest positions. This is the German system. Again, you may have similar classes, with the upper division recruited from university scholars of distinction who are expected to acquire the necessary legal knowledge *while* serving their apprenticeship. This is the system which was finally adopted in England and has proved very successful, especially where the legal knowledge—*e. g.* in the higher clerical work of the Inland Revenue—is incident to general administrative and clerical ability and a high order of general intelligence. There is a third method in vogue in Australia—that of attracting a single class of young men of sound high-school education, and giving them, either entirely in government offices, or partly in government offices and partly in university evening courses, the necessary academic and technical education.

The American system is, to attract a very miscellaneous and often ill-educated division of clerks by quasi-competitive examinations of the lowest conceivable standard, and to wait in vain for them to develop first-rate administrative ability.[1]

_____

[1] The Department of Justice is a conspicuous exception. In the first place the duties here are entirely legal—hence only men with legal

The most interesting, and indeed conclusive, evidence as to actual experience of open competition was that of an ex-official of the Privy Council Office.   He showed that in an obscure, roundabout way open competition had already been vindicated in the civil service.   It seems that Mr. Chester and others were much interested in an examining and prize-giving institution known as the Society of Arts—which was founded to spread knowledge through the middle and lower classes.   Its examinations were absolutely open; the competitions were large; and the prizes and publicity stimulated extraordinary efforts.   Among the successful candidates for Society of Arts' certificates were merchants, artisans, bookkeepers, engineers, laborers, clerks, mechanics, etc.   A chimney sweep got a certificate in geometry; and a first prize in Latin was awarded to an ambitious butcher.   Palmerston, Derby and others fostered this movement by giving several nominations in the civil service—presumably in the Privy Council Office— to the Society of Arts; and the men whom the society chose to compete for the final civil service examinations were not only always successful, but almost always first and second on the list, and became exemplary clerks.   Mr. Chester pointed to this record and pressed home the conclusion that an experiment which was so successful on a small scale certainly deserved further trial.   Mr. Chester made no secret of his adherence to open competition. Everyone, he thought, had a *prima facie* right to be a candidate.   But he desired to combine open competition with a direct stimulus to popular education through institutions

training are admitted; but the standards of examination and personal qualifications recently introduced by an Assistant Attorney General are admirable—in fact, if they are adhered to under the new administration, the Department of Justice should within the next decade be almost on a level with the German departments of justice.

like the Society of Arts; and he thought that his improvement once carried out by the government, would be adopted by almost all private employers and public companies.

Where the spirit of patronage rules, the appointments are given, to a great extent, as a reward for political services, without the least reference to the ability or knowledge, or fitness of the person appointed; but I have no doubt that private persons will find it to their interest, by and bye, to institute competitions of this kind, in order that they may get the best clerks; and, indeed, very large numbers of public and private persons, merchants, bankers, directors of railroads, and managers of public companies, have signed a declaration, approving of the scheme of examination instituted by the Society of Arts, and stating that in the distribution of their appointments, they will regard the certificates of the society as testimonials worthy of attention.[1]

Mr. Chester's imagination, coupled with his interest in the Society of Arts, carried him a little too far. The idea that the youth of the lower classes would compete furiously for all kinds of employments by the methods of the correspondence school and the village debating society, and that employers would unhesitatingly accept the resulting certificates of merit with effusive cordiality, had an unsuspecting element of humor to which *Punch* might have devoted a page or two with advantage.

It remains now to consider the official suggestions of the Civil Service Commission itself. They complained that a minimum standard could not be maintained in the face of several successive rejections;[2] that moral qualities did not

---

[1] *1860 Report*, p. 288.

[2] The number of candidates who received absolute nominations in 1858, after being rejected for similar or lower positions within the preceding year, was 53; 35 passed the second examination, and one persistent individual was rejected after four attempts.

enter into nominations.   However, the commission thought
that it was not wise to adopt open competition at once.
Two extensions were suggested, one by the commissioners,
the other by the secretary to the commission, Horace Mann.

Horace Mann had a scheme of open competition limited
by nominations by persons of approved positions, members of Parliament, magistrates, clergymen, ministers,
schoolmasters, etc., that is, open competition with certificates from approved persons.   After a first general
examination, the names of acceptable candidates were
placed in order; then examinations were held in subjects especially prescribed for different departments, and
these marks were added and persons qualified for each
department were put down in order of standing.   That
Mr. Mann was not a thorough-going democrat can
be seen in his Machiavellian suggestion that first divisions clerkships could be restricted to the higher classes,
where necessary, by raising educational standards or adding a subject like Greek.   Mr. Mann suggested a similar
course of preliminary and final examination for the second
division.   In case this plan should seem to the committee
too radical, Mr. Mann put forward an alternative plan: in
case limited competition were retained, there should be a
preliminary examination between nominees, followed by
a final competition between qualified candidates for all departments, a proportion of four candidates for each vacancy
being maintained, resulting in a single list of successful candidates from which the heads of offices might choose at
will.[1]

[1] To Mr. Mann, among others, the English civil service owes the
suggestion of a scheme which has had the most unfortunate consequences—the blind-alley employment of boys to do mechanical work.
He advocated hiring boys between fifteen and eighteen, because they
were *more tractable and docile*.   These should be kept only for a few
years and should not enjoy increasing salaries—12 or 15 shillings a
week would be quite enough.   This might interfere with the careers of

Sir Edward Ryan and Sir John Shaw Lefevre, the civil service commissioners, favored Mann's alternative plan and suggested nomination and a preliminary examination, followed by a final examination between at least three qualified candidates for each vacancy, as many vacancies as possible being grouped together in a single competition. In the final examination more latitude should be given to candidates. A wide range of subjects was suggested, and the Macaulay scheme of deducting marks to discourage smattering was adopted.

The committee in its finding sought the points common to the Ryan and Mann plans, but first they dealt with the old question of a division of the service.

What is demanded of a candidate for a junior clerkship in the office of a Secretary of State may appear unnecessary if we look only to the duties which he has to perform at the time of his first appointment; but when it is remembered that in the course of some years he will be placed in a position of great responsibility, and will have a large share in the conduct of affairs requiring much tact and discretion, it will be evident that it is important to take security for his general intelligence, and for his having received a liberal education.

The clerk in the Revenue departments, the Audit Office, the Somerset House branch of the Admiralty, and similar departments, are mainly occupied with accounts; and their qualifications for appointment may be more directly tested; yet even in these cases the difference between men of intelligence and mere machines is very considerable, and the public are gainers by the introduction of men of good education into these

some, but many boys are idle at this age, and others could prepare for higher civil service places in the evening, or could, by being given twenty pounds extra for each year in service, save enough to go out to the colonies. Thus the government gets its work done cheaply and well, and saves superannuation. Mr. Mann estimated the saving, exclusive of superannuation, at £30,000.

branches of the service, provided they are not repelled by the unattractive nature of the work required of them.

With regard to inferior appointments, while there is no doubt that the better educated men, if equal to their fellows in all other respects, will be the more valuable servants, yet, considering the nature of the duties they have to discharge, the importance of physical and moral qualifications is in these cases much higher than that of intellectual attainments.[1]

The committee decided that there should be a final competition among at least three qualified candidates for each vacancy, but that this examination system should not apply to positions where the qualifications were mainly physical—such as postmen, laborers, etc.; that the final examination, being calculated to test relative merit with respect to intelligence and industry, should allow more latitude in subjects as in the Indian civil service, and guard against smattering. On the strict maintenance of the rule of the preliminary pass examinations it depended whether the subsequent competitive trial would be real or illusory. Several vacancies were to be competed for at once, but the Mann suggestion of a single general list was repudiated. More stimulating arrangements for promotion were urged, and a suggestion was made that nominations to lower positions be used to stimulate the work of elementary schools and educational societies. Finally the committee suggested that open competition should be tried gradually, beginning with one or two departments. Thus a ground for comparison would be afforded and the ultimate extension determined.

The conclusion of the report shows the weakness of the compromise as well as its strength—the weakness of supporting the prescriptive right of perquisites, and the strength

[1] *1860 Report*, p. ix.

of a slow and deliberate advance of open competition, conquering by the overwhelming force of logic and fact.

Already the Civil Service in India, the Medical Service, the
Public Works Department in India, and the scientific branches
of the military profession, both in regard of the Imperial and
of the Indian army, have been thrown open to all competitors; nor does there appear, either in Parliament or among
the people, any disposition to regret or to draw back from the
large concessions thus made to public opinion at the expense
of private patronage.

But Your Committee, for the very reason that leads them to
desire the ultimate success of the competitive method, are
anxious to avoid such precipitancy in its adoption as might
possibly lead to a temporary reaction of public feeling. They
do not conceal from themselves that, in proportion as the
practice of simple nomination is departed from, private interests are disturbed, the prescriptive custom of political patronage is broken in upon, and many persons exercising local influence find themselves no longer able to obtain for relatives
and dependents that ready admission into public offices which
was formerly within their reach. If to these causes of natural
jealousy be added the prevailing and not unreasonable dis-
trust of administrative changes, proceeding on a principle
which, until of late years, has received no general recognition,
it is evident that much deliberation and prudence are necessary
before proceeding to carry out to its full extent the system
recommended by the Commissioners of 1853.[1]

As a result of this report the Civil Service Commissioners
at the invitation of the Treasury advised (1) a preliminary examination, including orthography, handwriting,
arithmetic, composition, bookkeeping, and in solicitor's
offices, Latin. This examination might be from a list of
special nominees, or open to all with a provision for nom-

[1] *1860 Report*, p. xiv.

inations from the successful list.   The Treasury, of course, chose the first scheme and thus retained patronage from the beginning.   The preliminary examination marks were not to count toward (2) a final competitive examination with an average of five or at least three candidates for each vacancy, including the preliminary subjects and in addition the present final subjects; (3) a *prima facie* evidence of character, health, etc., on the part of each candidate, but no physical examinations.[1]

These suggestions of the Civil Service Commissioners, together with the suggestions embodied in the report of 1860, were adopted by the Treasury and by most of the other departments.   The results were most gratifying. Thus in the competition of 1865, two out of every five candidates were rejected *in the preliminary examination;* in 1866, 196 out of 411; and in 1867, 244 out of 540 official nominees vindicated the disinterested good judgment of their patrons by failing in the most elementary subjects. Up to 1869 the Civil Service Commissioners had rejected on the written examinations 8,169 out of 66,519 candidates and they said, significantly:

" If the subjects of examination be divided into two classes, one

[1] *1861 Report,* xix, *Sixth Report of Civil Service Commissioners.* Furthermore, the commissioners stated that they would emphasize the physical requirements for lower Customs' positions, and regretted greatly that the Duke of Argyll, who had promised to raise the physical requirements and to institute open competition in the Post Office, had given up this idea on taking office and had allowed the old patronage to go on.   The commissioners also referred to the increasing numbers of copying clerks, who occupied anomalous semi-permanent and often responsible positions in several departments.   They even outnumbered the permanent clerks in the War Office and Admiralty, some being promoted to permanent clerkships in the former office after repeated attempts at the examination.   There were too many messengers, office helpers, etc., who, having previously been in domestic service, were appointed at a late age and kept in the service long after they became inefficient.

including reading, spelling, handwriting, arithmetic, and (in the case of each department), the subjects connected with the practical work of that office; the other comprising those which are prescribed as tests of general intelligence and cultivation; the number of rejections caused by failures in the latter class of subjects has been only 271, as against 7899 cases of failures in the former class." [1]

We have seen that real limited competition after a preliminary examination had been introduced. The system had been extended to the dockyards, to the public services of Ceylon and Mauritius, to the Irish constabulary and to the inspectors of schools. Wherever the new rules were accepted, there was an improvement in clerks, or at least a further elimination of the unfit. As the success of competition became more manifest, the ideal and practical value of patronage declined. The heads of offices could not fail to ridicule a system of patronage which introduced so many incompetents to be "plucked" at a childish preliminary examination; and politicians ceased to attach importance to their patronage when they could no longer insure their nominees the certainty of appointment.

Everyone was tired of the patronage system. In 1870 the Treasury, by a famous Order in Council, abolished patronage and set up open competition. This Order in Council is of great importance—with certain slight modifications it remains in force today. Its outstanding features were these: (1) open competition; (2) two divisions.

No person was hereafter to be employed in any department, unless tested and reported qualified by the Civil Service Commission after competitive examinations.

Schedule A contained the famous programs for class I and class II. In class I it created a list of departments

[1] Eaton, *op. cit.*, p. 26.

which were willing to subscribe to regulations for a staff of highly trained university men distinct from the ordinary clerks.

The clerkships to be filled up under the scheme for Class I were designed to be a new creation, not necessarily coinciding with any of the clerkships already existing in public offices. The initial salary was to be in all cases £100 a year, and the successful competitors were to rise by seniority to £400 a year, being subsequently eligible for the highest permanent posts in the Civil Service. A certain proportion of them, too, on whom the more responsible duties devolved, were to get, in addition to the ordinary maximum of £400 a year, extra or duty pay, not exceeding £200 a year in any case. These Class I clerkships were to be few and far between, one or two being calculated to be sufficient to direct intelligently the work of an entire office.[1]

The program for Class II was to supersede the innumerable schemes of examinations then in force for the various offices, and from candidates successful under it the vast body of existing clerkships were to be filled. But no attempt was made to equalize the salaries in the departments. Hence, as the initial salaries and prospects of promotion differed marvelously—and, it may be added, illogically—in different offices, these certificates were, in the order of their position on the successful list, allowed to select the Department to which they wished to be appointed, and there was for the most part an astonishing gap between the respective prospects of the first and of the last of the successful candidates.[2]

It is important to note that the Order in Council provided in its famous Clause VII a means by which specially qualified outsiders might be admitted to the service without

[1] W. J. Chetwode-Crawley, LL.D., D. C. L. (London, 1890), *Handbook of Competitive Examinations.*
[2] *Ibid.*

examination, upon the recommendation of the Treasury and the head of the office in question, and certificated by the Civil Service Commission. Moreover, situations to which the holder was appointed directly by the crown were exempted, and also those exempted under the Superannuation Act of 1859,[1] which, it will be remembered, denied pensions to those not examined and passed by the Civil Service Commission. These two acts all taken together —the Superannuation Act of 1859 and the Order in Council of 1870—have closed the English civil service to patronage, insured competitive examinations, and introduced vital distinctions in educational standards, without excluding exceptional appointments without examination of persons engaged in other pursuits, and peculiarly or professionally qualified.

It is needless to comment at length upon the deficiencies of this class I and class II system. Neither the Civil Service Commissioners, the Treasury, nor the Privy Council had any power to determine what offices had need of the Schedule A clerks. This list was fixed by consultations with the heads of offices. The Civil Service Commissioners, India Office, Board of Trade, Treasury, War Office, and Post Office signified their willingness to adopt the Schedule A rules. But this bargaining with department heads had very bad effects. Those heads who refused to adopt a first division, simply gave first division clerkships to second division men.

This, together with the existing differences of pay and prospects amongst the various grades of second division clerks in different offices, resulted in confusion, discontent, jealousy and bitterness, together with a loss in money and efficiency to the government which was none the less real because it could not be exactly calculated.

The following decade of civil service history marks

[1] Under Schedule B.

the attempts to remedy this state of affairs, and the important events of the decade are the findings of two commissions—one in 1873 on economy, the other in 1875 on the efficiency and standardization of the service.

Before turning to the work of the commissions of 1873 and 1875, it is worth while in passing to note the birth of the flourishing organ of civil service opinion, *The Civilian.* The first issue of *The Civilian* appeared in 1869. It was published as a weekly journal for civil service clerks in the Revenue departments, but is now, as its sub-title claims, " the accredited organ of the Civil Service." It has had a most honorable career. Apart from civil service news and editorials, it has always had considerable literary merit. Though at times somewhat pretentious and imitative, the best issues have not been inferior to those of the English political weeklies. It is hardly necessary to draw any comparisons between *The Civilian* and the writings of American civil servants. Washington clerks are quite incapable of such a publication.

From 1869 to the present time, *The Civilian* has exercised considerable influence in molding the opinions of the servants of the state, so that today they form a corporate body with a distinct program of rights and, for better or worse, a growing consciousness of the possibility of political action in their own behalf.

It would be a mistake to suppose that *The Civilian* is a democratic paper, in the sense that the publications of the French socialistic or syndicalistic civil servants are democratic. The editors of *The Civilian* are and have been higher second division clerks, who constitute the *haute bourgeoisie* of the civil service, and are just as anxious to preserve their distinction from the lower ranks of the service, as they are to break down the barriers which separate them from the first division. Moreover, *The Civilian,* besides agitating for reform and discovering abuses, has had an honorable record for benefit insurance and charitable work, has stimulated discussion and writing, and has been, in general, the source or organ of every honorable movement among the clerks and the rank and file of the civil service.

CHAPTER VI

FURTHER INVESTIGATIONS—THE REACTION—THE DECADE OF SCEPTICISM

THE period between the Order for open competition in 1870 and the third great investigation into the civil service from 1873 to 1875, is one of gradual adaptation.

In 1873 Sir Stafford Northcote, now Chancellor of the Exchequer, appointed a select committee " to inquire whether any and what reductions can be effected in the expenditures for the civil service." [1] Every class of officers and employees from the Chancellor to the post boys was examined.

The prior investigations had been directed to the best means of selecting and promoting officers, to the discipline, duties and methods best adapted to secure honest and efficient administration. This had for its object retrenchment and economy, in harmony with the new system. Nothing is more significant, in connection with this inquiry, than the fact that it could be ordered with such breadth and carried forward with such completeness and severity. When members could see that retrenchment might abolish places they wished to fill, send back to them their poor dependents, or cut down the salaries of partisan henchmen to whom they owed a debt of gratitude—[to say nothing of the scandals which such results might disclose]—how could they be expected to have courage for economy? But limited competition, from 1855 to 1870, having excluded most of the unworthy, and open competition, since 1870, hav-

[1] *Parliamentary Papers,* 1873, vii.

ing closed the doors of patronage and favoritism, members of Parliament had no longer the same interest to resist retrenchment. The investigation of 1873 was, therefore, a natural outcome of the new system of selections." [1]

The investigation filled three volumes and included 5,000 questions. It extended to the whole subject of organization —subordinates, discipline, hours, health, efficiency, pride of service, promotions, salaries, pensions, age of entrance, etc. The investigation included patronage in the hands of judges, and in particular discovered the shameless extravagances and sinecures of the old Bankrupts Court (not unlike those abuses in Chancery to the end of Eldon's day).

The select committee reported that the rates of salaries were not excessive; but *excess lay in the number of clerks* —due partly *to insufficient work required of a large number of employees and to the waste of time by employing well-educated men on merely mechanical duties.* [2]

Disputes about the authority of the Treasury in delimiting necessary establishments of other civil offices had prevented uniform reforms, and the committee urged the Treasury to extend its supervisory power.

It will be recalled that the famous Order in Council of 1870, besides instituting open competition, had provided that there should be two divisions of clerks with different schemes of entrance examinations. It was expected that, where high intellectual attainments were desirable, the head of an office would adopt both divisions, and that an office in which only average ability was demanded would be enrolled under scheme II. But there were heads of offices who disliked the idea of scheme I, and resolved to keep their clerks under scheme II rules, but to promote their best second division clerks to higher positions and pay them

---

[1] Eaton, *Civil Service in Great Britain*, p. 239.

[2] *Parliamentary Papers,* 1873, vii.

as if they were first division men. The results were most
unfortunate. In 1874 [1] we learn that ten departments were
to hold competitive examinations for vacancies under
scheme I and twenty-six under scheme II. The chiefs
of departments not named in the list, had either declined
to accept the principles of open competition, or had not yet
settled under which of the two schemes of examination
situations vacant were to be classed. Huge departments
like the Inland Revenue and Local Government Board admitted exclusively second division clerks.

In offices where both schemes were employed, the pay and
opportunities of first division men varied greatly.[2] But

[1] *London Times,* April 17, 1874.

[2] The following table shows the distribution of first division men in
five offices in which open competition was used; the classes referred to
being, of course, merely promotion stages in the first division: *

	3rd Class.			2nd Class.			1st Class.			Princ. Clerks, Ass't Secy's, etc.		
	Number.	Salary.	Increment.	Number.	Salary.	Increment.	Number.	Salary.	Increment.	Number.	Salary.	Increment.
Civil Service Commission.	....	....	....	6	£100–250	10	5	£300–500	15	1	£700	
India Office.	20			18	500–700	20	13	700–1000	25	6	1200	
	6	£100–400	15	3	350–650	15	1	700	..	....	....	
	10			9	500–700	20	3	700–1000	25	....		
	13			6	500–700	20	1	700	25	1	1200	
Board of Trade.	23	200–400	15	10	420–600	20	12	625–800	25	4	1000–1200	
										1	1000	
										1	900	
Treasury.	....	....	....	13	250–600	20	7	700–900	25	1	1500	
										4	1000–1200	50
War Office.	123	100–400	15	....	....	..	55	420–600	20	[1]10	800	
										[2]17	650	
										1	1500	
										1	1200	
										1	1000	
										1	900	
										1	800	
Post Office.	19	150–250	10	19	260–380	15	8	400–600	20	5	500–600	20
										6	625–800	25
										1	900	
										2	900–1000	33
										1	900–1200	50

[1] Principal Clerks.   [2] Assistant Clerks.

* *Parliamentary Papers,* 1873, lii.

these inequalities amongst first division clerks were as nothing compared to the amazing differences in pay and services
rendered by second division clerks.   In an office entirely
under scheme II, the pay, increments and opportunities of
the second division were of course much greater than where
both schemes were employed.   In one office a second division clerk might reach an insurmountable first division
barrier at £300 a year; in another a more fortunate second
division clerk might rise to a principal clerkship at £1200.

The results of this inquiry we need not review at length.
Many offices were abolished, work and pay were more
fairly and uniformly distributed, and a beginning was made
of a logical two-division clerkship system.   The aim of the
commission was economy and standardization.   The more
intimate and subtle questions of civil service reform, those
of class and democracy, of opportunities and contentment,
of influence on national education, etc., etc., were not within
the province of this commission.   They were reserved for
another great investigation under Gladstone's successor.

The most remarkable feature of the 1873 inquiry is one
which we are apt to lose sight of—the striking absence of
questions of corruption and dishonest patronage.   Mr.
Eaton, who was sent from the United States to report
on the English service, comments enthusiastically on the
effects of open competition and its accompanying efficiency
and economy, contrasting at all times this happy condition
with the motley rout of office holders and lobbyists at home:

" Under competition, you have no patronage, and there is
therefore no motive to increase establishments beyond the
strength which is required for the work; ... on the contrary,
there is a very strong motive in the departments themselves
to keep the establishment down, so as to have the credit of
economical estimates." ... There is one more important consid-

eration connected with this report to which I must refer. The
thorough and fearless scrutiny of the committee extended
over several months and into every office, without respect of
station, high or low—a scrutiny that brought the head of the
Treasury and the Lord Chancellor to their bar, not less than
the humblest clerks and doorkeepers—a scrutiny which invited
and received the complaints of every discharged or discontented official who chose to appear or to write—and yet such
a scrutiny did not, so far as I can discover, disclose a single
instance of peculation or fraud, nor was there any evidence or
charge that illicit gains or corruption ... anywhere existed or
were *by anybody believed to exist in the public service.* And I
am unable to find any other explanation of a condition of things
so striking, except selections and promotions based on merit, a
tenure not disturbed for political reasons, retiring allowances,
and the various methods ... for promoting self-respect and respect for the government on the part of those in its service. It
is only when we contemplate the full significance of such freedom from even the suspicion of corruption or dishonesty, and
compare it with the pervading venality and malversation which
had prevailed in earlier generations, that we are able to com-
prehend the scope and the blessing of administrative reform in
Great Britain.[1]

Shortly after the economy report appeared, the Gladstone Administration fell. The civil service rejoiced [2]
greatly. Gladstone's Cabinet officers as heads of departments were extremely unpopular, especially Childers and
Lowe. *The Civilian* claimed that they denied justice to
public employees, which was untrue; but added significantly: " they went further and withheld those small cour-

[1] Eaton, *Civil Service in Great Britain,* pp. 242-43.
[2] *The Civilian,* January 2, 1875.

tesies which cost so little, and are yet so highly esteemed
by their recipients." [1]

Disraeli's Government was often charged with the too
frequent practice of evading responsibility by referring em-
barrassing subjects to a royal commission or select committee. [2]

However obscure and temporizing may have been the
work of some of Disraeli's commissions, the new inquiry
into the civil service was meant to be both searching and
effective.   Sir Stafford Northcote became Disraeli's Chancellor of the Exchequer.   It was he who appointed the
committee and outlined its scope of inquiry; but it was a
Northcote who was no longer an eager enthusiast for free

[1] The grievances of civil servants against heads of departments were
of considerable importance. A ministry could be much hampered by
the attacks of civil servants in the press, and by the votes of civil servants. It is interesting to note that at this time the old act disfranch-
ising Revenue employees was repealed. As regards outside influence
exercised through the press, an instructive incident occurred in 1875.
Lord John Manners, the Postmaster General, attempted to prevent
Post Office employees from using the press to air their grievances
and personalities. He tried to stop the promotion and increments of
the whole division concerned, so as to make the culprits come forward.
The results of this childish expedient were howls of anger from the
innocent and guilty civilians, the derision of the press, the discounting
of a popular ministry and a general weakening of efficiency and loyalty.
Of course Lord John had to back down. In such cases an English
minister can only trust to the ultimate *esprit de corps* of the service,
to the intelligence of the public and to the English laws against gross
and wanton aspersions on private character.

[2] See cartoons in *Punch,* March 11, 1876, called "Civil Service Stores."
Disraeli is at the counter with an obsequious salesman's manner:
"What can we do for you, Madam?—Royal Commission? Select
Committee? Papers? Careful consideration. Official Enquiry? Anything to oblige!" April 10, 1875. "Dizzy" returns from the country,
still somewhat weak and shaky, and is questioned by Mr. Punch about
his health. One of his crutches is labeled " Majority", the other " Select Committee ".

and open competition, but rather a cautious and tried Conservative politician who now looked at the service from the perhaps higher vantage of practical efficiency, and had a suspicion that the existing methods of recruiting the service were not to be sustained at the expense of the best Conservative administration.

The members of the 1875 commission, known as the " Playfair Commission ", were: Rt. Hon. Lyon Playfair, M.P., Lord Claud Hamilton, M.P., Sir W. H. Stevenson, K.C.B., Sir F. R. Sandford, C.B., Rt. Hon. C. W. Fremantle, T. H. Farrer, Esq., T. Walrond, Esq., C.B., Herbert Joyce, Esq.

The subjects of the inquiry, as outlined by Sir Stafford Northcote, were: (1) selection of civil servants in the first instance; (2) principles of transfer from office to office, especially where numbers have been reduced, so that redundant employees can be employed in other departments; (3) grading the civil service as a whole; (4) employment of writers and temporary clerks.[1]

In Sir Stafford's instructions to Dr. Playfair there is a sentence which is significant as showing that the new Cabinet was by no means convinced of the permanence of open competition as a principle:

[1] The discussion of civil service history in the next two decades, the decades of the Playfair report of 1875 and of the Ridley report of 1888, will be largely confined to the chief problems before the two commissions, their recommendations, and the actual adoption of these suggestions by the Treasury. The earlier history of civil service reform has been treated at greater length because the general character of the service and the tendencies of growth and change are clearly indicated in the period between the first report of Trevelyan and Northcote and the Order for open competition in 1870. Having sketched the Playfair and Ridley reports, we shall pass on to the present-day civil service, examine more striking and decisive evidence collected by the present Royal Commission, and attempt to prophesy the course of immediate changes.

While the Government desire as a general principle to uphold a system of selection according to merit, as opposed to selection by simple exercise of patronage, they are anxious that the Commission should look thoroughly into the action of the present system of competitive examinations, and should give their opinion *upon any modifications* which they may find it desirable to recommend in it with perfect freedom.[1]

The Playfair Commission made three reports.[2] The first dealt with the ordinary clerical establishments, the second with technical branches, such as the British Museum,[3] the third with the outdoor establishments of Revenue and Customs.[4] Only the first Playfair report need be treated in detail in this chapter.

The leading principles established in the clerical civil service in 1870 were under fire. Open competition, the intellectually aristocratic division of the service, uniformity of requirements throughout the service, and the

[1] *Parliamentary Papers*, 1875, vol. xxiii, pp. 3-4; hereinafter referred to as *First Playfair Report*.

[2] *Parliamentary Papers*, 1875, xxiii. *Index*, 1876, xxii.

[3] The Revenue and Customs report recommended that there should be no artificial divisions of classes carrying different scales of pay; that promotion should be general; that there should be free transfer and periodical increments; and it was urged that there was too much specialization in the Customs.

[4] The more important recommendations of the committee in regard to the offices requiring special and technical qualifications, and to such establishments as the British Museum and Department of Science and Art, were that most of these places should be ploced under regulation I, being recruited like other clerical officials dealt with in the main report, or under clause 7 of the Order in Council of 1870, and that there should be a regrading of these departments, together with equalization of pay, duty pay, etc. Specific recommendations were made as to the South Kensington Museum and the British Museum, where the staffs were too small and too poorly paid.

absence of any free choice on the part of heads of departments—such principles as these, which had been successfully established, were attacked bitterly by the irreconcilables. A few quotations chosen at random will make this clear.

Sir Louis Mallet, C.B., rose from junior clerk in the Audit Department to Permanent Under Secretary of the India Office. He did not believe in open competition, but preferred to select his own men, those who were adapted to the work of the India Office, not those whom he must adapt. He did not believe in division I and division II, on the ground that a man's career should not be decided at twenty, and that the heights should be open to all. At the same time he wanted to be able to select men according to their fitness for intellectual and for mechanical work at the outset. He thought that each department must be considered as separate and that no uniform system of pay was possible.[1]

On the other hand, Mr. Knox, then a principal clerk, who rose to be a Permanent Under Secretary of the War Office, believed in the division of the service and favored the promotion of second division clerks only after an academic examination.

A. I would not have promotion secured at all, but I would leave an opportunity for exercising an extreme selection to promote a very good man from one class to the other, assuming that he was willing to take upon his shoulders also the liability to come up to the educational test (not in competition) of the senior establishment. You must maintain the status of the senior establishment.

Q. You would not allow a man to go from the lower to the upper division merely by official merit?

[1] *First Playfair Report,* p. 161.

A. No, not merely by official merit.

Q. You would not allow it without examination?

A. No, not without examination. *I think he should pass such an examination as would give him educationally the status of a gentleman.*[1]

The Rt. Hon. Robert Lowe expressed the same frank opinion: The first division was necessary, separate and closed, not because the men were of higher ability, but because, through their superior style of education and different ideas, they were fitted for dealing with members of Parliament and people from outside to whom they were socially equal. This, Lowe thought, could not be brought about by promoting clerks, however able and meritorious, from the second division. Lowe believed in a rigid two-division system recruited by strictly competitive examinations, without opportunity to rise from division I to division II. He advocated a third class of low-paid clerks—permanent and pensionable. He claimed, with justice, that there were far too many first division men, and advocated a committee of the Cabinet to remedy this. He did not believe in grading the whole service as to pay and promotion.[2]

Sir Charles Trevelyan, discussing the triumphs of open competitive examinations, said:

The Home Civil Service does not stand alone; the competitive system has been successfully applied, first to the artillery and engineers, and since that to the rest of the army . . . to the Indian Civil Service, and . . . in several of the colonies. . . . Appointment to the public service by open competition has been accepted as a national institution and is regarded as an

[1] *First Playfair Report,* p. 9.

[2] *Ibid.,* pp. 125-127.

inestimable privilege by the great majority of persons of the upper and middle class in every part of the United Kingdom. While the system was quite new it was twice brought to issue in the House of Commons,[1] and greatly to our surprise on both occasions a majority . . . was in favor of maintaining competition; when we inquired, it was found that a large and important class of clergymen and retired officers and persons of the middle class of all sorts . . . are in the habit of giving a good education to their sons. . . . And when the new system was in jeopardy, they wrote letters in shoals to their members, and that accounts for the majority. . . . Such a strong root has the system already taken . . . in one generation.[2]

Still there were a number of prominent people who thought that competitive examinations might be a way they had in the army, the navy, and the 'varsity, and eminently calculated to obtain jolly good fellows—but manifestly incapable of producing clerks in the home civil service.

Among these perennial sceptics on the subject of written examinations was Sir Arthur Helps, of the Privy Council Office, a distinguished man of letters of the day:

I contend that by this system the best men are liable to be shut out; and that success in a competitive examination is often an indication of the successful person's unfitness for the duties of practical life. . . . This system of competitive examination seems likely to prove very injurious to the general education of the country. . . . [It tends to destroy love of study and desire for knowledge.] [3]

An important question argued at great length before the Playfair Commission was that of employing a class of

---

[1] *Cf.* Chapter III, *supra.*

[2] *Second Playfair Report*, Appendix F, pp. 101-102.

[3] *First Playfair Report*, p. 361.

writers and temporary clerks to do the most mechanical and unimproving work of the civil service. This has been an ever-recurring and difficult question throughout the history of the English civil service.

A committee of 1865 had recommended the abolition of the supplementary clerk class, the founding of a government copying office near Whitehall, and the setting up of two classes of assistants, one of boys selected by open competition and employed only for a short term of years, without superannuation, and with only a weekly wage, the other of men enjoying superannuation, a yearly salary, and recruited from the boy division, extra vacancies being filled by open competition. This scheme was later approved by both the Playfair and the Ridley commissions. But between 1865 and 1875 other schemes were tried. An attempt was made to employ writers on weekly wages, without permanent tenure, superannuation, or prospect of advancement, but with wages rising by seniority or merit. This large class felt that it had a claim on the government. It aroused public feeling and attempted to bring political pressure to bear to gain holidays, sick-leave, superannuation, and, above all, a permanent tenure. By an Order in Council of August 19, 1871, this class was abolished; and the writers subsequently employed were given to understand at the outset that they were strictly temporary, were to be paid by the piece, and were to have no claim to get into the established civil service.

A commission, known as the Otway Commission, arranged the new terms and made some concessions to the old writers employed before 1871, whose prospects and hopes had been shattered by the Order in Council of that year. After Mr. Otway's Commission, the same old writer trouble appeared again. More writers were employed, some on superior work, and all claimed a

right to get on the establishment. It was the duty of the
Playfair Commission to settle this problem. The commission found that writers and supplementary clerks were employed in a number of cases upon really difficult and important work.[1] As was indicated in the special report of
1865, every improvement in their qualifications made the
distinction between them and the established clerks more
odious.[2] On the other hand, there were strong objections to
promotions to permanent clerkships from the writer class,
a practice in the Admiralty Department. As Horace Mann
put it, a little crudely:

To recruit, to a large extent, the permanent establishments
from a force of men admitted, at any age, on the test of a
National-school boy's examination, and with the defects of
character implied in Micawberish antecedents, would be not
only to starve competition, but to weaken and continually dis-
turb the service.[3]

If the writer class was to be abolished who were to do
their work? The objection to writers had already led to
the appointment of too many clerks under regulations II,
a practice bound to cause overcrowding, dissatisfaction and
needless expense.

Another great problem before the Playfair Comission
was that of equality of opportunity among second division
clerks, and the unnecessary and unfair extension of the
first division to posts which should properly have been a

---

[1] Cf. evidence of Brand and Clayton, First Playfair Report.

[2] At a later date it was suggested quite seriously that the Fenian out-
rages were really the work of starved and fanatic government writers.
Cf. Heads and Tails of the Civil Service (London, 1887), bound in
Political Tracts, 1865-1896, in the British Museum Library.

[3] First Playfair Report, p. 366.

goal and incentive to second division men. As an example of the anomalies of pay and opportunity in the civil service of this period, we have the following evidence: In 1862 A, B and C were 1, 2 and 3 in competition for Internal Revenue offices. Three appointments declared to be of the same value were offered them. In the absence of information, A took the Receiver General's office, B the Register of Warrants's office, and C the Solicitor's Department. In 1875 A and B were getting £220, with no likelihood of rising above £250 for years, while C was getting £370, rising by annual increments to £450. Again, in 1862, D and E were bracketed equal in competition for two vacancies in the Internal Revenue. It was suggested that they toss for jobs. In 1875, D, who won the toss, was stationary at £150, while E was getting £220 and stood an excellent chance of promotion. There was chronic discontent amongst men like A, B and D who were confined to the narrow limits of small offices.

This discontent was voiced by many representative clerks who appeared before the Playfair Commission. In general, we may say of these clerks' representatives that their ideas of the fundamental constitution of offices, promotions, etc., were not very valuable. Only their specific complaints about their own offices were worth having. They all commented on their extraordinary responsibilities, on the variety of work in their office, and demanded higher pay and quicker promotion. Each representative[1] clerk

[1] The following words from *The Civilian* are worth quoting:
" It is above all things desirable that members of the Civil Service in their newborn prospects of having some kind of justice dealt out to them, should not allow their joy to override their discretion. From the information that comes to us . . . we fear that *harmonious combination* stands in peril of being overlooked in the frantic haste displayed by each office . . . to lay its own particular tale of woe before Dr. Playfair's Commission. In the Revenue Departments . . . it is

entered the commission room bursting with the news of his
unknown responsibilities and of the unrewarded labors of
his office, with lofty and impartial criticisms of the general
conduct of business, and exhaustive schemes accompanied
by architectural plans and Benthamite essays, showing just
how the whole civil service could be reformed and remod-
eled to suit the needs of modern England.[1]   Several weeks

especially necessary that no evidence and no witness should be ten-
dered to the Commission which has not been submitted to a commitee
or to one or two persons competent to judge what should be omitted
and what inserted."

[1] A junior inspector in the India Office had an elaborate scheme for
arranging clerks under three classes and promoting by merit through
an independent Board of Control, together with a plan for the shifting and exchanging from department to department of men of relative
rank, pay and age. The following quotation illustrates the conception
that some clerks had of their ability:

Q. "Do you find that the clerks are better for having gone through
experience of different kinds of work?"
A. "I find them infinitely improved."
Q. "Have you done so yourself?"
A. "My service is rather peculiar. I served in the West Indies
before coming to England. There is no branch of the Service with
which I am not thoroughly conversant, and I ascribe any ability which
I have to discharge the duties of the office to the general knowledge I
possess. I have been through almost all the branches."

The secretary of the Civil Service Association (a clerk) said that
the examinations for scheme II were not comprehensive enough. He
"abominated" the division into two schemes and knew "many good
men who woke up one morning and found they were Second Class
officers. They never knew it before and were told exactly the opposite.
They had been degraded, not graded." He wanted the scope of the
examination widened "so that anyone who has anything in him will
have the means of bringing it out."

Elaborate plans for increasing salaries were drawn up so that nine-
tenths of the men under scheme II would eventually reach £600.
Preference classes were to be arranged so that those who developed
late could overtake the precocious. A civilian who though he should
be thus preferred, contrary to the opinion of the head of the office,
could write to a Board of Appeal and demand an investigation. The

of such hearings are calculated to weary the most inde-
fatigable commissioner, but the expediency of airing all
grievances, and of lending a sympathetic ear to intelligent
suggestions, is unquestionable. In a free country, government employees cannot be forced to secret political agitation to get their grievances redressed and their feasible suggestions adopted. And in this case we must remember that
there were actually many cases of men not long in the service, holding superior positions and drawing higher pay
than older colleagues employed on the same work.

Such were the problems before the Playfair Commission.
Let us see how they were dealt with in the report. Dr.
Playfair's Commission commented on the unequal value
of situations under each of the regulations, and they
asked gloomily whether, after all, competition had not
failed. Formerly when the clerks looked to the heads of
offices as their patrons, they were satisfied with prospects
in their office, and did not set up odious comparisons. The
commission thought that any uniform competitive examination must be too high for some places and too low for
others, and they felt that examinations did not afford any
real test of ability. They commented on the current objections to the barrier between divisions I and II, and re-
marked how many offices had evaded it by having division
II and staff officers, and no division I at all.[1] The commis-

reason given for this appeal was, that a man often forms a better
opinion of himself than does his superior. A Board of Control was to
transfer men when and where they pleased. The secretary of the Civil
Service Association made this final statement: " Throughout the whole
service I would not have a single rigid line. I think that the nearer
we approach to nature in the service the better. We do not find any
rigid lines in nature. I have almost carefully thought this part of my
statement—no rigid lines should be placed above any class." *First
Playfair Report*, Appendix B, *passim*.

[1] The following is an example of the kind of difficulty which arises

sion doubted the wisdom of choosing important officers by a single, competing, literary examination at the very offset.

No better analysis of the Playfair recommendations could be found than that which appeared some years later in the second Ridley report.

The object of the commission was:

1. To separate from the superior service the class employed on work of a lower character.

The numbers of the superior service to be greatly curtailed.

2. To have different systems of examination for the two divisions.

Lower Division

3. The Lower Division of the Civil Service to consist of men clerks, admissible from 17 to 20 years of age, and of boy clerks, admissible from 15 to 17 years of age.

4. The Civil Service Commissioners to hold twice a year, or oftener if necessary, competitive examinations for men clerks under the present Regulation II, and for boy clerks in a more limited number of subjects.

5. Lists of those who are successful in the competitions to be made out in the order of merit, the number of names on such lists to be in excess of the number of permanent clerkships which are likely to be vacant.

in an office employing only lower division men, when the work of the office expands, and exceptional qualifications are demanded. The Local Government Board originally came in under regulation II (*i. e.*, second division only, no first division men). All promotions to class I in this office were to be from class II, the second division. Very high salaries were offered and thus the best second division men were attracted. But when business increased and several legal assistants were appointed, although it was understood that these were not to interfere with the promotion of other clerks, the latter were very dissatisfied. The second division men felt that they had a kind of vested right in all the higher positions in the office. This made it very difficult for the head to appoint men from outside. *First Playfair Report,* evidence of J. Lambert, C. B., secretary to the Local Government Board.

6. Each competitor named in a list to serve in any office under the State where he may be wanted.

7. From these lists the Civil Service Commissioners, on the application of the departments having vacancies, to supply, on probation, the requisite clerks, whether for permanent or temporary duty, as a general rule, according to their order on the lists, but with liberty to select a clerk who, in his examination, has shown special qualifications for any particular subject, if special application for such a clerk be made by any department.

8. The period of probation to be not less than one year, and if the clerk is rejected by his department within that time the rejection to be signified to the Civil Service Commissioners, with the reasons, and such Commissioners to decide thereon whether his name shall be struck off the list as unfit for the Service generally, or he shall be allowed a trial in another department.

9. Boy clerks not to be retained as such after completing their 19th year: but after approved good service to be allowed to compete under Regulation II among themselves for a limited number of men clerkships of the Lower Division.

10. Appointments may be made exceptionally to the Lower Division of clerks from the body of writers serving before 4th June, 1870, if thoroughly qualified, and from those subsequently registered by the Civil Service Commissioners, provided the age of these latter did not exceed 30 years at the time of their being placed on the Register, and provided they prove their fitness by a supplementary examination, and produce certificates from the heads of the departments in which they are serving that it is desirable in the interest of the public service to retain and employ them in the department.

11. The salaries of men clerks to commence at 80l. and rise by triennial increments to 15l. to 200l.[1]

---

[1] The commission decided that the pay of clerks in the civil service was as high, and of lower officers higher, than in private establishments. See statistics in appendix, *First Playfair Report*.

12 Extra pay, not exceeding 100*l.* per annum, to be attached to certain situations open to clerks of the Lower Division, which involve superior duties.

13. Official attendance to be of not less than seven hours per day.

14. Promotion from the Lower to the Higher Division of the Service to be a matter of rare occurrence, requiring a certificate from the Civil Service Commissioners, to be granted upon a special recommendation from the head of the department, and with the assent of the Treasury, and to be published in the " Gazette."

Higher Division

15. For the Higher Division the Civil Service Commissioners to hold a preliminary test examination, open to all persons above 17 years of age, four times in the year, in London, Edinburgh, and Dublin, at which the subjects should be—

(*a*) Handwriting.

(*b*) Arithmetic, including vulgar and decimal fractions.

(*c*) English composition.

(*d*) Geography.

(*e*) English History.

16. Candidates who have passed this preliminary test examination to be eligible for a second examination, to be held twice a year in London. This examination not to be so high as Regulation I, but to be competitive, and of such a character as to suit young men from 18 to 23, adequately trained at a public school, good private school, or university. The competition to be limited to a small number of subjects selected by the candidates out of a list of subjects prepared by the Civil Service Commissioners in consultation with the departments. The competition to determine the successful candidates, who shall be placed in alphabetical order, their success consisting in this, that they come up to a certain standard in a certain number of subjects, this standard being determined by experience with reference to the average supply of qualified candidates, and the average demand for them.

17. The number of candidates from time to time selected to be such as wil suffice to maintain a list somewhat in excess of the number of vacancies expected during the following six months.

18. Any successful candidate to be at liberty to offer himself for an examination in additional subjects, and, if successful in them, to have the fact noted against his name in the list.

19. Candidates placed on the list to be eligible for appointment in any department which has a vacancy, but to have no claim to an appointment.

20 As vacancies occur in the several departments, the head of each department to be able to select for the place any of the candidates on the list.

21. The heads of departments to have the power of making success in certain subjects obligatory for obtaining situations in them.

22. The successful candidates to have the liberty of refusing situations offered to them, and of retaining their names upon the eligible list until the completion of the 25th year of their age.

23. After a candidate has obtained his appointment, he is to remain on probation for a year. During this probation he is to be required to go through carefully and to master all the details of the more simple and routine work of the Lower Division. If his probation ends in his rejection, he is to be dealt with, up to his 25th year, according to the preceding Article 8.

24. The salaries of the Higher Division to commence at 100*l*., and rise by triennial increments of 37*l*. 10*s*. to 400*l*.

25. Extra pay, not exceeding 200*l*. per annum, to be attached to certain situations in the Higher Division which involve superior duties.

Staff Appointments

26. Above the Higher Division of ordinary clerks there are to be staff appointments, including such officers as chief clerks and principal clerks, of which the number and pay would be fixed by Order in Council with reference to each department.

27. The selection of men to fill staff appointments is to be left wholly to the chiefs of departments, who may select either from within their offices or from the outside. Within the offices merit, and not seniority, is to be the condition of selection.

Occasional Copyists

28. Below the Lower Division of ordinary clerks (including boy clerks), there are to be men and boy copyists, employed for mere copying and routine work under direct supervision, on the same conditions of service as those at present in force for men and boy Civil Service writers. Rates of pay 10*d*., or, in some cases, 1*s*. per hour, but piece-work whenever possible.

General Conditions of Service

29. Throughout the entire Civil Service, neither staff appointments nor extra pay are to be given by seniority, but by selection for merit.

30. Throughout the entire Civil Service, the increments of salary are to be triennial, and are only to be allowed in full upon a certificate from the immediate superior of each clerk, countersigned by the head of the department to the effect that the clerk's conduct had been in all respects satisfactory. In cases of great demerit, no part of the increment is to be allowed.

31. Throughout the entire Civil Service, transfers to be made, so far as practicable, from the less important to the more important offices, for the sake of encouragement; and generally to avoid compensations on abolition.

32. The general regulations affecting the Civil Service to be embodied in an Act of Parliament.

33. All appointments, promotions, and transfers to be published in the " London Gazette."

34. Introduction of new system to be accelerated by superannuations. Transfers difficult, and of doubtful economy.

Special Proposals Considered and Rejected

35. The following special proposals were considered and rejected, viz. :—

(a) To group offices, or divisions of offices, and to assign to each different kinds of examination.

(b) To make out the list of successful competitors for the Higher Division in order of merit.

(c) To reserve appointments for the sons of civil servants.

(d) To confine advancement to periodical increases of salary, abolishing all distinctions except staff appointments.

(e) To offer high initial salaries.

(f) To encourage the employment of discharged soldiers as clerks in Civil Service, except in the War Office, and its subordinate departments, and under military officers.

(g) To shorten the period at which clerks may claim to retire on superannuation.[1]

The commission claimed that no additional cost would be involved in the introduction of the above scheme.

In general we may say that the first Playfair report was neither clear nor convincing. Sir Stafford Northcote, then Chancellor of the Exchequer, called the recommendations sweeping and reactionary. Evidently he repented his own reactionary instructions to the commission. He said that transfers might be made so as to discourage rather than encourage merit, and that it was doubtful whether first class men would be attracted by the division I scheme. As a Treasury official, he decided to proceed by cautious experiment. Sir Charles Trevelyan was displeased with the report.[2] He was opposed to duty pay, to reintroducing nominations, and to special examinations for special positions. He said that an Act of Parliament should fix the civil service, and that the slipshod Order in Council method had caused the existing retrogressions from open competition.

---

[1] *Second Ridley Report*, p. 570.

[2] See *Second Playfair Report*, Appendix, p. 102.

He favored a standing committee for revision. Sir Charles Trevelyan had good cause for protest against the Playfair report. Division I requirements were to be lowered. The creation of a list of candidates for division I, from which heads of departments were to choose, was a return to patronage. Why should a candidate be more loyal or more tractable because he was chosen by the head of the office? In what way would the heads choose? The report would have gained if it had frankly aimed at pointing out the defects in the working of the old 1870 scheme, instead of speciously pretending to set up a new one. If the list of eligible candidates for higher positions was not to exceed the average number to be absorbed in six months, what choice would remain for the heads of less important departments? The examinations in extra subjects could only cause confusion. The service-and-duty pay idea was not bad, but increments for time service, like promotion by seniority, were inevitable. The writer question was left unsettled. The idea of transfers from office to office was impracticable. It was a dull report, and the enlightened faith in open competition which had appeared in previous reports was entirely lacking. The commission would undoubtedly have voted for patronage and nomination if they had not been constrained.

A Civil Service Consultative Committee on the first Playfair report opposed all the Playfair suggestions; and Dr. Playfair felt called upon to justify his report in an article in *The Spectator*.

The newspapers of the day were very generally against the Playfair report, and feared that patronage would be introduced.[1] Meanwhile the government was marking time. In answer to a question in Parliament as to the in-

---

[1] See *Times, Standard, Post, Echo, Observer, Hour*, etc., February 6, 7, 8, 1875.

troduction of scheme I and the reorganization of departments, Sir Stafford Northcote, the Chancellor of the Exchequer, said that each department must propose its reforms individually, and that the individual plans would then be considered by the Treasury, but that there would be no further Order in Council. A committee consisting of Dr. Playfair, Lord Mahon, and Mr. Stephenson of the Treasury, was then appointed to see how far the Playfair scheme could be introduced in the Treasury.[1]

Finally, the Treasury decided to regulate the rank and file of the civil service by a new Order in Council which would embody the less debatable Playfair recommendations. The Order in Council of February 12, 1876,[2] provided:

(1) The number of higher clerks to be reduced, and their places filled by lower division men.

(2) First division men to be appointed only very rarely for duties of a very high order. But their appointment to be left to the heads of departments and the Treasury, thus avoiding a single, straightforward decision on the Playfair upper division recommendations.

(3) The new lower division to consist of men and boy clerks, engaged as a class, and ready to serve in any department by appointment or transfer.

(4) Candidates for boy clerkships to be between 15 and 17, for men clerkships between 17 and 20; and a list to be drawn up in order of merit, upon which each boy competitor could remain until 19, each man until 25.

---

[1] As a result a new upper division was created in the Treasury somewhat on the lines of the Playfair higher division. See p. 157, *infra*.

[2] This Order in Council of February 12, 1876, and a subsequent Order of June 27, 1876, put the recommendations of the Playfair Commission affecting the Customs and Internal Revenue departments into effect.

(5) The number of probable vacancies for six months to be announced, and from the list of competitors positions were to be filled *in order of merit.*

(6) Boys to be retained in the service until 19, and then dismissed if not successful in limited competition for men clerkships.

(7) The salaries of men clerks to begin at £80, and rise by triennial increments of £15 to £200, the increments being strictly dependent upon the production of a certificate of merit from the immediate superior. But a higher scale rising from £90 to £250 to be provided for offices in which seven hours' work is required. Boy clerks to be paid 14s. a week, with a shilling per week additional per annum as long as employed. Extra pay not exceeding £100 to be given to lower division men employed upon superior or supervisory work.

(8) Promotion from the lower to the higher division of staff and other high officials to be granted only exceptionally after ten years' service, upon certification by the Civil Service Commission and special recommendation of the head of the department, with the consent of the Treasury, such promotion to be gazetted.

(9) A copyist class of men and boys, paid preferably by piece work, to be again instituted to replace the old writer class (and for no very good reason).

It will be seen that the Order in Council of February 12 did not decide the mooted questions of the Playfair scheme I. It did not go on to prescribe a new higher division, but proceeded to prescribe promotions from the lower division just as if a higher division had been constituted. The worst feature of the Order in Council was this vagueness and indefiniteness concerning the actual constitution of the new upper or higher division. The Order in Council carefully regulated the lower division, and referred to

the upper as an accomplished fact, but it left the regulation
of the upper division entirely to chance, the Treasury and
the heads of departments. A few quotations from the Ridley report of 1888 will give some idea of the confusion
which resulted:

May we argue from that that the Treasury disapprove of the
Playfair scheme?—Of the upper division, do you mean?

Have they ever disapproved of the Playfair scheme generally?—No, I do not think so. The Treasury have applied, and
are applying, the lower division part of the scheme as fully
as they can. The higher division is adopted, but it has been
a matter of very great consideration as to whether it is desirable to apply that part of the Playfair scheme universally.
So far I say there has been no determination come to by the
Government upon that point.

How do you get your upper clerks?—By open competition,
or, as I say in some instances, by transfer from one of the
other offices.

Then, in point of fact, it does come to this, that the
Treasury disapproves of the Playfair scheme as applied to
itself?—(*Lord Lingen.*) Perhaps the Chairman will allow
me to explain the position of the matter as it was settled
while I was at the Treasury. The Playfair Report has no
independent authority of its own; it is simply the recommendation of a Commission, except so far as it has been embodied
in Orders in Council. In the Order in Council of 12 February, 1876, the Government adopted so much of the scheme
as related to a lower division, but left the constitution of an
upper division undetermined, except so far as to indicate that
the number of clerks serving in the existing departments, with
salaries above the scale of the Playfair Lower Division required to be reduced. In the Treasury, in the Secretary of
State's offices, and in some others, the old system of salaries,
graded per class, without duty pay, was retained; in other
offices the Playfair scale with duty pay for the higher division has been introduced. When vacancies in the higher divi-

sion have to be filled up, they are announced by the Civil
Service Commissioners, and the terms of each of the situations are known; a single examination, the same for all, is
held, and the candidates are free to choose the office they
prefer according to their place as determined by the number
of their marks. (*Sir R. Welby.*) Lord Lingen has expressed
more clearly than I should have done the answer I was about
to give, namely, that the higher division has not been adopted
by Order in Council, which is the binding authority upon us.

That arouses a suspicion in my mind that the Treasury
have never approved of it?—I think I should rather say that
the question of the universal application of the upper division
of the Playfair scheme has not been considered by the Treasury for the whole service as yet.

But do not you think it is high time, if the Playfair scheme
is to be propounded as the one thing needful for the Civil
Service, that after so many years there should be a decision
about it one way or the other in all the high departments?—
Of course there must come a time when that question would
have to be considered. It is a very important question, and
the Government will have to take it into consideration.[1]

[1] *Parliamentary Papers,* 1888, xxvii, p. 2.

CHAPTER VII

THE RIDLEY INVESTIGATION, 1888-1890

THE purpose and personnel of the Ridley investigation [1] is seen in the patent of appointment:

Now know ye, that We, reposing great trust and confidence in your knowledge and ability, have authorised and appointed, and do by these presents authorise and appoint you, the said Sir Matthew White Ridley, Adelbert Wellington Brownlow, Earl Brownlow, Nathaniel Mayer, Baron Rothschild, Ralph Robert Wheeler, Baron Lingen, George Sclater-Booth, Henry Hartley Fowler, Sir Edward Cecil Guinness, Algernon Bertram Freeman Mitford, John Cleghorn, Alfred Spalding Harvey, Charles Edward Lewis, Arthur O'Connor, and Peter Rylands, to be our Commissioners for the purposes of the said inquiry.

And We do hereby authorise and empower you, or any five or more of you, to inquire into the numbers, salaries, hours of labour, superannuation, cost of the staff, and the administration, regulation, and organisation of the said offices.

You will state whether, in your opinion, the work of the different offices is efficiently and economically performed; whether it can be simplified; whether the method of procedure can be improved; and whether the system of control is deficient or unnecessarily elaborate.

---

[1] The volumes of the Ridley report are found in *Parliamentary Papers*, 1887, xix; 1888, xxvii; 1889, xxi, and 1890, xxvii. They will be referred to in this chapter as to *First Ridley Report, Second Ridley Report*, etc.

As ten years have now elapsed since the adoption of the scheme of organisation recommended by the Playfair Commission, the time has come when the working of the scheme may, with advantage, be reviewed. You will, therefore, report whether the scheme has been fairly tried; whether its provisions have met the requirements of the Service, and deserve confirmation, and whether any modifications are needed to give it complete development.

The report was in four parts. The first related to the organization of the War and Admiralty departments; the second, which is the one of greatest importance for this essay, reviewed the Playfair report, commented upon its effects in operation and suggested changes. The third report had to do with the organization of the Customs and Excise departments. The fourth and final report was on the Foreign Office and the diplomatic and consular services. We shall deal briefly with the first, third and fourth reports, and then pass on to the review of the Playfair scheme in the second report.

Constant reorganization in the War Office and Admiralty, without regard to economy, had resulted in an enormous overstaffing, and the commission recommended a new organization and greater Treasury control, together with the immediate reduction of the number of higher clerks. The remaining evidence in the first report shows that the War Office and Admiralty clerks had the same grievances as the clerical staff elsewhere. The classes tended to overlap, the lower class being employed on superior work, and vice versa, with resulting overpay on the one hand, and complaints about pay and prospects on the other. Below the permanent staff, the temporary draughtsmen complained that they really were employed on responsible work, and wanted to be established. As usual, the lower division clerks claimed that their work was difficult and supervisory; and they protested against the rule for ten years' service before promotion. The government attitude [1] toward these complaints was based on the theory that only a very few of the lower division clerks were fitted to rise to the upper division, because they lacked a sufficiently high education. This subject belongs properly to the third report. As we shall see, the questions of upper and lower divisions had been left in an extraordinary state of confusion and vagueness after the Playfair report.

In its third report the commission decided that so important an experiment as the amalgamation of the Customs and Excise departments was not justified. They feared that the amalgamation would result in a leveling-up of salaries and would create an unwieldy department, whose chairmanship would tend to become a political office. After hearing the complaints of employees, the commission wisely refrained from giving opinions adverse to those of the responsible heads of offices. They did, however, lay down the rule that no subordinate officer is entitled to compensation because the number of higher offices for which he has been eligible has been reduced. A minority of the commission, in a separate report, recommended the amalgamation of the Customs and Excise, agreeing with Mr. Gladstone— and their judgment has recently been vindicated. The long expected amalgamation took place in 1909, and the reorganization was completed in 1911 by the report of a committee of which Mr. C. E. H. Hobhouse, M. P., was chairman. This was known as the Hobhouse report, and was adopted by the Treasury.[2]

The fourth Ridley report on the Foreign Office recommended that limited competition should be maintained and

[1] See evidence of Sir R. E. Welby, *First Ridley Report*, p. 5.
[2] See p. 187, *infra*.

that the Foreign Office and diplomatic service should be, as far as possible, amalgamated by interchange of officials. It condemned the requirement of an independent income for diplomats. It urged two years' training for all diplomats in the Foreign Office before being sent abroad; uniform salaries for both Foreign Office and diplomatic service; and the regular system of pensions governing all other departments in place of a peculiar one. It recommended that consuls, hitherto appointed by patronage, be selected by pass examination of men of experience between twenty-five and forty years of age, who should first be employed in the Foreign Office, Board of Trade and Revenue departments to get specialized business knowledge. The writer has been unable to find that any of these recommendations were adopted at this time. None of the Ridley ideas appear in the new regulations of the Foreign Office for 1891. This is an example of the ineffectiveness of commission suggestions to departments not under the Treasury. In recent years something like the Ridley plan has been adopted, but the complete fusion of the two departments has not been realized, and is probably not desirable.

We turn now to the review of the Playfair scheme in the second report. The commission reported that an honest attempt had been made to comply with Dr. Playfair's suggestion, but that difficulties had been encountered. It was difficult to reduce numbers in the upper division, and many of the old upper division men were still hanging on, though performing only lower division work.

The commission pointed out that the key of the Playfair scheme was the division of work between a higher and a lower division, the small and highly educated higher division to do the work which involved "responsibility, discretion and power to direct work," and to be separate and distinct from the large lower division.

The commission then reported that:

Subject to the important qualification of the different needs of different offices, this principle of a division of labor has the sanction of almost every experienced administrator from whom we received evidence. In practice, however, the work has overlapped, and although the reasons of the failure to preserve this principle of a division of labour, lie partly in the fact, already alluded to, of the large existing number of highly-paid clerks both of the old establishment, and, in some cases, of the new Higher Division, and of the insufficient time as yet allowed for the new classification to develop, *it is undeniable that the line of demarcation has been drawn too low;* that the bulk of the Lower Division clerks are not contented with their position and prospects, and that, so far as can be judged from experience of the past twelve years, *i. e.,* since the date of the Order in Council of 12th February, 1876, a considerable proportion of those clerks are fitted to fill a large number of places now unnecessarily reserved for the Upper Division.[1]

We are of opinion that the purely *clerical* work of the service can be, and therefore ought to be, done by one class of clerks, viz., those entering upon the present lower examination, and we think that the door of promotion to all the upper posts should be open to any clerk who has shown that he possesses the necessary qualifications for discharging the duties of them efficiently.

We have, however, no doubt that it will always be necessary to introduce a very limited number of men by means of a higher examination, to fill directly some of the more important posts of the public service.

We think it an object of the most serious importance that men of the same standard of liberal education as those who now adopt the open professions should be attracted into the

---

[1] Note that "higher" and "upper" are used without discrimination. *Cf.* pp. 156-158 *supra* and p. 167 *infra.*

public service, and trained there, for selection for the highest permanent posts.

There need not be the same proportion in all Government offices between the two classes, and probably, in some, as *e. g.*, the Revenue Departments, it may be found that all the necessary supervision, and higher work, can be done by men admitted under the lower examination.[1] Upon this point we would draw special attention to the evidence given by Sir A. West and Sir C. Du Cane. Among the reasons which have led us to this conclusion, we may specify the technical character of most of the work in the Revenue Departments, and also the large number of officers from whom selection can be made. *Promotion by merit alone* is assumed by us in the adoption of any such plan.

There are departments, on the other hand, such as the Treasury, the offices of the Secretaries of State, and some of the other principal offices, in which it is clearly necessary to have a larger proportion than in others of men of more liberal culture in order to discharge satisfactorily the consultative and deliberative work of those offices. Generally, however, it cannot be too emphatically stated that the bulk of the work in all the Government offices can satisfactorily be done by clerks who have received an ordinary commercial education, and that Government *clerical* work does not differ materially from that done by clerks in large commercial establishments. Among men of this stamp we may fairly expect to find some capable of discharging the ordinary duties of supervision, while beyond the sphere of *clerical* work, the position meant to be occupied by members of the Upper Division, involves duties more nearly akin to those of *management*.

Bearing in mind these guiding principles, we recommend

---

[1] It is interesting to note that this opinion is no longer entertained. The Revenue Departments have required more and more highly trained clerks, and the result has been that two divisions above the old second division are now employed in certain offices of the Customs and Internal Revenue. (See discussion of intermediate and first division clerks in the next chapter).

that the character and special wants of each department should be carefully considered, and a normal establishment for each should be, so far as practicable, defined. In aiming at such a standard, use should be made as far as possible of existing material, both within and without the particular department.

We are not insensible to the objection that, for some time to come, there will be very few young men, if any, coming into the Service by means of the higher examination. Nor do we think that the work will be so efficiently done, as it will be when the system has had time to be thoroughly developed; but we have to deal with an existing Service, and we cannot recommend so large an addition to the non-effective charge as would be involved in the removal of a considerable number of the existing staff upon the only terms now open to the Government.

The commission added that an Order in Council, promulgated by the Treasury, should fix the normal establishments of all departments, that the best methods of effecting the necessary changes and all questions including pensions and increases in expenditures should in each case be determined by a permanent committee consisting of a Treasury official, a civil service commissioner, and at least one permanent official of the great Revenue departments. This committee should also review all offices periodically in the interests of harmony, economy and standardization. We shall see that the Lords of the Treasury first repudiated this suggestion, but soon after changed their minds and adopted it in an Order in Council.[1]

The commission commented on the difficulties of effecting transfers and of getting rid of redundants by transfer or pension. They said that the suspension of examinations

[1] It is interesting in this connection to note the recent attempts of President Taft and his Efficiency Commission to set up such a standardizing agency in Washington. See p. 256 *infra*.

for the upper division could not be helped, and trusted that these would be more frequent when prospects throughout the service had been equalized.

Passing on to the lower division clerks, the commission said:

As stated in our former Report, we are of opinion that the young men of this grade who have entered the Service since the Order in Council of 1876 have been of excellent quality and capacity. All the evidence we have received points in this direction. We are not surprised, however, to find that, partly owing to the keenness of the competition and the expectations aroused by success in it, there is, on the whole, considerable disappointment felt in regard to the prospects of promotion; and in some departments this is, no doubt, and must for some time remain, a serious evil. It is out of the question, however, to promote clerks when higher-paid service is not required, simply in order to provide advancement for them; and though individual men in this class are probably fit for, and are in fact employed in some instances upon, higher work than would appear to have been contemplated in the Order of Council, it is our opinion that this part of the clerical service is, on the whole, not inadequately remunerated.

We think that routine promotion by seniority is the great evil of the Service, and that it is indispensable to proceed throughout every branch of it strictly on the principle of promotion by merit, that is to say, by selecting always the fittest man, instead of considering claims in order of seniority, and rejecting only the unfit.

It is no doubt true that objections on the score of favouritism may arise in the application of such a rule in public departments, and the intervention of Members of Parliament also presents an obvious difficulty, but we think that such constant vigilance, tact, and resolution, as may fairly be expected on the part of heads of branches and of offices, will meet these objections, and we believe that the certain advantages of promotion by merit to the most deserving men, and therefore to the public service, are so great as to be sure, in the long run, to command public support.

We recommend that the Lower Division, constituting, as it now does, and as it will in a still greater measure in future, the *clerical* establishment of the various offices, should be recruited from young men of the same age as at present, and under the existing regulations.

That the character of the examination should not be raised, as it appears now to afford a sufficient test of a good commercial education.

The commission recommended several other second division changes:

That shorthand and a modern foreign language be included as optional subjects.

That the first year's probation be made real, since a competitive examination does not always insure fitness.

New salaries with annual instead of triennial increments —an initial salary of £70 rising by £5 to £100, and by £7 10s. to £190 with certificates of merit, and special reports of competence on reaching £100 and £190.

A seven-hour day. Abolition of duty pay and opening of more staff places to second division men, but only after ten years' service as recommended in the Playfair report.

That the lower division be called the second division—there being objections on the part of clerks to the existing name.

A very curious thing in connection with the organization of the civil service which appears throughout the Ridley report and in all the discussions of this period, is the confusion caused by the words " *upper division* " and " *higher division* ". There can be little doubt that Dr. Playfair used the terms "*upper division*" and "*higher division*" indiscriminately, to indicate the directing positions filled by university men who entered by a separate academic exami-

nation.   The Order in Council of 1876 did not embody the
Playfair scheme and salaries for the higher division.   Some
offices had adopted the higher Playfair scheme and salaries,
but the Treasury and other departments were employing
so-called upper division men at salaries greater than the
Playfair higher division men; and in other departments
the upper division probably consisted of superior, lower division clerks.   The Ridley report put an end to this confusion:

We recommend that, upon the occurrence of vacancies, all
new appointments to the greatly reduced Upper Division
which we propose, should be made on the scale set forth in
para. 56 of this Report.

*We are of opinion, that it is desirable to secure young men
of more liberal education for those posts in the Service, which
are not simply clerical, but demand a wider and more cultivated view of public affairs than can as a rule be expected
from youths entering by the lower examination.   We agree
with the Playfair Commission, that the best preparation for the
Upper Division is not to be found in the purely clerical routine
of the ordinary clerkships, though there may be exceptions;
and while we desire to leave the heads of offices a free choice
among all clerks in the service, we think that a strict line can,
and ought to be, drawn between the work of the two Divisions.*
The Upper Division, however, should be very much smaller
than at present, and in some offices need not exist at all.[1]

---

[1] A few quotations will show that the views of heads of offices, as
well as those of the lower division clerks, as to the desirability or
necessity of retaining a university-bred first division, were very similar
to those elicited in former reports:

The lower division clerks said:

" The necessity of conciseness precludes a full statement of the objections to a division of the clerical staff into severely defined classes
with a practically insuperable barrier between them.   This much,
however, may perhaps be said:—such a barrier is unnecessary to prevent incompetent men rising, its only possible object; it is unparalleled

We are of opinion that, on the whole, open competition is
in modern organizations of men; it is impolitic, in stifling instead of
stimulating effort; and ungenerous, in impeding men who are sufficiently handicapped in their career by their lack of a university
education.

The framers of the Playfair Scheme must have forgotten that no
machinery or supervision, however elaborate, can so well promote
economy and efficiency in large establishments as contented officials,
animated by hope and pride in their work.

The more sentimental though not less vital objection may be dismissed in a few words. The Class I. Clerks occupy separate rooms,
have a luncheon room, keep a record of attendance in a different
manner, use separate lavatories, &c., have nearly double the annual
leave of Lower Division Clerks, and are altogether treated as a superior race of beings. As a consequence, the Supplementary and
Lower Division Clerks are perpetually reminded of their inferior
status. That this has an injurious effect is obvious." (*Second
Ridley Report*, Appendix, p. 528.)

The permanent heads of offices, defended the division into classes
as follows:

" The contention on the part of the lower division clerks that there
should be no distinction between the higher and the lower division,
that all clerks should be admitted by the same examination, and that
the higher should be solely recruited from the lower, cannot be too
steadily resisted. There should not be any bar to the selection for the
higher division of a clerk of the lower division who is thoroughly
competent to discharge its duties. Nor is there any such bar except
for a short period. But to admit a presumptive right on the part of
every clerk in the lower division to rise into the higher, would be to
land the Government unnecessarily in largely increased expense, to
interfere most seriously with the efficiency of the administration, and
to bring back and make general throughout the service all the discontent and stagnation of promotion which existed in these offices, such
as the War Office, Admiralty, and Customs, in which formerly there
was only one homogeneous class of clerks. As is pointed out in the
paragraph of the Playfair Commission Report, to which I have directed special attention, the performance of routine duties is not only
not a good training for the higher posts of the service, but, as a rule,
it is a bad training, and the State would, in my opinion, act very
foolishly if, with the whole world to choose from, it contented itself
with the very moderate material for the higher posts in the service,
which the lower division can supply." (*Ibid.*, p. 423.)

" (*Chairman.*) Supposing there was an adequate flow of promotion

the best method of selection, and that the limits of age should

in the office, and 'supposing there was not this stagnation which kept the lower division clerk on at the same daily work all his life, if you can imagine that out of the way could you see any reason why in the work of the War Office there should be any distinction between the work of the upper and lower division clerks such as exists between the commissioned and non-commissioned officers in the army?—Certainly; and for this reason, because, more particularly in the War Office than in the other offices, the present War Office is amalgamated out of a large number of offices, and a great portion of this department is superintended by military officers, men of good social position and education, and considerable intelligence and ability, selected to superintend the rooms of the military branch. The War Office men to hold their own against those men in argument and discussion must be men of the same kind socially and in ability and I believe that you cannot attain that by means of the lower division.

Taking a man who has passed the competitive examination of the lower division and been trained for some years in the War Office, and who thoroughly understands the detail, what is there to disqualify him from discharging the duties of principal in the department in which he would be placed?—I think he has not been educationally trained to take that breadth of view that is necessary for a man who is in a responsible position of principal or even a lower position than that." (*Ibid.*, p. 392.)

" Then, is the introduction of men of university standing under the Playfair schemes in your opinion, a good thing for the Service?—Yes, I think it is.

Do you think that such men are really a valuable addition to the public service, and necessary to the public service?—Yes.

(*Mr. Cleghorn.*) Am I right in supposing that you think their numbers should be few?—Yes. I think that the number of the higher division clerks could certainly be reduced." (*Ibid.*, p. 397.)

It is interesting to note the following summary of the work of the Upper division (corresponding to Playfair's first division) men in the Treasury submitted by the Treasury heads to the Ridley Commission. The necessity of a high order of intellectual training is evident. The only question which would immediately strike a German or American observer is, whether a training in economics and finance should not be a requisite for Treasury positions. Thus far, however, the English Treasury has been successful in selecting first class university men without special economic training, and giving them the necessary practical experience in the first years of apprenticeship in the service.

be 20-24. As a rule, the older men will be successful, a result

" The *Upper Division* are charged with the deliberative and executive work of the Treasury.

The work is divided as follows:—

First Division.

Finance generally. Banking and Currency. Mint. Exchequer and Audit. Paymaster General (including the Irish Branch). Queen's and Lord Treasurer's Remembrancer, Scotland, for financial business. Bank of England. National Debt Commissioners. Public Works Loan Commissioners. Ordinary applications for issues from the grants of Parliament, or the Consolidated Fund, or the Treasury Chest Fund. Treasury Audit. Treasury Chest abroad. Estimates for Civil Services, Revenue Departments, and Votes of Credit. Metropolitan Board of Works. Local Loans. Guaranteed Loans. Sinking Fund Accounts. Moreover, the Accountant and his staff keep the accounts of all Exchequer receipts and issues: direct the issues: prepare the Consolidated Fund Charge: keep the accounts of the Votes administered by the Treasury, and of the Civil Contingencies Fund, &c., &c.

The head of the First Division is especially the clerk of the Chancellor of the Exchequer. His *main* function is to see, under the direction of the Chancellor, that money is at all times ready to meet Imperial demands at home and abroad.

The First Division is the point of contact between the annual Select Committee of Public Accounts and the Treasury; one of the most important duties of the Principal Clerk being attendance at the sessions of that Committee, when he occupies a special position and is expected to be ready to state the views of the Treasury upon all points which may arise. For this reason, as well as from finance being its special domain, it belongs to the First Division to suggest and enjoin the principles which the other divisions are to apply in their dealings with the spending departments.

One of the First Class Clerks is specially charged with the preparation of the Estimates for Civil Services and Revenue Departments: and it is his duty to attend all sittings of the House of Commons when these Estimates are under discussion, and to prepare information to enable the Financial Secretary to answer questions and give explanations thereon.

Second Division.

Correspondence with Foreign Office, Colonial Office, War Office, Admiralty, Chelsea Hospital. Woods and Forests. Duchies of Cornwall and Lancaster. Municipal Corporations. Slave Trade." (*Ibid.*, Appendix.)

which we should prefer.   A marked distinction in age facilitates the working of an Upper Division.

We are disposed to doubt whether undue weight is not now given in the examination for the Upper Division, to extensive information, as distinguished from accurate knowledge, and we suggest that the subjects for examination should be grouped in some such manner as they are in the Final Schools at the Universities, and that no candidate should be admitted to more than two groups at most.

To attract men of this standing and capacity, we think that 200*l*. should be the initial salary.   And that the scale should be:—

	£			£	£
3rd grade	200 by an annual increment of			20 to	500.
2nd "	600 by	"	"	25 to	800.
1st "	850 by	"	"	50 to	1,000.

There should be no duty pay for the First, any more than for the Second Division, and the hours of attendance should in future be seven, at the least.   *It must be borne in mind that the new First Division will be very much smaller than the present Upper Division, and that the salaries now suggested will be paid only for the same kind of work as is now being done by the higher grades of the Upper Division.*

There should be a strict probation for two years, during which time it may reasonably be expected that a man's official aptitude, or the reverse, will be discovered.   There should, however, be no hesitation in getting rid of any man who does not show the requisite qualities for official work within this period.   This condition is absolutely necessary in order to guard the public service against the introduction of men who have no other aptitude than that of being able to succeed in a literary examination.

It should therefore be clearly made known to all competitors that fitness for office work will be necessary to secure them continuance in the public service.

The same test of fitness should, in principle, be applied at each of the steps or grades, and it should be recognized that advancement to a higher grade is not a matter of right. The numbers in each of the grades of the First Division should be laid down for each office; and promotion from each grade should only take place upon the conditions (*a*) that there is a vacancy in the grade above; (*b*) that the work of the department requires the vacancy to be filled up; (*c*) that the particular clerk proposed to be promoted has been reported fit to discharge the higher duties he will have to undertake. To some men, 500*l.* will be the limit, to some 800*l.*, whilst only the best will attain to the maximum of the scale.

The scale of salary we have suggested is, in our opinion, sufficient to secure good candidates for all the competitive upper posts in all the offices, without exception. And open competition should therefore, in future, be universally compulsory, wherever men of this class are required.

There will still be certain special appointments requiring professional or technical knowledge, which cannot be satisfactorily filled by open competition. These should be scheduled, and it might be desirable to fix a minimum and maximum of age, say 25-40.

As regards the distinction between the work of the present Upper and Lower Divisions, it is alleged that difficulties have arisen, and must arise, from the fact that the Upper Division clerks are, as it were, apprenticed for a time to work with the Lower Division, thereby causing jealousies and a sense of inequality, especially when the latter are much older men. It appears to us that with a very small Upper or First Division, such as we now propose, it will generally be possible to employ the probationers with their seniors in that Division; and we conceive that if certain work be clearly defined as Upper or First Division work (such, *e. g.*, as dealing with papers which have arrived at a certain stage), there ought to be no difficulty in apportioning it to men of the calibre we have indicated.

Finally, the Ridley Commission dealt with the old question of the employment of copyists and their grievances, regretted that the Playfair recommendations had not been carried out and that over 1,200 copyists were still employed, many upon superior work and for long periods, and suggested that in the future their work be turned over to junior second division clerks, and to boy clerks recruited by competition. They suggested that the employment of women should be extended, especially as typewriters. The concluding pages of the report deal with questions of superannuation. The commission recommended that the existing system be maintained,[1] excepting that there be a compulsory deduction of 5 per cent from all future salaries. They denied that pensions, as then constituted, were deferred pay, and they suggested that the law[2] which gave the Treasury power to pension off useless, inefficient or redundant employees, should be revoked. Compulsory retirement at 65 was suggested, and the practice of adding a

---

[1] On the history of pensions in the English civil service, see the memorial by Sir Herbert Maxwell in the Appendix to the *Second Ridley Report*; also the *Report of the Commission of 1857* on the Superannuation Act; also a *Report* of President Taft's *Commission on Economy and Efficiency* by Herbert Brown, 1912; and the appendix of the *Civil Service Year Book of Great Britain*, published annually by Sheppard, Cooper & Company, London. Before the Ridley Commission it was claimed that pensions *are* deferred pay, that the existing system was illogical, unfair to the individual and uneconomical for the state, that it prevents the dismissal of incompetents and encourages men to stay in the service until the retiring age, etc. This is the view adopted in the United States. See p. 256 *infra*.

Since the Ridley report the theory that pensions are deferred pay has been generally accepted, and provision has been made for compulsory retirement at 65, and for lump sums to dependents; but the method of payment is still that of " straight pensions." The present regulations, revised in 1909 by the Courtney Commission, are substantially those of the old Act of 1859.

[2] Act of 1887, 50-51 Victoria c. 67, s. 2.

number of years to the actual service of professional officers appointed from public life at a mature age was condemned.[1]

In general, we find in the Ridley reports no undercurrent
of opposition to open competition, and no stifled sighs for
the good old days of executive choice and prerogative. On
the whole, the improvements suggested by the Ridley Commission on the reorganization scheme of Dr. Playfair were
considerable. The Ridley scheme standardized the service
and put an end to the confusion caused by the Order in
Council of 1876. The old two-division system was retained, and second division men were given greater opportunities but less pay.

A Treasury minute of 1889 approved most of the recommendations of the second Ridley report, and Orders in
Council of February 1, 1890, March 21, 1890,[2] and August
15, 1890,[3] adopted the Ridley recommendations, together
with the old Playfair background. A new program of
study for division II was made, retaining the idea of a
sound commercial education. Later on, the Ridley recommendation of shorthand as a subject was adopted, but time
showed that this test of a commercial education was not
calculated to attract as efficient men as a purely academic
examination. Schoolmasters complained of the bad effects
of the examination in demanding "'a superficial polish
upon a rather low, though useful order of accomplishment,"

[1] This condemnation was ignored.

[2] Constituting the second division. See also Order in Council of
Nov. 29, 1898.

[3] Constituting the first division. All these Orders in Council have
been repealed, having been consolidated and amplified in the Order
in Council of Jan. 10, 1910. See Appendix A.

and finally the academic examination now in force was substituted, the difficulty of the test being materially increased.[1]

The Treasury Minute of 1889 and the Orders in Council of March 21 and August 15, 1890, substantially govern the civil service today. A compact digest is therefore given here. The Ridley scheme could not be adopted in its entirety immediately. It will be seen that the Treasury had to continue temporarily some of the old Playfair arrangements. The ultimate adoption of the Ridley scheme had to wait until time had removed the Playfair generation of clerks.[2]

TREASURY MINUTE ON THE SECOND RIDLEY REPORT

1. The Playfair scheme has been fairly tried and reductions in numbers have been made, but My Lords of the Treasury agree with the Ridley Commission that only time can bring about a complete reduction. Compulsory retirement is unfeasible because very expensive and very invidious.

2. The Ridley Commission recommends that, in order to extend the Treasury control, a general Order in Council for the organization of the civil service be passed; that every department regulate its normal establishments in accordance with this Order in Council, and that the establishments thus formulated be referred to a committee of the principal Treasury officials and other permanent officers,

---

[1] Lowell, *Government of England*, vol. i, p. 166. President Lowell adds: " The result in the future will no doubt be to make proficiency in regular school work the real test for appointment, and thus, in accordance with Macaulay's principle, to base selection upon general education instead of technical knowledge." See also Appendix E, *infra.*

[2] The suggestion that the government could dismiss redundant or superfluous clerks, since no clerk has a contract in the government for a life tenure, was, of course, not acted on by the Treasury. Such a procedure would be cruel, and even if legal, highly injudicious.

one representing the Civil Service Commission and one the great Revenue departments, this committee to report to the Treasury, and final authority to rest, as now, with the government. My Lords cannot agree with these recommendations. Friction between the Treasury and other departments would be avoided if decisions were made by a body representing the whole civil service, but such a committee must consist of heads of departments who are too busy for such work. Therefore the Treasury must go on with this work with the assistance when necessary of a special committee. When the Treasury and a department disagree, the cabinet must decide. My Lords agree that there should be periodical reviews of the departments by a committee like that recommended by the Ridley report, this point to be embodied in an Order in Council.

3. Regulations affecting the lower grades of the service are to be made uniform by an Order in Council in accordance with the Ridley report, but only the lower grades.

4. A seven-hour day is agreed to.

5. Uniform holidays and sick leave throughout the services are agreed to, but not the same for all classes.

6. Technical and professional posts not recruited by open competition are to be scheduled.

7. Redundants will be transferred where possible.

8. The classification proposed by the Ridley commission will be carried out, and the number of clerks of the upper division reduced.

9. Copying work will be done mechanically by junior second division and by boy clerks wherever possible. Other copying work will be done by piece work, or by contract work in open market. Boy clerks and boy copyists will be amalgamated, and a way will be opened to the second division by examination. Women typists will be employed wherever possible.

10. Wherever necessary, groups of men below the second division, *e. g.*, for statistical abstraction, will be employed, but a general class will not be created.

11. In the second division promotion will be by pure merit. There will be a uniform scale of salaries. Duty pay will be abolished. There will be a year's probation. The initial salary will be £70 and will rise by £5 to £100. The Playfair Commission gave triennial increments, which were rarely withheld, and annual increments are not likely to be withheld either. Therefore after £100, a satisfactory certificate in writng must be given by the head of the division before promotion. Then the clerk rises by £7 10*s.* to £190, but instead of another certificate above this as recommended by the Ridley commission, My Lords have decided on a higher class (class one, division two), with small numbers to be reached by promotion for merits—£200—£10—£350.

12. Second division clerks may reach division one for exceptional merit, on very strong recommendations of the head of the department. Eight years' service in the second division is required instead of ten as formerly. [The Ridley Commission wanted this term abolished entirely.]

13. Reductions in minimum salary and duty pay are considerable, but on the whole there is a considerable increase in expenditure on the second division.

14. First division. The Playfair scheme of salary and duty pay for the first division has only been adopted in the Admiralty, Customs, Internal Revenue, Irish Secretary's office, Lunacy Commission, Patent Office, Science and Arts departments, and War Office. In other departments pay like that hereinafter proposed by the Ridley commission is given. The Ridley provisions are for a first division of very limited numbers chosen by open competition. The salaries will be as follows: 1st grade—£200-£20-£500; 2nd grade—£600-£25-£800; 3rd grade—£850-£50-£1,000.

The probation period is to be two years. There will be no duty pay, and vacancies will be filled only where required. My Lords will have a first division in a department only when they and the head of the department agree that it is necessary. There will be a seven-hour day. They agree about the other recommendations; but the Ridley salary scale is to represent a *maximum,* and not to be universally applied, at least until the upper establishment has been reduced. Meanwhile where the Playfair scheme of salaries has been adopted (offices above), it will be maintained and second division clerks promoted to the higher establishments. Instead of duty pay, clerks of the Playfair division will have a higher class, £400-£20-£600,[1] appointed by merit only. The age of first division competitors is to be from 22 to 25. There will be open competition except in the case of the House of Commons, House of Lords, and Foreign Office clerkships, and Legal Offices. When a staff office falls vacant, no appointment shall be made without the approval of the Prime Minister after conference with the Chancellor of the Exchequer. New staff offices or increases in pay will be determined by My Lords of the Treasury with the Prime Minister. Changes are to be effected gradually. The immediate object of an Order in Council will be to substitute second for first division clerks wherever practicable.

ORDER IN COUNCIL MARCH 21, 1890

This regulates the second division according to the final Treasury Minute on the Ridley report. Special provision is made for those in office who must work seven hours instead of six, and who formerly received duty pay.[2] The

---

[1] It will be remembered that the Playfair scale was £100—triennial increments £37-10s—£400, with duty pay not exceeding £200 per annum.

[2] The question of an "implied contract" between government and

other provisions of this Order in Council are described in the Treasury Minute above. This revises the existing Order in Council of February 12, 1876, which followed the Playfair report.

ORDER IN COUNCIL AUGUST 15, 1890

This regulates the first division and follows in most respects the Treasury Minute above. Following the Ridley recommendations, officers may be forced to retire with pensions at 60, and provision is made for the yearly return before Parliament of officers whose services are prolonged beyond 65, with reasons.[1] The Ridley plan for a consultative committee, repudiated in the Treasury Minute, is after all adopted. A consultative annual committee is formed to advise as to staff salaries and organization, consisting of the permanent Under Secretary of the Treasury or the Assistant Under Secretary, the First

civil service fixing a six-hour working day, came up before the Ridley Commission. Though it was decided that there was no such contract, the difficulty of increasing the hours and work of the civil service, without granting extra pay or creating an uproar and political pressure, was commented on. The duty pay of the Playfair report was given largely for an extra hour's work each day. Sir T. H. Farrer of the Playfair Commission stated before the Ridley Commission that he now regretted the extra pay for a seven-hour day. See *The British State Telegraphs*, by Hugo R. Meyer (New York, 1907), p. 327; see also p. 205, *infra*.

[1] An Order in Council of November 29, 1898, provided for compulsory retirement throughout the civil service at 65, subject to the power of retention for five years in very exceptional cases. Three cases are mentioned where removal may be detrimental:

(a) When the number of officers aged 65 in a department is large and removal would cause grave inconvenience.

(b) Peculiar qualifications.

(c) Where officer has been entrusted with the execution of a particular duty which is approaching completion.

In 1901-1902, for example, only fourteen men were so retained.

Civil Service Commissioner and two other principal officers of public departments, and a representative of the department under consideration if the department is not represented. If the department is represented, then one more principal officer of another department. Disputes between the Treasury and heads of departments may, with the consent of the Chancellor of the Exchequer, be referred to this committee. There shall be quinquennial inquiries into pay and numbers.

CHAPTER VIII

The Civil Service To-day

THE PRESENT ROYAL COMMISSION

The Question of Intellectual Aristocracy

During the last two years a Royal Commission on Civil Service has been again successfully performing the monumental task of inquiry.[1] Statically and dynamically the

---

[1] " GEORGE R.I.

George the Fifth, by the Grace of God, of the United Kingdom of Great Britain and Ireland and of the British Dominions beyond the Seas King, Defender of the Faith, to

Our right trusty and well-beloved Counsellor Antony Patrick, Baron MacDonnell, Knight Grand Commander of Our Most Exalted Order of the Star of India, Knight Commander of Our Royal Victorian Order;

Our right trusty and right entirely beloved cousin and Counsellor Victor Christian William, Duke of Devonshire;

The Right Reverend Father in God Hubert Murray, Bishop of Southwark; and

Our trusty and well-beloved:—

Sir Kenneth Augustus Muir Mackenzie, Knight Grand Cross of Our Most Honourable Order of the Bath, one of Our Counsel learned in the Law, Permanent Secretary to the Lord Chancellor, Clerk of the Crown in Chancery;

Sir Henry Primrose, Knight Commander of Our Most Honourable Order of the Bath, Companion of Our Most Exalted Order of the Star of India;

Sir Donald MacAlister, Knight Commander of Our Most Honourable Order of the Bath;

Sir William Guy Granet, Knight;

Harold Trevor Baker, Esquire;

Alfred Allen Booth, Esquire;

Arthur Boutwood, Esquire;

machinery and personnel of the civil service have been ex-
posed to view. From the Lord Chancellor to the office boy,
every one has again been invited to describe his duties, air
his grievances, and suggest changes. In many ways this
is the most remarkable document in the history of civil service in any country. In keeping with the spirit of the age,
this inquiry is conducted in a manner at once scientific, open-
minded, and sympathetic. The new sociology, the new
democracy, and the advanced ideals of national education
are evident in cross-examinations which are no longer pains-
taking and perfunctory. The commission is, we may say, a
conservative one, in that the majority belong to the upper,
highly-educated class of administrators, university professors, and members of Parliament—but there has been a

> John Robert Clynes, Esquire;
> Samuel John Gurney Hoare, Esquire;
> Richard Durning Holt, Esquire;
> Percy Ewing Matheson, Esquire;
> Arthur Everett Shipley, Esquire, Fellow of the Royal Society;
> Philip Snowden, Esquire;
> Graham Wallas, Esquire;
> Elizabeth Sanderson Haldane, Spinster; and
> Lucy Anne Evelyn, wife of Granville Edward Stewart Streat-
> feild, Esquire, Greeting!

Whereas We have deemed it expedient that a Commission should
forthwith issue

To inquire into and report on the methods of making appointments
to and promotions in the Civil Service, including the Diplomatic and
Consular Services, and the legal departments;

To investigate the working and efficiency of the system of competitive examination for such appointments, and to make recommendations for any alterations or improvements in that system which may
appear to be advisable; and

To consider whether the existing scheme of organization meets the
requirements of the Public Service, and to suggest any modifications
which may be needed therein: etc, etc."

(At the date of this writing the commission is still hearing evidence,
and has issued no report. Three volumes of evidence have appeared).

noticeable disposition on the part of the whole commission to bring the civil service into line with modern needs, and to look upon new experiments without shuddering.

In writing this chapter an attempt has been made to combine quotations from the most noteworthy evidence submitted to the Royal Commission with facts concerning the civil service obtained elsewhere—in such a way as to give a clear idea of the conditions, tendencies, and prospects of change in the civil service.

Before turning to the questions of education, class distinction, and opportunity, which are the most important features of the Royal Commission's inquiry, we shall sketch as briefly as possible the developments and changes which have taken place in the recruiting and organization of the civil service since the Ridley report.

(1) The first division examinations have been standardized and incorporated with the Indian civil and Eastern cadetship examinations.[1]   The first division, following the recommendations of the Playfair and Ridley reports, has been greatly reduced in numbers.   Certain offices, as indicated below, have been entirely removed from division I, a new intermediate class being substituted.   In some offices only division II men are employed, and very frequently higher staff appointments have been exclusively reserved for second division men.   On the other hand, the need of highly intelligent men to administer new and complex measures has resulted in the employment of first division men where they were previously superfluous.[2]

[1] The candidates highest on the list generally prefer the Home civil service; those next in order go to India, and the lowest successful candidates accept eastern cadetships.   The first two or three men on the list usually go into the Treasury, the most desirable department. For a list of subjects and specimens of examinations, see Appendix C.

[2] For example, the Customs Secretary's office now employs an in-

(2) A new class has been created between the first and second divisions. This intermediate scheme was introduced into the civil service by a Treasury Minute, without authority from Parliament, and without an Order in Council. The appearance of such a division in certain offices for which the first division represented too high and too academic an education, and for which the second division did not represent a sufficiently high education, was foreshadowed in the Ridley report by Sir S. A. Blackwood. His suggestion is worth quoting in full:

What would be your suggestion to improve the state of things? It cannot be a good thing to have men come in that way who are above their work, can it? — I ought, perhaps, to preface what I say, by saying that I have not given a great deal of attention to questions of organization. My work has been much too hard to allow of my doing so. I have had to carry on the work of the secretary of the Post Office, which is a constant drive, and to work with the instruments that I find at my hand, and therefore I have not become a doctrinaire at all with regard to questions of the organization of the Civil Service. At the same time, of course, I have come in contact with all classes of officers, both in my own office and in a good many other departments of the Government, and I have formed certain opinions about them, but I should not like the Commission to take them as those of a man who has devoted a great deal of thought or attention to the subject, or endeavoured to plan out schemes under

creasing number of university men. The Lloyd George budget introduced complex machinery where the Balfour budget was quite simple. Thus, in the case of liquor licenses, there are now ten or twelve persons employed where formerly only three or four were needed, and instead of a simple uniform tax there is a tax which varies, and there must be taken into consideration the total proceeds of the restaurant or hotel, the relations which the liquor receipts bear to total receipts, and the total receipts to the rental, etc.

which the Civil Service generally could be ultimately constituted. But my own impression, with that preface and pro-
viso, is rather that as these men are often too good and too
old for the work, we should get a very fit class of men if we
took a lad at the time he leaves a public school at 18,—when
he leaves the sixth form,—where he has had what we call a
liberal education. We should then have men not above their
work. They would be more teachable; they would not be
discontented with their work as not being equal to their abilities, and they would be capable, therefore, of more thorough
effective training for the regular work of the office. If I were
the head of a branch in my office, and had to do the regular
current work, and were to be asked which I would prefer, a
double first-class man at 24, who has been out in the world,
and been engaged in other occupations, or a lad of average
ability from a public school at 18, I should say certainly—
" Give me the latter." He will be quite as good for all my
purposes. I shall find him more amenable, more susceptible
of official training, and he will make in the long run as good
a public servant, if not as brilliant a one; and my impression
is that the Civil Service does not want brilliant men, except
in very rare cases.

The conclusion we are rather inclined to draw from what
you have said is this, that you are perhaps going rather too
far when you say that a good deal of the work that is done
by this enormous staff of upper division clerks could not be
done in the lower portion of it by clerks promoted from the
lower division, and entering upon the service by the lower
division examinations, especially if that examination were to
a certain extent raised by languages being added, or something of the sort perhaps?—That might make all the difference.
The lower division examination is certainly not what you
would ordinarily regard as answering to the general accepta-
tion of a liberal education. It is considerably below that.
Nor is the lower division recruited from the social class,
which, I think, men in the service of the Government, occupy-
ing responsible positions such as those in the upper grades of

the Civil Service, ought to have come from, and been brought up in.[1]

The intermediate class was first introduced in the Naval Stores Department of the Admiralty. In this department there was a great deal of difficult routine work of great detail, work too high for all but the best, older second division men and of a kind repugnant to the first division men. Though they could do it well enough, the first division men all felt that their education was wasted on such labor, and tried to get themselves transferred. Hence the intermediate division was introduced from boys at the age of graduation from Public Schools (18 or 19), and was very successful.

The idea of the Treasury in founding the intermediate scheme was that it should supplant both first and second divisions in the offices in which it was used.[2] There are now no intermediate division men employed side by side with second division clerks, but the existence of the intermediate class above them, with only slightly higher qualifications, is one of the grievances of second division clerks. The new Insurance Commission is eventually coming under the intermediate scheme. There are at present about 1,400 members of the civil service who have entered by the intermediate examinations as against 700 first division and 4,000 second division men. Transfer of intermediate clerks is nominally free, but rarely exercised.

(3) The Hobhouse Committee of 1909 on the amalgamation of the Customs and Excise departments standardized classes, pay and promotions. Apart from the central clerical service, recruited by division I, intermediate and division II examinations, there is now one entering examination

---

[1] *Second Ridley Report*, 1888, p. 273.

[2] For a list of offices in which the intermediate scheme is employed, subjects and specimens of examinations, see Appendix D.

for the whole general Customs and Excise department, indoor and outdoor. Yearly increments to salaries are provided, with certain efficiency bars which are passed only on special recommendation, inspection of books, and written examination. Beyond the grade of surveyor, the highest positions of inspectors and collectors are recruited by promotion by merit.

(4) Women and girl clerks, and female learners and sorters are recruited by open competition, but are thus far employed only in the Post Office.[1] Female typists are employed in several departments. On marrying they must resign, and they receive a bonus, more, it is said, as a sign of commiseration than from any desire to promote matrimony.[2] The further employment of women is a subject urged by several witnesses before the present Royal Commission,[3] but the objections to employing men and women side by side, the grave doubts expressed by superior offi-

[1] The Board of Agriculture and the India Office, however, employ some women.

[2] Lowell, *Government of England*, vol. i, p. 172.

[3] *New York Times*, June 2, 1913.

"Several distinguished men and women have sent Premier Asquith a memorial urging an increase in the number of women employes in the civil service, and asking that women clerks be made eligible for promotion in the same manner as men, and also allowed to enter the higher divisions of the service, especially those departments which are concerned with women and children, with many conditions of home life, and with the domestic management of institutions.

The memorial also urges that women should be eligible for scientific and other specialist appointments, especially in State museums, and, finally, that a woman should be appointed a member of the Civil Service Commission."

Women inspectors of factories, etc. under the Home Office have given great satisfaction, but they have been paid much less than men inspectors doing the same work. The usual arguments—*e. g.* absence of family and dependents, and market price of female labor—are used against equal pay, but in this context they are not very convincing.

cers as to the ability of women to compete with men in
efficiency in the long run, and as to their physical capacity,
and the probability that they will leave the service by early
marriage, all indicate that the employment of women on a
large scale above the typist class is not contemplated. The
examinations open to women have been largely attended—
in fact, the proportion of candidates to vacancies is often
as high as twenty to one.

(5) The " blind alley " employment of boy clerks, sanctioned by the Ridley report, by which boys of 19 are turned
out of the civil service into the world without a calling, has
recently become an acute question. To its solution the present Royal Commission has devoted much time and questioning, and as a probable result only as many boys will be employed in future as can be absorbed into the higher classes.
A standing committee on boy labor in the Post Office has
evolved a scheme of educating boy messengers who enter
the Post Office at 14. For two years they will be required
to attend classes under the local educational authorities. At
the end of this period they will be examined in the subjects
taught, *viz.*, handwriting, spelling, English, arithmetic,
geography and history. Those who pass highest will be
allowed to compete amongst themselves for positions as
sorters and telegraph learners, the latter positions being
hereafter removed from open competition and reserved for
boy messengers. Those who are not successful at this second examination will continue as messengers until they are
19, and will then be appointed postmen without further
tests. As yet the compulsory classes are available only in
large towns; but the system will eventually extend throughout the country.

It is probable that the Royal Commission will suggest
further educational plans of this kind in other departments,
so that as few boys as possible will be dismissed from the

service, and as many as possible educated up to further and higher usefulness.

(6) Unfortunately, the employment of a temporary writer class, supposedly discontinued by a Treasury Minute in 1886, and condemned by both the Playfair and the Ridley reports, has again been resorted to. Probably there always will be fluctuating work of this kind. Perhaps the present Royal Commission may discover some satisfactory scheme for a permanent, unattached writer class. At present the tendency is to do away with this class altogether.

(7) It is of the greatest importance to bear in mind that, although unlimited competition has increased with the growth of the civil service since the Ridley report, it is still used *for only about one-third of the situations in the English civil service.*[1] About 2,500 positions are annually recruited by open competition. In general, we may say that all division I clerkships, staff clerkships, second division clerkships, intermediate clerkships, and assistant and boy clerkships—that is, all the general clerical staff—are recruited by open competition. Limited competition has been extended in keeping with early tendencies, to cover a great many technical, professional positions, such as positions in the British Museum, engineers, and also a very miscellaneous lot of offices such as clerks of Parliament, the Royal Irish constabulary, assistants to factory inspectors, clerks in the Foreign Office and consuls, junior inspectors of mines and quarries, naval cadets and clerks, police court clerks, Post Office supplementary clerks, sorters, etc. In some cases (as in those of junior inspectors of mines) the competition is really open, all applications being considered on their merits, and in others (*e. g.,* Metropolitan Police Court clerks and Post Office supplementary clerks

[1] *Cf.* Appendix B.

and sorters) the competition is amongst clerks already in the service who are nominated by their superiors. It is, however, obvious that some of these positions might with greater fairness and no danger be recruited by open competition. Nomination and limited competition for clerkships in the Duchy of Lancaster, House of Lords, and House of Commons, will probably not survive the report of the Royal Commission. The remainder of the positions in the English civil service are still filled by simple nomination, either with or without examination. This class is, of course, largely composed of dockyard workers, messengers, prison employees, and outdoor workers of many kinds, for whom competition has been thought undesirable or impossible. The Royal Commission has certainly brought out that there is no very sound reason why female typists and Post Office employees such as telegraphers, postmen, and numerous other clerks and technical officers, need be recruited in this way.

(8) With the introduction of new paternalistic measures of government, entirely new methods of initial appointment have been found desirable, owing to the necessity of employing experts to get things under way. In the case of the labor exchanges a committee was appointed to sift applications. 13,000 application blanks were received; 800 were selected, and 200 candidates were interviewed. As a result, 100 were finally recommended, the committee being unanimous as to all but one man.[1] This is, however, a method open to grave suspicion of patronage. In the case of the National Health Insurance Commission a somewhat similar plan was adopted, there being, however, a qualifying examination before appointment. Further appointments under the Insurance Commission are to be made by promotion

---

[1] Women candidates were similarly interviewed.

and transfer of civil servants or through the intermediate
scheme of examination.   In general, it may be said that this
method of appointment by consultation has been very favor-
ably commented on by many witnesses before the Royal
Commission, the consensus of opinion being that this is a
desirable way of recruiting managing officials of new departments in an emergency.[1]

(9) It is difficult to generalize about methods of promotion in the civil service.   In spite of the fact that successive
commissions, Orders in Council, and departmental regulations insist upon promotion by merit alone, seniority has,
and always will have, great weight.   As between two men
equal in ability, the senior of course goes ahead; as between
a junior clerk and a senior a little inferior to him, the
senior is probably preferred.   The practice of jumping a
man over the heads of a number of seniors is, of course,
exceedingly unpopular in the service itself.   Herein the
government is always handicapped as against a private employer.   This question of seniority and merit is of little im-

[1] The Civil Service Commission in its report of 1911 says: "All these
posts are at present temporary and unpensionable, and are included
in Schedule B of the Order in Council of 10th January, 1910. They
are not, therefore, under the jurisdiction of our Board; but should
any of the candidates recommended by either of the Committees come
up hereafter before us for certificates of qualification for the posts
for which they were recommended, we shall have no difficulty, after
learning that they have discharged their duties to the satisfaction of
the Board of Trade, in certifying from personal knowledge that they
are qualified in point of experience and ability for these posts.   This
procedure constitutes a new precedent; and in view of the number
of posts that are being created, for which special experience and
capacity in dealing with practical affairs are of more importance than
attainments such as can be tested by open or limited competition, we
regard with satisfaction the apparent success of this novel method of
selection.   It is, in fact, a new kind of open competition, in which
tests are applied such as men of business use in the choice of their
employees."

portance where there are written examinations for promotion; but except in the Revenue departments (and, of course, promotions from boy clerks to assistants, and assistants to the second division), examinations for promotion in the civil service are rare, and within the clerical establishments almost unheard-of. Efficiency bars and certificates from superiors seem to be effective in preventing shirking, in stimulating effort, and in insuring the requisite ability for promotions.

In the United States there is a marked tendency to trust to written promotion examinations and to complex efficiency records, especially in municipal governments. The Chicago Civil Service Commission, for example, has drawn up elaborate step pyramids in each department, showing how, by promotion examinations and efficiency records, the lowest clerk may rise from stage to stage to the highest post at the apex of the official Sakkara. This system has been successful in Chicago, but it is difficult to see what virtue there can be in successive examinations once a man's mental calibre, ability in the discharge of present duties, and general qualifications for higher place, are patent. In all cases there are " personal marks " awarded on past record, etc., and the examination itself seems to be merely a way of avoiding any suspicion of partiality in the final choice. Something like elaborate efficiency records were proposed in the 1853 report, but were never adopted in England. There seems to be more need of taking precautions against laziness and inefficiency in the United States, especially in city governments. The great danger is that such records may result in a system of espionage at once meticulous and tyrannical.

(10) It may be well to indicate briefly the existing exceptional methods of entering the civil service without examination.

I. Under the Superannuation Act of 1859, sec. 4, the Treasury may, by order or warrant, declare that for certain offices professional or other peculiar qualifications not ordinarily to be acquired in the civil service are required, and may exempt such offices from the Civil Service Commission entirely.

II. Clause 7 of the Order in Council of 1910 (re-enacting Clause 7 of the Order in Council of 1870 [1]) provides that if the head of a department and the Treasury propose to appoint a person of peculiar or professional ability acquired in other pursuits, the Civil Service Commission may, if they think fit, dispense with examination, age limits, etc.

III. All positions to which the holder is directly appointed by the crown. [2]

[1] *Cf.* Appendix A.

[2] This list is as interesting as it is miscellaneous and anomolous.

"APPOINTMENTS HELD DIRECT from the CROWN.

The First Lord submits names for His Majesty's approval, in respect of the following appointments (Ministerial and Civil Service), held direct from the Crown and paid out of public moneys:

(a) *Appointments by Letters Patent:*—
Commissioners of the Treasury.
Commissioners of Admiralty.
Commissioners of Inland Revenue.
Commissioners of Customs.
Comptroller and Auditor-General.
Assistant Comptroller and Auditor-General.
Clerk of the Parliaments.
Clerk of the House of Commons.
Registrar-General.

(b) *Appointments by Warrants under the Royal Sign Manual:*—
Paymaster-General.
Commissioners of Public Works, Ireland.
Commissioners of Woods and Forests.
Charity Commissioners.
Deputy Clerk Register.
Clerk Assistant and Second Clerk Assistant of the House of Commons.
Secretary to the Charity Commissioners.

IV. Cases in which the necessity of obtaining a civil

(c) *Appointments by Order in Council:—*
    Civil Service Commissioners.

The First Lord also appoints on behalf of the Lords Commissioners of the Treasury (in some cases specifically in conjunction with the Chancellor of the Exchequer) to the following appointments, completed by Treasury Warrant or Minute. In some cases the approval of the King is required to be obtained:

Permanent Secretary to the Treasury.
Assistant Secretary to the Treasury.
Auditor of the Civil List.
Solicitor and Assistant Solicitor to the Treasury.
Treasury Valuer.
Solicitors to Inland Revenue and Customs.
Special Commissioners of Income Tax.
Secretary and Assistant Secretary to Board of Customs.
Assistant Paymaster-General.
Assistant Paymaster-General for Supreme Court.
Treasury Remembrancers.
King's and Lord Treasurer's Remembrancers.
Crown Receiver for Scotland.
Controller of Stationery Office.
Secretary to Office of Works.
Director of Kew Gardens.
Inspector of Ancient Monuments.
Deputy Master of Mint.
Directors of Suez Canal.
Astronomer Royal.
Law Agents, Scotland.
Registrar of Friendly Societies.
Secretary to Civil Service Commission.
Superintendent of Statistics (Registrar-General's Office).
Parliamentary Counsel.
Keepers of National Gallery, Tate Gallery, and Wallace Collection.
Government Chemist.
Insurance Commissioners.

The First Lord also submits to the King the names for appointment as Ambassadors after consultation with the Secretary of State for Foreign Affairs.

The Chancellor of the Exchequer (in his capacity as National Debt Commissioner) appoints the Controller of the National Debt Office.

Both First Lord and Chancellor appoint to vacancies in their staff of Office-keepers or Messengers which occur at their respective residences during their term of office."

Royal Commission, 1912, vol. i, Appendix IV (b).

service certificate is specifically excluded by statute, or by enrollment in Schedule B of the Order in Council of 1870.

It is impossible within the limits of this essay to discuss at length the back door methods of entering the civil service. Such methods are necessary, and when adopted in good faith and with sufficient publicity are highly desirable. The evidence before the present Royal Commission has, however, made it palpable that one back door into the civil service is enough. A new Order in Council or statute will probably be drawn up combining the advantages of Section 4 of the Superannuation Act and Clause 7 and Schedule B of the Order in Council of 1910. Under the Superannuation Act there is not enough publicity, although announcement is made in Parliament, and there is no provision for consultation with the Civil Service Commission.[1]

The desirability of consulting with the Civil Service Commission when an exceptional appointment from outside is to be made to an important position, was recently conspicuously illustrated in the appointment of Sir Matthew Nathan as Secretary to the General Post Office.[2] There was difficulty in finding anyone to fill the secretaryship. The Postmaster General felt that he had no one of requisite qualifications in the department to promote. Sir Matthew was a Colonel of Engineers and had been a successful colonial administrator as Governor of the Gold Coast and of the Straits Settlements. The Postmaster Gen-

---

[1] There are a number of other anomalies to be abolished by the coming Order in Council, *e. g.*, the Post Office has never been enrolled under Schedule A (providing for open competition), and yet open examinations are held regularly by the Civil Service Commission for the Post Office as under Schedule A.

[2] Sir Matthew has since been appointed, by the Crown, Chairman of the Board of Inland Revenue.

eral wanted to appoint him to the vacancy, but under the
Order in Council of 1910 he had to get the consent of the
Civil Service Commission. The Civil Service Commission
inquired into the record and fitness of Sir Matthew Nathan,
and certified that his qualifications were such that the ordinary requirements of examination and promotion might
be waived. If this method is universally adopted, the public will never be suspicious of exceptional appointments to
high positions in the civil service from public life.

(11) In recent years the question of "influence" and
patronage in appointments and promotions to high positions
has received much public condemnation. Investigation dis-
closes how little undue influence is exercised, and how much
public opinion has been educated up to an almost rigid insistence upon the letter of the once abominated civil service law.

So far as the writer can judge, the "jobs" of this kind
perpetrated by ministers and the Treasury in the last decade
have been very few. Very rarely a man is appointed from
outside on account of family or political connections to a
post for which he is not particularly fitted; again, charges
are made about favoritism in appointments to new departments, but apparently without much ground. There is,
however, a kind of promotion, called the "private secretary
scandal," which is worth investigating. It seems that a
number of first division clerks, who have served as private
secretaries to political heads of offices, have so impressed
their chiefs that these have found means to promote them
to really high and responsible positions in their own or in
other departments.

On investigation it appears that in some cases these promotions are really "jobs"; in others, that exceptional men
have demonstrated their right to rise to high positions. As
an example of a palpable job, we have the case of Mr. G. E.

P. Murray, a young man of thirty-one, who in 1912 was made a Commissioner of Excise at £1,200 a year.   Mr. Murray's father was the highest official in the whole civil service, the Permanent Secretary to the Treasury.   The younger Murray entered the civil service in 1903, through a back door, as a " temporary examiner " in the Education Office.   After eight years' temporary, if somewhat responsible, service, Murray was suddenly appointed to the £1,200 commissionship.[1]

In this connection it is well to remember that a private secretaryship is an admirable agency for bringing out the exceptional qualifications and abilities in a young man which mark him for high place.   The secretary to the political head of an office comes into contact with great men and measures; he prepares papers of great importance and is alert to supplement and expand the work of his chief.   The private secretaries to Mr. Lloyd George have had to assist a man who is brilliant in evolving schemes, in popularizing them, and in defending them in Parliament, but in matters of formulation and detail at once impatient and insatiable. The private secretary to Mr. Lloyd George must have, not only wide knowledge, adaptability, patience, tact, and insight into character, but also the ability to work indefinitely without regard to official hours or personal convenience, and always with a fresh and curious mind.   Such a man develops wonderfully in a short time, and the success of great national measures, such as the Insurance Act and the Budget of 1909, are not a little owing to him.   And when the great measures are once in force and a high position elsewhere becomes vacant, is it surprising and reprehensible if the Chancellor of the Exchequer points to his tried private sec-

---

[1] Other "cases" are quoted in the *London Magazine* of October, 1912, and in *The Civilian*, November 23, 1912.   These "cases" must be taken with several grains of salt.

retary as just the man for the vacant place? It is indeed a bold outsider who sees graft and patronage in the appointment of a secretary to Mr. Lloyd George as a member of the Council of India. Usually it is the jump from a modest salary to £5,000 a year which takes away the breath of the man in the street.[1]

[1] "The following is a list of those gentlemen appointed to lucrative positions in the Civil Service after serving in the capacity of Private Secretary to Members of the Government. The list does not pretend to be complete, and it, of course, excludes Private Secretaries of Ministers, who have received substantial Departmental promotion, according to custom:

Mr. Mark Sturgis, Private Secretary to Mr. Asquith, appointed to be Special Commissioner of Income Tax.

Mr. F. N. Rogers, ex-Liberal Parliamentary candidate and ex-Private Secretary to Mr. McKenna, appointed to be Small Holdings Commissioner.

Mr. Max S. Green, Private Secretary to Lord Aberdeen, appointed to be Chairman of Irish Prisons Board.

Mr. Lionel Earle, Private Secretary to Mr. Lewis Harcourt, appointed to be Secretary to Office of Works.

Mr. L. Neish, Private Secretary to Lord Loreburn, appointed to be Registrar of the Privy Council.

Mr. E. P. Murray, Private Secretary to Lord Morley, appointed to be Commissioner of Customs.

Mr. E. G. Soames, Private Secretary to Mr. Churchill, appointed to be National Debt Commissioner.

Mr. W. R. Davies, Private Secretary to Mr. James Bryce, appointed to be Assistant Secretary, Education Office.

Mr. Vaughan Nash, Private Secretary to Mr. Asquith, appointed to be Vice-Chairman of Development Commission.

Mr. H. J. Houlihan, Private Secretary to Lord Portsmouth (ex-Minister), appointed to be Secretary to Irish Insurance Commissioners.

Mr. G. E. Baker, Private Secretary to late Parliamentary Secretary of Board of Trade, appointed to be Principal Clerk, Board of Trade.

Mr. H. G. Maurice, Private Secretary to Mr. Runciman, appointed to be Assistant Secretary, Fisheries Department, Board of Agriculture.

Mr. W. H. Clark, Private Secretary to Mr. Lloyd George, appointed to be Member of Viceroy of India's Council.

Mr. J. Rowland, Private Secretary to Mr. Lloyd George, appointed to be Welsh Insurance Commissioner.

Mr. E. A. Gowers, Private Secretary to Mr. Lloyd George, appointed to be Chief of Department of Insurance Inspectors."—*The Civilian.*

(12) On January 1, 1912, the English government took over the whole telephone business of the country. Without any hitch and without public demonstration, the Postmaster General assumed the administration of this huge department:

The change means that capital amounting to over £16,000,-000, and 18,000 employees are transferred to the state—that, in short, the nationalization of the telephone service is an accomplished fact. Of these additional civil servants at least 12,000 will have the right to pensions under the post-office. The staff has not been transferred in its entirety. Certain members, such as the solicitor, the secretary, the general superintendent, the chief engineer, the assistant engineer, and six provincial superintendents, will not come under the Government. The highly-paid officials will receive compensation from the company's fund established for that purpose.

An idea of the extent of the service taken over by the state may be gathered from the following statistics: There are over 400,000 subscribers, 1,571 exchanges, 500,000 exchange stations, and 36,000 private stations. Before the transfer the post-office controlled about 500,000 miles of telephone wire with 120,000 subscribers. By the change it will control 1,253,-890 miles. The additional mileage brings the capital value of the system owned and worked by the state up to £25,000,000. The change, so smoothly accomplished, is the result of a decision in Parliament in 1905. The old company worked under a license from the Government granted over thirty years ago. It was resolved that the license should not be renewed, and that on its expiration the telephone service should be conducted by the state.[1]

It is impossible to look into the future, with its prospect of immensely increased numbers of civil servants, without

[1] *Literary Digest*, Jan. 27, 1912, p. 154.

feeling that the question of the relation of these employees to the government is one of the first national importance.

With the expansion of departments like the Post Office, and the further development of state and municipal owner-ship, there arises the great question of the rights and powers of civil servants as against the state. When the telephone employees enter the civil service, is their relation to the state exactly the same as was their relation to their old private employers? Or, in other words, is the state under the same dangers of trades unionism, hostile organization, and strikes as the private employer? The conservative and the state-socialist say no. The socialist and syndicalist say yes.

It is not possible here to discuss the many differences from the point of view of the public welfare between the status of civil servants and the status of workmen in private employ, when there is a question of enforcing demands by trades-union methods and by strikes. The general tendency is certainly [1] to regard government employees as a pecu-liar class, and to regard political agitation as dangerous and unwarranted, and strikes against the government as being like strikes of the army or navy, treason and mutiny. *The Outlook,* in an editorial on the strike of the municipal street cleaners of New York said:

"Men who are employed by the public cannot strike. They can, and sometimes do, mutiny. Then they should be treated not as strikers, but as mutineers."

The strike of the French telegraph and postal employees in 1909, and the resulting conversion of the erstwhile advo-cate of the general strike, M. Briand, to a saner policy of repression, is still fresh in our minds. The reply of the French postmen's organization to repressive measures is

[1] Walling, *Socialism As It Is* (New York, 1912), p. 392.

" that the administration of the Post Office is an industrial and commercial administration; that it is a vast enterprise of general utility; that the notion of loyalty or treason is entirely misplaced in this field." [1]

No doubt the postal and telegraph employees in France have some just grievances. The writer is not sufficiently acquainted with their needs to know how pressing these are. But certainly as regards the English postal employees, the writer believes—in spite of Mr. Walling and his socialistic brethren—that the civil servant may safely depend upon the public and parliamentary recognition of the justice of his cause, upon the fairness of the Treasury or a minister (who have none of the selfish interest of private employers), and upon royal commissions which act as a kind of arbitration board, to get real grievances redressed and reasonable demands granted. However, developments of trades unionism in the English civil service are likely to prove very interesting in the next decade.

It will be recalled that at one time a large group of civil servants were disfranchised in order to keep the civil service out of politics. This radical act was repealed after serving a useful purpose, when the examination system had replaced patronage. It seems very improbable that disfranchisement will be attempted again. " Democracy gives back none of its victories." It is, however, interesting to note that the disfranchised civil servants resident in the District of Columbia seem to be satisfied with their voteless interest in the government which they serve. It

[1] *Op. cit.*, p. 395. Mr. Walling believes that " the gulf between those who consider the collective refusal of the organizations of government employees to work under conditions they do not accept, as being ' treason ' and ' mutiny,' and those who feel that such an organization is the *very basis* of industrial democracy of the future and the sole possible guarantee of liberty, is surely unbridgeable."

will be remembered also, that an Act of Anne had
threatened with fine and dismissal any postal servant who
should persuade a voter to vote for or against any candidate. This act is unrepealed, but practically useless. Recently civil servants have developed organizations to further
their welfare, which, beginning like the trades unions with
philanthropic and benefit work, have gradually developed
into civil service unions with programs of pay, promotion and prospects which they seek to enforce by political
pressure, publicity and agitation.[1]

The English Post Office has been the home of many serious agitations, and now that it includes the huge telegraph
and telephone services of the kingdom, the danger of political pressure and strikes is one which calls for serious consideration.

A few quotations will illustrate this civil unionism. At
the time of the Ridley inquiry in 1888, Sir R. E. Welby offered testimony which briefly and clearly states the problem:

You say you have not taken any steps to put down what is
virtually a trades union among the Lower Division clerks.
Do you think it advisable that no step of that sort should be
taken?—I think that a very difficult question to answer. I do
not like the combination of civil servants to obtain by parliamentary action increase of pay, but I dislike, if it can possibly
be avoided, any measure of authority which appears to preclude people from making known their grievances.

In the interests of the public service, do not you think it
would be in a certain degree inadvisable to prevent these men
expressing what they believe to be their grievances and simply
let the discontent foment in the office?—I should be anxious
that any body of men, who really think that they have griev-

---

[1] *Cf.* Lowell, *Government of England*, vol. i, pp. 147-153.

ances, should have assurance that those grievances should be considered. I am anxious to go as far as that, but I think that each case must be judged by itself. I should be the last person to say that any amount of combination or any use of parliamentary influence is to be permitted. There must come a point at which it would be necessary to check it; but I do not like expressing a general opinion beforehand, which might be interpreted as unfavourable to the reasonable making known of grievances.

Are you aware that repressive action has been taken in the Post Office amongst the Postmen?—The circumstances are not known to me. . . .

I should like to ask you whether it is not known to you that of course electioneering action is forbidden to civil servants at the present time, that is to say, they are not allowed to appear on political platforms.—I am not aware of any general minute forbidding civil servants interfering in elections, or rather I should say not interfering but taking part in elections.

(*Mr. Freeman Mitford.*) There is an unwritten law, is not there; it always was an understood thing that civil servants did not take part?—It is relaxed very much. You must recollect that the whole tendency has been to remove disabilities.[1]

As a result of constant agitations, there were at least three committees on Post Office salaries in a single decade—in 1897, in 1903, and in 1906. After the Tweedmouth report in 1898 on the Post Office establishments, when the government had been forced to compromise with the Post Office employees, members of this and of other parliamentary committees which did not give satisfaction to the civil service became marked men, and every effort was made to secure their defeat at elections.

The debates in Parliament in opposition to this pressure, though they magnify the dangers of political agitation, cer-

[1] Sir R. E. Welby, *Second Ridley Report*, p. 18.

tainly show that future governments must be prepared to deal quickly and thoroughly with undue political activity of civil servants.[1]

In 1912 the postal servants demanded that the Prime Minister immediately appoint a committee to redress their grievances on pain of a strike during the Christmas rush. The report of the *Morning Post* on this situation is worth quoting in full:

Sections of Post Office workers are threatening that unless the Government concede the demand of the postal servants for an immediate inquiry into their alleged grievances, they may strike during the period of the Christmas rush. No actual decision has been made on this point, and though extremists are in favour of drastic and immediate action, it is hoped that wiser councils will prevail at a fully representative meeting in Birmingham of postal servants, to be attended by 70 delegates, representing all branches of the service, which has been

[1] Concerning the civil servants in the telegraph departments, Mr. Hugo R. Meyer, an American opponent of public ownership, says: ". . . Organized in huge civil service unions, the telegraph employees have been permitted to establish the policy that wages and salaries shall be fixed in no small degree by the amount of political pressure that the telegraph employees can bring to bear on members of the House of Commons. . . . To a considerable degree the State employees have established their demand that promotion be made according to seniority rather than merit. In more than one Postmaster General they have instilled 'a perfect horror of passing anyone over.' . . . . The civil servants have been permitted to establish to a greater or a lesser degree a whole host of demands that are inconsistent with the economical conduct of business. Among them may be mentioned the demand that the standard of efficiency may not be raised without reimbursement to those who take the trouble to come up to the new standard; and that if a man enters the service when the proportion of higher officers to the rank and file is 1 to 19 he has an 'implied contract with the Government that that proportion shall not be altered to his disadvantage though it may be to his advantage.'" *The British State Telegraphs and Public Ownership* (New York, 1907), pp. 380, 381. *Cf.* also pp. 385-386.

called for Sunday exening next, and at a further meeting at the Memorial Hall on the following day. Briefly, the contention of the disaffected workers is that while there has been an increase in the cost of living, there has been no corresponding increase in their rates of pay. The Postmaster-General has decided that no inquiry shall take place until after the Board of Trade inquiry into the cost of living; and this, in the opinion of the postal servants, means that no redress can come for three or four years. Another grievance is that the men are worked at higher pressure than was the case a few years ago, and are consequently more liable to breakdown.

The situation from the men's standpoint was explained yesterday to a *Morning Post* representative by Mr. W. B. Cheesman, the secretary of the Fawcett Association. " The National Committee of Postal and Telegraph Associations," he said, " consisting of postal, telegraphic, and engineering branches, and representing 70,000 in the Federation, have been negotiating for an inquiry into their grievances on the questions of pay and conditions of service. This inquiry has been conceded by the Government, but they decided not to appoint a Committee until 1913. The Prime Minister was asked to receive a deputation, as it was felt that he could not be in possession of all the facts bearing on the case. But he declined to meet us, and his refusal has precipitated the present trouble. The 70,000 men I have mentioned would represent a great proportion of the established staff of the Post Office, but similar societies are in entire sympathy with the movement, and would doubtless throw in their lot with us. They have been holding protest meetings on the same lines as ours. So far the National Committee has been in favour of ordinary lines of procedure, but they feel that they have not been treated quite fairly by the Postmaster-General and the Government. Personally, I do not approve of striking, but you must remember that in many industries the executives of the men's Unions have been driven beyond the policy they were advocating. This has happened in the case of the boilermakers, the engineers, the railwaymen, and the miners, and it is the pressure of the rank and file which may cause extreme action to be taken in the present crisis."

Mr. Cheesman was asked what conditions of service the men particularly objected to. " The speeding up and other practices in recent years," he said, " have added largely to the unrest. Then there is the question of wages. In 1904 the Bradford Committee reported in favour of considerable improvements in the wages scale of existing staffs; but the report has been entirely ignored by both Governments which have been in power since then. The Hobhouse Committee recommended certain scales of pay, which have also been denied to the existing staff, being made operative only for new entrants and for officers of twenty-one years of age and under. The increased cost of living is a very big factor in the question. The Postmaster-General on September 28th recognized that food-stuffs alone had gone up in London 4 per cent since the Hobhouse Committee reported, and that is one of the main factors for fixing wages in the postal service. We are promised an inquiry in 1913, but next year will be a critical one for the Government, and no one can say with certainty that they will be in power when the time comes for them to fulfil their promise."

In the London Branch of the Postal Telegraph Clerks' Association, it is pointed out, the position is more acute. A strike here would mean an almost complete dislocation of the telegraph service of the country, since such an action would affect 2,500 men and women employed at the Central Telegraph Office. Their grievances refer to rates of pay and cost of living, and include a complaint as to maximum salary. They also complain of understaffing, espionage, and maladministration. A special meeting has been called for Monday evening next in the Memorial Hall to consider the following proposal submitted by some of the members: " That this meeting of the members of the London Branch P. T. C. A. hereby expresses its intense dissatisfaction at the reply of the Postmaster-General to the demand for an early increase in wages; and further condemns the policy of the National Joint Committee which led up to this defeat. We are of opinion that the action of the Postmaster-General has been determined by the fact that the Postal Trade Unions, in their present divided state, are incapable of sustained effort, and we therefore instruct our Executive immediately to take such steps as may be necessary in order to secure the abolition of the sectional nature of our organisation and the substitution of one common organisation for the whole of the workers in the Civil Service." As an amendment to this the Committee will move the deletion of all words after " an early increase in wages."

It is pointed out that at present there are six unions for postal servants operating in the United Kingdom, . . . between them representing about 80,000 employees of the Post Office. The total number of men employed in the course of the year by the Post Office is about 200,000, but about 90,000 of these are supernumeraries, and the total permanent staff directly employed numbers a little over 100,000. The difficulty heretofore appears to have been to secure concerted action among the different unions. It is doubtful if they will succeed at the present time. One postal servant with whom a *Morning Post* representative discussed the question was strongly of opinion that they would not. " There is a union in every grade of the service," he said, " but you will never get them to combine together, and I very much question if any particular union would unanimously support a strike movement. The men know when they are well off. If the Fawcett Association called a strike to-morrow I venture to say that only half the men would come out." It is also pointed out that should a strike take place the public would not be unmindful of the inconvenience caused thereby when the postmen make their annual appeal for benevolence as soon as Christmas Day is over. This factor ought to weigh in the question.

The strike policy in this case was probably not approved by a majority, but nevertheless Mr. Samuel, the Postmaster General, bowed to the demand for a committee. The report of this committee has stirred up another rebellion, most of the employees' claims having been disallowed. *The Times*[1] describes the resulting deadlock as follows:

A special conference of the Postmen's Federation was held at Birmingham on Saturday to consider the Holt Report. There were 480 delegates present, representing a membership of 43,000. . . .

Mr. G. H. STUART, general secretary, moved, on behalf of the executive, " That this conference declines to accept the Report of the Select Committee as a propr verdict on its just and moderate claims. It emphatically states that no juggling with pence will dispose of the admitted increase in the cost of living, and regards the proposals to increase the working hours of the staff under the guise of a concession as an insult to the intelligence of the Post Office employees. It calls upon the Government to take immediate steps to deal with an acute and dangerous situation."

The resolution was carried by a large majority.

Mr. F. M. P. CAMPBELL (London) moved, " That this conference declares in favour of a strike policy."

Mr. STUART, general secretary, supported the resolution. His reason for doing so, he said, was that their possessing a " no-strike " policy had influenced the Holt Committee. He did not think they were ready to come out on strike, but by passing the resolution they would let members see that they were ready to take up a more vigorous policy.

On a card vote the resolution was carried by 549 votes to 175, the result being received with enthusiastic cheering.

On Monday and Tuesday a joint conference of the Postal Telegraph Clerks' Association and the United Kingdom Postal Clerks' Association was held. About 500 delegates were present, including for the first time representatives of wireless telegraphists.

The conference passed a resolution rejecting the recommendations of the Committee in their entirety, and adopted by a

[1] Sept. 25, 1913.

large majority a motion instructing the executive committee to take steps immediately to form an emergency fund. An instruction to take a plébiscite of the members was also agreed to. It was further resolved by a large majority to instruct the executive committee to institute an agitation for an all-round immediate increase of wages commensurate with the increased cost of living. The resolution demanded a 15 per cent increase in wages for manipulative grades of the service, the increase to take effect by January 1, 1914; and an increase in the annual increments of all classes according to a scale agreed upon. It was agreed that, failing a satisfactory solution within six weeks, a further special conference be called within three weeks from such failure to decide the further action of the unions. . . .

The Post Office on Monday issued a reply to the criticisms which have recently been passed on the proposals of the Holt Report by the various postal servants' organizations and their leaders.

It is pointed out that the claims put forward by the staff would, if granted, involve an additional expenditure of £10,-000,000 a year. The Select Committee, the Report of which is now under consideration, recommends improvements in pay and conditions of service which will increase the expenditure of the Post Office on wages, pensions, &c., by upwards of £1,000,000 a year. On the complaint that the increases of pay are not commensurate with the recent rise in the cost of living, attention is called to the statement of the Select Committee that the cost of living is still at about the same level as in 1884. A comparison is made with the wages and conditions which prevail in occupations similar to those of postal servents, and emphasis is laid on the fact that established servants of the Post Office have security of tenure, prospect of a pension, generous holidays on full pay, and in some cases free medical attendance.

It will be surmised that the " strikers " are not very sure of themselves, and it may be prophesied that, in the last analysis, they will probably not carry out their threat. It is not, however, safe to generalize from this situation that none more serious will arise. For the immediate future English traditionalism, patriotism, and genius for compromise, lead us to suppose that the first bitter fruits of the general strike will be enjoyed on the Continent.

On the whole, the organizations of civil servants—like the organizations of trades unions—seem more terrifying in their hot-headed revolutionary youth than in their mature and responsible development. There can be no sense in attempting to gag civil servants. A reasonable amount of discussion and even agitation must be allowed. For the rest, heads of departments must prepare to recognize and encourage the responsible committees of civil service organizations,[1] to treat their moderate suggestions with the utmost open-mindedness and respect, and to send their recommendations to the Treasury, with such remarks as may seem pertinent. Any suggestion of a permanent arbitration committee, with representatives of the clerks and of the government, to decide differences between employees and ministers, is at present simply unthinkable. There should be a royal commission every decade to inquire into all irreconcilable differences.

The most interested and mooted question before the Royal Commission is that of the division of the upper clerical service into separate classes upon the basis of academic entrance examinations. We have seen the genesis of this

---

[1] The Treasury has long since (see *Parliamentary Papers*, 1883, xxxviii, p. 543) made rules forbidding subordinate employees to appeal to the Treasury directly or through members of Parliament, for promotion, rise in salary, etc. These applications must come from heads of departments, Lords of the Admiralty, and commissioners of Internal Revenue.

division and its development. We have seen that at the time of the Playfair and of the Ridley reports, the lower division clerks had demanded the removal of a bar which they claim unjustly discriminated against them. They claimed that the superior education of the aristocratic class of university men was of little use to the service, and that this class, though nominally employed upon a higher order of work, was really drawing higher salaries for work which was done or could easily be done by lower division men. It has been indicated that this contention of the second division, except in so far as it applied to mere numbers in the first division, has not been supported by Parliament, ministries, or royal commissions, and that time has merely shown how farsighted was Macaulay's original plan.

We have seen also that an intermediate division has been created, and we shall see that the assistant clerk class, partly recruited from boy writers, and possessed of considerable education, has inherited the grievances of the old writer class against poor pay and has become infected with the second division virus for free promotion and no classes. The situation is indeed curious. There is a second division which claims that it is capable of filling all the highest places in the service; there is an assistant division, which claims that it not only can do as well as the second division, but that it is really employed on second division work already and in some cases even upon intermediate work. Then there are boy clerks who are supposed to be about as good as the assistant men clerks, and writers who demand to be established on the ground that they are quite capable of better things. And, finally, there is the beginning of the employment of women typists who, it seems, have as yet no pressing grievances.

The Royal Commission has published voluminous evidence on the subject of democracy and classes. The testimony is almost complete. It remains to quote some of the leading evidence on each side before the Royal Commission, and, in the absence of the verdict of the commission and the Treasury, to estimate how much change is likely to be made in the class system, and what new schemes of educational requirements and of promotion in the service are likely to be adopted.

Before presenting the memorial of the second division clerks, it is essential that the present possibilities for promotion from the second division be understood. The rule laid down by the Order in Council of 1890, following the Ridley report, is that there is promotion from the second division to the first only upon special recommendation of the head of a department, followed by the consent of the Treasury and the Civil Service Commission, and only after the clerk has been at least eight years in the service. In nineteen years (1892-1911) there were only 73 such promotions; and there were in addition a few second division clerks who entered the first division after taking the first division examination. Second division men are allowed to exceed the usual age limits for the first division examinations.

But we must bear in mind that there are a number of offices in which there are only second division men and in which *all* higher appointments are made from them; and that in almost all offices some staff appointments with high salaries are reserved for second division clerks.[1] Thus, there have been in the last twenty years some 1,500 promotions of second division clerks to positions equivalent to division I posts, at least in point of salary. It is considered by the Treasury that there is a real distinction between the work done by these staff officers and the work done by first

[1] Notably in the Admiralty, Inland Revenue, Local Government Board, Board of Trade, and War, Estates' Duty, and Post Offices.

division men, an intellectual distinction, though the two kinds of work may have the same market value and earn the same salaries. Thus, the assistant director of stores at the Admiralty, a promoted second division clerk, receives from £800 to £900, while a first division senior clerk in the Treasury receives about the same amount; but it is claimed that the work of a Treasury first division clerk requires a kind of education and intellectual background not at all necessary or even desirable in an efficient director of stores.. This is no disparagement of the work of the latter. He is paid equally well, but for a different and, on the whole, more easily obtainable ability.[1]

There is a Treasury rule that a second division clerk promoted to the first division, does not carry his old salary to his new position, probably because he enters upon an entirely different kind of work. Thus a promotion of this kind would probably imply a fall in salary, since a second division man of eight years' or more standing is sure to be receiving more than the initial first division pay. It is somewhat difficult to see what justification there is for such a rule, beyond that of economy. Certainly a second division man so exceptional as to deserve promotion to the first division is also capable of earning more than green first division men.

[1] " By way of illustrating possibilities it may be stated that the undermentioned important posts are now held by promoted Second Division Clerks, viz.:—The Assistant Directorship of Stores at the Admiralty (£800 to £900), a Principal Clerkship at the Admiralty (£850 to £1,000), a Commissionership of Income Tax in the Inland Revenue Department (£850 to £1,000), the Secretaryship in the Estate Duty Office of the Inland Revenue Department (£1,200), an Acting Principal Clerkship at the War Office (£900), two Chief Accountant-ships in the Army Accounts Branch (£850 to £1,000), the Secretary-ship of the Irish Land Commission (£1,200), the Accountant-General-ship of the Navy (£1,500), and the Receivership of the Metropolitan Police (£1,200 to £1,500)." See *Civil Service Year Book*, 1912.

Let us turn now to the claims presented to the Royal Commission by the Association of Second Division Clerks in a remarkably clear and lucid memorial.[1] Their arguments are directed mainly against the system of patronage in making appointments and against a class barrier. We have already touched on the patronage question. The memorial makes a straightforward plea for open competition, a plea which is probably unanswerable in the case of numerous offices now anomalously filled by limited competition and nomination; but the obvious objections to filling clerkships in the Foreign Office by open competition are not considered by the second division clerks, and in the further discussion of patronage there are a number of unsubstantiated charges, including unjustifiable aspersions on the impartiality of the Civil Service Commission, and of the Selection Committee for Labor Exchanges who are accused of "notorious cases of jobbery". The second division clerks seem to think that every promotion from the unestablished group of writers which exists in various parts of the service, is a case of patronage. With more cogency they complain because a very efficient Liberal whip, Sir Ernest Soares, has been appointed from political life to be assistant controller of the National Debt Office.   •

We come now to the question of the barrier. The claim of the second division clerks is " that a sufficient standard of education is attained by the Second Division to enable them to fill any post in the Civil Service ", and that, if anything, their attainments are too high for their work and are not utilized. This claim is based on the belief that there is no possibility of distinguishing between administrative and clerical work, and that there is no real distinction between offices in which the higher posts are open to second

[1] See Appendix V, *Second Report of Royal Commission*, 1912, p. 483 *et seq.*

division men, and offices in which they are filled by the first division. For example, the memorial claims that the work of the Customs Secretary's Office was being efficiently discharged by second division men when, in 1909, for no good reason it was decided to divide the office and recruit the upper part by first division examinations.

The memorial states that the intermediate division was founded merely to bring in Public School boys. The official reason has already been stated. There seems, however, to have been some injustice done to second division clerks who were transferred to other offices when the intermediate scheme came into effect.

The second division clerks unquestionably show that they are as a class highly intelligent and ambitious. They quote the example of second division men who have devoted their leisure hours to the study of government and law, sometimes with conspicuous success. The writer is acquainted with a second division clerk in the Board of Agriculture who took a B. Sc. degree at London University in political science, with first class honors. He is, as we shall see, in an office in which there is no higher division; he is eligible for staff posts and technical positions there; but it is felt by many that he ought to be eligible for a first division appointment elsewhere.

The second division memorial quotes with approval this statement by Professor Edwin Cannan of the London School of Economics:

" I have been rather struck myself with the ability of the Second Division Civil Servants. I daresay, as an average, their ability is not very high, but the ability of the people who come to us, who are, of course, a picked lot, is very considerable."

In answer to further questions: " . . . I have had a good many of these Second Division Civil Servants, who are really very capable, so much so that it makes me doubt whether the present chasm between the two divisions is expedient."

On being questioned regarding the difference between a man trained at Oxford and an evening student at the London School of Economics, Professor Cannan replied: " . . . the difference between them is rather like the difference between men and women . . . it is a thing very difficult to define and give a satisfactory account of. It is a question of previous education and surroundings very largely. You get rather more intelligence, perhaps, out of our people than you do out of the young man at Oxford. On the other hand, the young man at Oxford has a better literary education, his power of expression is greater, and your feelings are not violated by a number of things which are rather annoying in the work of others."

(*Sir Robert Morant.*) " . . . You do not think, *a priori,* there would be much difference between the one and the other? "

(*Professor Cannan.*) " . . . I am not prepared to say so. I do not think I should send my own son here in preference to sending him to Oxford. . . . I say that is a question of social environment. When a man has been at one of the older Universities he feels he is one of a class which, he believes, enjoys some public esteem, and it gives him confidence, which is always something." [1]

In support of its contentions the memorial also quotes from a high colonial official:

It cannot be said that their [the Second Division] position is altogether satisfactory, and it is, in fact, one of the most difficult questions with which the heads of an office have constantly to deal. It is a general understanding that their work is of a different class from that of the Higher Division; and,

---

[1] Extract from *Third Report, Appendix, of the Royal Commission on University Education in London.*

not having passed the higher examination, they are naturally shut off from the higher appointments.

But it is inevitable, especially in such a department as the Colonial Office, that some of them should occasionally be called upon to perform work that, while it can hardly be distinguished from that of the Higher Division, nevertheless does not carry with it the same advantages, and I am afraid that the consciousness of this has been productive of a growing feeling of discontent.

It seems to me, in fact, that some revision of the existing regulations will before long become absolutely necessary. Many of this class in the Colonial Office have served directly under me, and I can unhesitatingly testify to the valuable nature of their services.

I should be only too glad to see their position improved, and I trust that it will not be long before some improvement takes place.[1]

The clerical reorganization proposed by the memorial is this:

The first division to be abolished as a separate class.

In future to be two classes—a first grade into which will be merged the present first, intermediate, and second divisions, and a second grade, composed of boy clerks and assistant clerks.

The first grade to be recruited at the normal age of leaving a secondary school—$17\frac{1}{2}$ to $19\frac{1}{2}$ years.

The intermediate scheme of examination to be used, but so modified as to offer equal chances to boys " leaving any type of school."

The memorial magnanimously consents to allow university men to enter the service by a higher examination, so arranged that Oxford and Cambridge men will have no advantage, the university men thus chosen to count five years'

---

[1] Appendix V, *Second Report of the Royal Commission*, p. 490.

seniority, but to be otherwise on a level with the ordinary first grade men.[1]

The boy clerks, who are all to be absorbed into the assistant clerk class, to be recruited at about 14 or 15½ years, the elementary school-leaving age, and to be compelled to attend compulsory continuation classes for three years, then to be eligible for assistant clerkships, specially well-paid supervisory positions, and for exceptional promotion to grade I.

This is an ingenious leveling-up-and-down scheme in the interests of the second division, which is calculated to remove distinctions between the three upper divisions and perpetuate new distinctions between grade I and grade II; and the question arises as to what grade II think and may be expected to think of their new status.

The assistant clerks also handed in a memorial.[2] Their present opportunities of promotion into the second division are very fair. After six years' service they may rise by or without examination to the second division. Their claims are curiously like those of the second division; but unlike

[1] Apart from the question of the actual value and need of first division men, it is palpable that university men would not enter the service under such conditions as this memorial proposes. It will be remembered that, in 1853, there were many critics who denied that the best university scholars could be attracted into a profession so ill-paid, obscure and uninteresting. This anticipation was not realized; but it is still a source of wonder to political heads of offices that talented university men are willing to remain in the restricted field of the civil service. These are frequently men who might have had greater scope in the open professions. They must adjust themselves to first division routine, just as there are men of more modest endowments below them who must at present accustom themselves to the four walls of the second division. The existing attractions to university men are not too great. If they are reduced, the best men in universities will not enter the civil service.

[2] Appendix VII, *Second Report of Royal Commission*, p. 495 *et seq.*

the second division,[1] it is palpable that they are scandalously underpaid and that this grievance must be redressed. They show that the wage at 21 is not sufficient for a decent living, and that marriage before 30 is quite out of question. The government is not in this respect a model employer.

The economy responsible for the institution of the Assistant Clerk Class results in the passage from youth to manhood of a large number of boys, educationally well equipped and specially selected, being made in poverty-stricken circumstances. Forced to exist amid the dismal environment obtaining amongst that section of the community which, in large cities, has to preserve respectability of appearance under the most trying economic conditions, what real happiness in life can be theirs? Unable to marry at a proper age, and when married to bring up a family under decent conditions, the course of time brings but little relief. Such economy cannot be regarded as worthy of the dignity of the State, and is not, therefore, to be commended.[2]

The assistant clerks also claim that they are too well educated for the work they are paid for, that they are frequently employed upon second division work, and that " there is no real difference between the work allotted to the Second Division and [that allotted to] some Assistant Clerks ". They claim that they have even more than the " ordinary commercial education " which the Ridley Commission said constituted the bulk of work of the government departments; and they claim that there was no authority in the Playfair or Ridley reports for the creation of an assistant clerk class. They demand a proportionate sys-

[1] It is claimed by high officials that the second division clerks are paid more than the corresponding clerks in private employ. It is calculated that if the wealth of the nation were equally divided, each man with a family would have £150, exactly the salary of an ordinary second division clerk between 27 and 30.

[2] *Ibid.*, p. 498.

tem of promotion to the second division, one for every three vacancies arising. " It is obviously impossible, short of cast-iron rules, to keep a body of men, so educated and trained, permanently in the service on these ' copying and simple duties ' which have been so lightheartedly assigned to the class." Just as the second division insisted that administrative and clerical work could not be separated, the assistant clerks claim that " excepting copying, the clerical work cannot be divided so as to be done by different classes."

The assistant clerks' scheme of reorganization is, therefore, that the first division be retained for high administrative work, but that the second division (intermediate ?) and assistant clerks be in one clerical division recruited by a single entrance examination, with a standard something like the present assistant clerks' examination standard. The boy clerks would be abolished and democracy introduced.

National Fairness.

It is submitted that the method of recruiting by means of one entrance examination, besides making for efficiency, is more democratic. Certainly under it the very poor classes would continue to be at a great disadvantage, but not to such an extent as is at present the case, while on the other hand the better classes of working people, the lower middle, and the middle classes would be put upon more equitable terms with the upper middle, and wealthy classes.[1]

Let us see now what some of the superior officials think about the necessity of class distinctions and of the work of first division men. Viscount Haldane, formerly War Secretary, now Lord Chancellor, who brought to the investigation not only his parliamentary, administrative, and legal experience, but also a wide knowledge of German education and government, gave the most profound and significant, if

[1] Appendix VII, *Second Report of Royal Commission*, p. 502.

not the most topical, evidence submitted to the commission.
A few quotations will show his position on the first division
and class questions. He believes that the intelligence, the
cultivated tastes, the outlook on life, and the university associations of the first division are indispensable. He is not
a blind admirer of the older universities. He looks forward
to the successful competition of men from the new universities, but holds that at present the leading scholars of the
older universities, and particularly those who have taken
honors in the Humaner Letters, have the finest equipment
for superior work in the civil service. He wants, however,
to see other kinds of ability and education attracted into
the service, and recommends the appointment without examination of students distinguished in graduate work. He
would employ more first division men on original work. In
the last quotation it will be seen that Lord Haldane is convinced that the present inequalities can only be remedied by
a complete development of popular education.

Then might I alter my question and say that an education
at a resident university and the general atmosphere of a university gives you the type of man you want for the higher
division?—Yes, emphatically.

But do not you think that a second division clerk who has
had a few years' experience in business before he entered the
Civil Service would be quite as likely to develop the power of
handling men and to administer as a person of similar age
whose time has been spent at the university?—I do not think
so. In the Civil Service, when a Civil servant comes in contact with an outside citizen he does not bully him or command
him; he has to persuade him and make the outsider see that
the point of view which the system of the Civil Service represents is a reasonable one, and that depends on the power to
take a large view and to get at the principle and reason of the
thing as distinguished from what is laid down in the Regulation; and my experience now, which is considerable, is that

the highly trained first division clerk is quite admirable for
getting alongside the mind of the soldier, for getting alongside
the mind of the civilian in the county association, for getting
alongside the minds of the one hundred and one people you
have to deal with in a complicated organisation such as I have
had to preside over for some years past.[1]

If you have no other remarks to make on the Class I. examination perhaps you will say something, if you desire to do
so, on the lower examination for Class II., especially on the
multiplicity of examinations in the lower division?—I should
like to say something about that. The Class II. man is very
often an admirable man, and you get a very good quality of
man. His difficulty is that he has not got education in the real
sense up to his age. If he is going to be examined at 17 or 18
he has too often left the secondary school prematurely in order
to prepare for the examination, and the result is that the examination never can approximate at that level so closely to
the teaching as is the case with the higher examination. For
the higher examination the class of question that is more and
more put is a question designed to show whether the candidate
has an original view of some sort. It does not very much
matter whether it is his original view or that of his teacher,
or whether it is the university's original view or his own; it
does not matter so much whether he is right or wrong in the
opinion of the examiner as whether he shows that he has been
trained to think and to observe, but that is because the uni-

---

[1] Appendix, *Third Report of Royal Commission*, see question 1770,
1781. *The Civilian*, criticizing this evidence, said: "Lord Haldane
not having passed through the lower ranks of the Service will never
know much that undeniable fault is the result of the very system he is
inclined to support.

"If he had had that experience he would have discovered to what
extent thinking for oneself is penalized in the lower and larger divisions, and how much the uniformity and lack of imaginativeness is impressed on the workers by the routine nature of their duties. It is
largely a matter of scope. Any thinking man with leisure could
devise a hundred plans for governing a country, but only a genius
could find two methods of boiling an egg."

versity is essentially different from the school. In the university teacher and taught are together on a voyage of discovery, exploring regions which to both of them are unknown, and the stimulating personality of the teacher leads on the student and stimulates him; but he does not impose upon him an authoritative view, and very often the student does not accept the authority of the professor. But the lower you get in education the more mechanical is the process when a statement from a book or an authority is given and the pupil has to accept it; consequently the examination is always based more or less on what has to be taken on authority and on what depends on memory as distinguished from what depends on originality and trainedness of mind on the part of the pupil. The result is that a pupil who leaves the secondary school, say, at 15, or perhaps has not gone there at all, in his preparation for the examination has to anticipate all the possible authoritative questions—and you know why I use the term " authoritative " now—which the examiner may put to him, and the tendency to cram becomes more and more serious and formidable than in the case of the higher class examination. I am not underrating cramming, I am not underrating even cramming for examinations, because they do provide for concentration, and they set a man to work. I have known men who were made by having to prepare for an external examination; it is good of its kind, but it is not education in the best sense of the word, nor does it produce the best quality of an educated mind. That is my criticism upon the machinery by which we produce the lower division; and the more examinations there are the worse it becomes.[1] . . .

[1] Appendix, *Third Report of Royal Commission*, see question 1675. An extreme example of this suspicion, almost fear, of cramming, and also of the Macaulay-Haldane insistence upon a liberal academic education as a better test of fitness than any mere technical text book knowledge of the duties ahead, appears in the appointment of inspectors and assistants of inspectors of factories in the Home Office. The two classes are distinct and separate. For the assistants, a number of years of actual working experience in a factory or workshop is required. For the inspectors

I was very much interested to hear your remarks with re-

only a difficult academic education is set up, and they are expected to learn their duties and their factory law while on probation. The idea, of course, is that the man of sound general education will get his practical knowledge quickly in office, while the assistant must have practical experience beforehand because, in the absence of education and mental training, this is the only security that he is fit for the job. An excerpt from the evidence of Sir Edward Troup, K.C.B., Permanent Under Secretary of the Home Office, will show, at any rate, that this system is somewhat hard to defend under cross-examination:

"At one time was practical acquaintance with factories and workshops a subject of examination?—No, never. At one time a knowledge of factory law was; but I do not think you could possibly have an examination in practical acquaintance with factories and workshops."

"But at one time a knowledge of factory law was necessary at the first examination?—Yes, for a long time, up till in fact quite recently, but it was found to be a regular cram subject, and it was dropped and deferred until after two years' service."

"That change was made by Mr. Gladstone, I believe.—Yes."

"An inspector can be appointed now without having given any evidence that he has any knowledge of factory law?—Yes, that has been one of the great improvements that have been made."

"And he is at once put upon the work of inspection of factories?— Yes, he goes round with an inspector and learns his work with him."

"And he has given no evidence whatever that he knows anything about factory law, or about sanitary laws governing factories?— Quite so. It is his business to learn that during his first year or two of holding the office. If he does not make himself an expect in factory law and sanitary law within his first two years he would be dropped out."

"But in these two years he is doing the work of inspector of factories?—Quite so."

"Although he does not know anything at all about factory law?— Although he is rapidly learning about it."

"And he is expected to find out violations of the factory law?—He is certainly expected to. He goes first with another inspector, and then as far as his knowledge goes, which is rapidly extending, he discovers infractions of the factory law."

"But long before the two years he is inspecting on his own?—Yes, and long before the two years, if he is worth anything, he is well qualified in factory law. . . ."

"Then you had an examination for English composition. They were asked to write an essay upon 'Corporations have no conscience,' or

gard to the new universities. Would you be surprised to hear

'Algeria and Australia are different types of Colonies,' or 'The ideals of trades unionism.' One of the optional subjects is English literature and English history. Again, bearing in mind that the object of the examination is to get the man who shows the possession of knowledge and ability to enable him to undertake these very important duties, I suppose I am right in saying that the scheme of examination has been framed by the Home Office.—Yes, the scheme of the examination."

"With the sanction of the Treasury?—The Civil Service Commissioners have a good deal of say in it. However, I think the Home Office must take the responsibility for the subjects but not for the Papers."

"In English history, this aspirant for the position of inspector is asked: 'When, and under what circumstances, did Milton write "Paradise Lost"?' Do you think the answer to a question like that indicates the possession of knowledge that is likely to be of great service in discharging the duties of a factory inspector?—If the object were to test his knowledge which he is likely to bring to bear on his inspection duties, it would be absolutely useless; but that is not the object of the examination. The object of the examination is to find a man who has sufficient intellectual capacity and adaptability to make a good factory inspector."

"Do you think a question like that is calculated to bring out a man's intellectual adaptability?—Taken by itself, of course not, but taken as part of a Paper on English literature probably it is."

"Let us pass away to modern history. He is asked to sketch the career of William the Silent. Do you think a man who could sketch the career of William the Silent is more likely to become a good factory inspector than a man who could answer questions bearing upon factory law and sanitary law?—Yes, to sketch the career of William the Silent you want a good general knowledge of the history of that period. To answer a question on factory law, such as would be set in these Papers, you would only want to cram for three months."

"Would not the same thing apply to his knowledge of history?—No, I do not think so—not to the same extent. I know history is rather a cram subject too, but I certainly think the question about William the Silent would be a much better test question of a man's capabilities than a stock question on factory law."

"But if the man did cram on factory law and sanitary law he would have acquired the knowledge by cramming?—Yes, a knowledge which he could acquire very much better in connection with the practical work of inspection." Appendix, *Second Report of Royal Commission,* p. 122 *et seq.*

that the new universities are providing practically no candidates at all for the higher division of the Civil Service?—The reasons for that is, I think, not very far to seek. The new universities, in the first place, are only getting their students together, and in the second place, their students go largely into the professions; but, I can only say, knowing a great deal of the new universities (I am chancellor of one and had something to do with the foundation of others), that, looking through the Civil Service examination papers, there is teaching going on in the new universities which fits a man to pass on these papers quite as well as the teaching of Oxford or Cambridge.

You would not say, then, that the examination papers give a special advantage to those who have an Oxford or Cambridge degree?—Certainly not. I will make this qualification, that I think if you take the Scotch universities, where lately Latin and Greek have gone, I will not say in the background, but are not so prominent as they were, the Latin and Greek papers here would be more easy for somebody who has got the very fine teaching in Latin and Greek which is given at Oxford or Cambridge; but that is altering itself, too. In the new universities there is very fine training on the arts side growing up, which ought to make candidates quite as capable of taking that examination. . . .[1]

After a good deal of observation, both while I was at the bar and while I was in charge of an administrative department, I have come to the conclusion that as a general rule the most stimulating and useful preparation for the general work of the higher civil service is a literary training, and that of this a classical education is for most men the best form, though not exclusively so. No doubt, men vary, and science or modern literature may develop the mind, in the case of those who have aptitude for them, better than Latin or Greek literature. But, as Goethe said long ago, the object of education ought to

[1] Appendix, *Third Report of Royal Commission*, see questions 1764-1765.

be rather to form tastes than simply to communicate knowledge. The pedant is not of much use in the conduct of public affairs. For the formation of tastes and of the intellectual habits and aptitudes which the love of learning produces, the atmosphere of a highly organized university life is a tremendous power, and we cannot do without it. And, therefore, while I am not without sympathy with the complaint of democracy that the entrance to the higher positions in the Civil Service is by far too much the monopoly of a class, I reply that a highly educated clerk is essential for a particular kind of work which the State needs. . . .[1]

The best products of Oxford and Cambridge are the best products, so far as education goes, in this country. The ideal kind of training for the Bar I used to think was an Oxford or Cambridge training, and on the whole by preference, though not by any means exclusively, a classical training. I say that, not being a classical scholar in the proper sense myself, but as the result of observation, I should have said that the very best training for the Bar was a really high training of scholarship at Oxford or Cambridge. . . .[2]

. . . By what means would that superior education be best attained? — If I were dealing with an ideal system it would be this: I never was myself at either Oxford or Cambridge. I was brought up under the influence of German universities, and I spent a great deal of time at the University of Edinburgh. I was Ferguson Scholar of four Scotch universities, so that the universities I know best are the German universities and the Scotch universities. At the same time I have had a great deal to do with both Oxford and Cambridge, particularly Oxford. I have had relatives who have been professors there; and I have lived there a great deal, and been an examiner there, and have received honorary degrees from both Oxford and Cambridge; so that I know them pretty well.

[1] From a speech by Lord Haldane at Bristol, quoted by the *New York Evening Post.*

[2] Appendix, *Third Report of Royal Commission; cf.* questions 1668-1671.

But the ideal system of university education would to my mind, if it were possible, be what I have been familiar with in Scotland. There, the son of a working man, thanks to the old rooted system of elementary education and the much more complete system of secondary education than exists in England, has a chance of rising from the ranks through the secondary school, or through the extension of the primary school that we have there, to the university. There are scholarships and bursaries, as they are very often called, by means of which he gets to the university. I have sat side by side in class rooms with the son of a ploughman, and a very clever fellow very often he was in many cases. I have also seen the son of a ploughman rise up and get a university degree, and come back to be doing manual labour because he was at any rate not a sufficiently clever fellow to make full use of his opportunities. I have known men who have been at the university working at manual work in Scotland; they come back to the circumstances out of which they rose. If you could have that system developed very much you would get the perfect system. You would get an equal opportunity for everybody, which I think is the real foundation of democracy. You would get the son of the workman with his chance, if he had it in him, to get the highest university training, and to go into any of the professions or become one of the highest division clerks; you would get the breaking down of the distinction between classes in many cases. I need not say that we are very far from that in England at the present time; but we are improving. In the last 14 years ten new teaching universities have been organized in England and Ireland; the four Scotch ones remain as they were; the Welsh University I am not taking into account—it was there before. You have got these ten new universities, and you have Oxford and Cambridge doing their work and making great changes, and I think these new universities will presently begin to pour out the class of highly-educated persons you want to get, and to pour them out with more access from what I may call the poorer stratum of the community. Until that comes I think, in the interests of the State, which must prevail over the interests of any class, however great, if we are to get the most efficient type of Civil servant for the highest work in the Civil Service, we must look to such universities as there are, and no doubt Oxford and Cambridge, where the training in some respects is very admirable, to supply us with a very good stream of them. I may say that I have had large experience at the Bar, as well as six years' experience of the War Department, and there I saw men competing side by side. The Bar is a very democratic place; all sorts of people come up there and fight side by side—men of natural capacity who rise very high; but there, too, I saw the barrister handicapped if he had not come through the mill of a really high type of univeristy education first. In the main the people who come to the top and make the finest lawyers, the finest men of the world, and the finest managers of men, were the highly-educated men; but there again, also, exceptional men, with a touch of something like genius in their individuality, made up for it and rivalled and even beat them.[1]

. . . I was suggesting whether it would be possible for the State, as one way of recruiting the service of the State, to get a certain number of men in at a somewhat later age and by post-graduate work?—I would like very much to get men who could write a thesis, say, for some of the very difficult work that there is at the Treasury, for instance; and the comment which occurs to me to make upon what you say is that there come into the Civil Service through Class I. a certain number of men who really do pursue privately post-graduate work and could produce your thesis, and they do. I know, for instance, first-rate economists who have become such in the Treasury, and I think you know some too, who have become so by their Civil Service work, and I doubt whether you could get better than that if you took a man at a later age on a thesis. That there are such men I do not doubt, and these are just the class of men I want still to retain the power to bring into the Civil Service under section 4 of the Superannuation Act, for instance. . . .

[1] Appendix, *Third Report of Royal Commission, cf.* question 1660.

But you know the reason, of course, why boys leave the secondary school at 15 or 16 instead of continuing two or three years longer; that in almost every case it is the poverty of the parents.—But in these days there are a good many scholarships (and there ought to be a great many more), and if the misfortune of the poverty of the parent is the reason, and they ought to get sufficient education to qualify them for the service of the State, then, I say, the interests of the State must preponderate over the interest of a class. But my reform would be to do everything to remove the disability and difficulty of a class while preserving the standard of the State. . . .[1]

I take it, it is your view that we cannot devise a thoroughly democratic system of entering into the Civil Service until we have very much widened the education ladder?—That is exactly my view, and I should like to join hands with you, Mr. Snowden, to-morrow, in saying that the great mode of access to a democratic system in this country was to put other things aside and to deal with the education system from its foundation.

The opinion of the permanent head of the Colonial Office, Sir John Anderson, G. C. M. G., about division I is summarized in the following quotations:

I gather on the whole you are satisfied with the first division men?—That is so.

Have you any suggestions as to the method of recruiting them. Can you see any better system than the competitive system at present in force?—Certainly not. I am entirely satisfied. If there was an attempt to recruit by any other system we should certainly get men who were not on the whole equal to the men we get by open competition. . . .

Are we to assume from that that all the higher division men are of high capacity and of a high level of intelligence, ability,

[1] Appendix, *Third Report of Royal Commission*, cf. question 1708, 1777.

and attainment?—I should say with regard to our existing staff that is so.

Are there no failures amongst the higher division men?—No.

None?—I have not known any in my office.

You must, within the last 30 years you have been in the public service, have known a great many higher division men from one department or another. Do you mean to tell us that you have never known one who was a failure as regards efficiency?—I would not say that; we have been very fortunate in our office. We have not had one whom I could describe as a failure. We have had men of greater ability than others undoubtedly, but the general average is distinctly high.

(*Bishop of Southwark.*) Was my impression correct, after my visit to the Colonial Office, that a good deal of the work which a first class clerk of junior standing does when he first comes into the office is very much of the same character as is done by staff officers?—Staff officers attached to the General Department immediately under the chief clerk.

It is the same sort of work?—It is regarded as less responsible, really.

That is to say, when they first come into the office as first class clerks and are of quite junior standing, they are doing very much the same sort of work as the staff officers?—That is so.

The staff officer is a man who has had long experience of the routine of the office.—Yes.

These new men would have had no experience at all?—No.

Do they do it as well?—After the first two or three months I should think they do it as well, if not a little better.

That is to say there is something about them either of natural ability, or due to their previous training, which enables them to do in three months what another man has taken 20 years to learn?—Of course they have had very different training, but there is no doubt they have a wider outlook. The training of a second division clerk and his social opportunities are naturally restricted, and, of course, that is bound to affect his outlook.

The power of getting a grasp of what they have to do is the sort of capacity which you think best fits a man for the responsible work he will ultimately have to do in the first class?—That is so. . . .

Then why do you consider that certain second division men are fit to be promoted to posts carrying a salary of 500*l.* a year, but are not fit to be promoted into the first division with perhaps 300*l.* or 400*l.* a year, seeing that you have already admitted that the salary is fixed according to the importance of the work that has to be done?—The work to which the staff officer promoted from the lower division is put is work which requires certain experience, and he has to exercise certain supervision probably over men junior to himself. In respect to that he is entitled to be paid more. The higher division clerk, as soon as he comes in, is set to work which really comes to this, that he is advising the Secretary of State on matters of public business that come into the office.

Is a young man of 23 who comes fresh from the university, who has never had any work to do, and no business experience whatever, competent at once to advise the Secretary of State on matters of policy?—He is allowed to try. . . .

But your general impression would be that as long as the education suitable to a first class intellect had been of a high and stimulating character, it does not matter very much what the education is?—It does not matter whether it has been science, classics, or mathematics.

And that it is better for a man up to 22 or 23 years of age to have had that kind of training rather than a technical training in the details of the office?—Undoubtedly.[1]

Mr. Harris of the War Office emphasizes another familiar distinction between division I and division II, a distinction of course well illustrated in the training of army officers.

---

[1] Appendix, *Second Report of Royal Commission*, p. 138.

I think that Class I. requires absolutely different qualifications from those to be normally found in Class II. There are two ways always of regarding a particular grade in the Service; one is to look at it from below as the reward of faithful service in the lower ranks, and the other is to look at it from above as a recruiting ground for the next and higher grades, and, although from the second division, as it stands to-day, you would by selection get a considerable number of officers who were competent to fill the lower grades in the higher division, I do not think you would get heads of departments of the necessary quality by further selection from those lower grades.[1]

A high official of the Inland Revenue agrees with the second division men that they have not enough opportunity for promotion:

But may I express your view in this way: Although you consider that the first division is necessary to furnish you with what I may call a *corps d'élite* in the service, yet it may be most usefully supplemented by promotion from the second division?—Yes, by exceptional merit.

And you yourself are acquainted with particular instances in which such promotion has been justified?—Speaking off-hand, I remember four promotions being made; there may be others, but I remember four.

Then I want to ask you whether from your experience you think these promotions are sufficiently numerous.—That is rather a matter for the head of the department, knowing his department and acquainted with it.

I want your own opinion. You have had a large experience of the service, and I am asking your own opinion whether you consider that these promotions have been made sufficiently frequently?—On the whole I should think scarcely sufficiently;

---

[1] Appendix, *Second Report of Royal Commission,* p. 343.

and that was the feeling which actuated me at Somerset House. [1]

It is very interesting to note that Sir Thomas H. Elliott, who himself rose from boy clerk to head of the Department of Agriculture, is most decided in his demand for higher scholarly attainments than the second division examinations insure. In his department there is no first division, but a large and miscellaneous class of inspectors and assistant inspectors with qualifications very much like those of the first division,[2] staff officers and second division men. Sir Thomas demands advanced study before a second division man may be promoted.

Then on the second sheet of that same document there is this paragraph: " Strong objection to any arrangement which would exclude men who go to universities and take good degrees there. Board's organisation does not do this." Does that refer to your outdoor staff particularly?—No; I am speaking there mainly with reference to the question of the promotion of second division men to the higher clerical staff. I have a very strong feeling that the entrance examination for the second division is not in itself a sufficient test of fitness for the higher posts, and I should be very sorry indeed to see any arrangement made which would not give the public service a certain number of the best men of their year at the universities. . . .

I suppose from what you have told us, and especially from your memorandum of February, 1895, we may take it that you think it is a good thing to have the work of an office so graded that in different ways it invites the men of the junior staff to

---

[1] Appendix, *First Report of Royal Commission, cf.* questions 906-909.

[2] Sir Thomas insists upon special examinations of a division I standard because he wishes to lay emphasis on certain special subjects, such as law, political economy, and English composition, and because through nomination he has a personal choice.

qualify themselves for higher appointments. There is no such thing in your office as a hard and fast distinction of kinds of work, but there is a sort of gradation that invites a man from one stage to another?—I think there is a natural and proper distribution of work between the higher and the lower posts, but I also feel very strongly that the men who come into what is at present known as the second division ought to have the opportunity of rising above that grade, and I tried in that memorandum of February, 1895, to indicate in what way they could rise above their grade. I stated in that memorandum that the important fact to be borne in mind in connection with these higher posts is that mere length of service, however blameless, and the possession of the attainments indicated by success at the second division or lower examination were insufficient qualifications for the discharge of the higher work of the office. Then I endeavoured to show, in the case of the different branches, in what way men could qualify themselves for that higher work. . . .[1]

You made a statement in your memorandum of 1895 which seems to me to be sligthly inconsistent with the opinions you have expressed here to-day. On the last page of the memorandum you say: " The important fact to be borne in mind in connection with these upper staff posts is that mere length of service, however blameless, and the possession of attainments indicated by success at a second division or lower examination, are insufficient qualifications for the discharge of the higher work of the office." Would you think that the educational qualifications of a second division clerk, coupled with experience in the office and fairly good natural ability, are sufficient qualifications for the discharge of the higher work of the office?—No, I do not, speaking generally. It is that view which, of course, underlies the whole of that memorandum. I think that a man who has done the same routine work for a considerable number of years and has not shown much power of initiative, organisation, or imagination in regard to

[1] Appendix, *Second Report of Royal Commission*, p. 227.

the saving of labour, cannot with any advantage be placed in higher places. I may perhaps put it in this way, that the maximum salary in the second division is 300*l.* a year, and there are many men who are worth 200*l.* to 300*l.* a year who never become worth more than that.

(*Chairman.*) What about the exceptional men?—They show qualities which enable them to be put in higher positions, but one has to be on the lookout for those qualities. They are to be attained sometimes by education, sometimes by special training, and sometimes by a sort of natural power of acquisition. . . .[1]

(*Chairman.*) One question of a general character I would like to ask you. You know the Civil Service from the top to the bottom, and have had experience of all classes recruited into the Civil Service?—That is so.

What is your appreciation of the average men recruited by the Class I. examination and men recruited into the second division? Do you think there is a very marked difference between the mental calibre or mental powers in the two types of men?—Speaking of classes I should say, yes.

Have you known many men in the second division equal to the Class I. type?—The difficulty is to speak generally and without regard to the many exceptions which occur. I have known men who have entered the service as copyists who have become distinguished Civil servants. I may mention, for instance, a gentleman who is now representing this country in the Turkish Customs Service—Sir Richard Crawford. He was a copyist when he entered the service of the Board of Agriculture, but became head of the Intelligence Branch of the Board of Agriculture. He then became Commissioner of Customs, he is now a high officer in the Turkish Customs Service; and he has quite recently received the K. C. M. G. I mentioned him as a type of the one class. On the other hand, one has known Class I. men of whose abilities one has had a very poor impression. Speaking in classes, I should say I

---

[1] Appendix, *Second Report of Royal Commission,* p. 230.

should prefer to have the man who has had a longer and more extensive education than a man who, unfortunately, very often from no fault of his own, has had a less extensive education. And it must be remembered also that in these days the universities are really very democratic institutions. A young man in the class from which the second division is recruited has ample opportunities, and very often utilises his opportunities, of going up to the universities and coming into Class I. It is not to be supposed that Class I. does not include many men of the same social grade as the men in Class II.

I make no reference whatever to social divisions, I merely wish to learn your opinion as regards the type of men produced by a university education, which gives you the great majority of the Class I. men. I have put to you the question with this object. I ask you whether you have known in the second division men who were much better than their fellows and deserving of promotion, and I want to find out from you whether you think the opportunities now available, or the methods of administration are such as to bring these exceptional men out of Class II., and whether they have at present a sufficient opportunity of making their way up to the higher class?—I think it would be improper for me to express any opinion except with regard to my own department.

I am asking your opinion as an experienced and distinguished Civil servant who has passed through all the grades, and I think we are entitled to ask you that opinion.—I can only say that, as regards my own department, I have made every possible effort to familiarise myself with the second division men who showed any capacity at all, and to give them every opportunity of remedying the deficiencies which, from no fault of their own, they have suffered. But, on the other hand, one has to admit that the men coming into the second division do suffer from a certain deficiency as regards education. They have not had the long and extensive education at a period of their life when they can probably put it to the best account. It must be much more difficult in a large department to give opportunities to the second division men to emerge from their rank. I do not know what could be done in order to improve those opportunities. In comparatively small departments like mine I think it is comparatively easy; but where you have large blocks of second division men it must be very much more difficult.[1]

The permanent head of the Admiralty was questioned as to the claims of the second division clerks in their memorial.

(*Mr. Shipley.*) Would you agree with the statement in the document which has been put in on behalf of the staff clerks, on page 2, in the paragraph headed " No distinction between so-called administrative and clerical work," that men who were formerly staff clerks and second division clerks are now merged with men who were formerly first division clerks?— No, I should not agree with that statement.

You do not think that the further statement is true " that first division, staff, and second division clerks divide the work indifferently between them "?—No, except as qualified by what I have said in answer to a previous question, that the younger higher division clerks must learn the business of the department, and they must necessarily, therefore, for a time, at any rate, be doing a certain amount of work which would be being done also, perhaps, by second division clerks. . . .

I suppose I need hardly ask you whether you agree with the general conclusion of this paper [a memorial of the Admiralty second division clerks], namely, that there is no adequate reason why you should have, putting it in a word, any higher division men?—Speaking quite deliberately, it would, in my opinion, be a serious blow to the administration of the Admiralty if the services of men of the highest educational qualifications were debarred.

(*Mr. Boutwood.*) I have only one other question to put to you, which is really suggested by what happened when I

[1] Appendix, *Second Report of Royal Commission*, p. 234.

visited the Admiralty with other Commissioners. What happened was this: We saw in succession two men. One was a
clerk who had entered by the Class I. examination, and the
other was a clerk who had become a Class I. man by promotion
from the second division; we saw them within the same five
minutes, and my own mind received a very definite impression, and I will tell you what that impression was: that if any
sudden emergency or any emergency arose which called for
prompt action, or initiative, or entailed new responsibility, or
anything of that kind, you might have got some help from the
Class I. man; you certainly would not have got any help from
the promoted man. I want to ask you what is your impression
of the promoted men, the men who have been promoted from
the second division in the Admiralty—whether you think that
impression of mine is simply individual, or would you think it
could be generalised at all?—It would be a little difficult to
answer that question without having in one's mind certain particular cases; but undoubtedly the Admiralty have not found
among the men so promoted quite the same capacity—I will
put it in that way—to respond to all conditions and to the
higher responsibilities that devolve upon them later, as among
the class of men who come in at a later age after a university
education.[1]

Let us see what the permanent head of the Admiralty,
the department in which the intermediate scheme originated, has to say about the need of such a division and the
possibility of getting this work done by second division
clerks.

Then the comparison will be between the selected men of the
second division, and the men who came in by the intermediate
examination. Is there a great difference between these two
classes of men?—A great difference, no; but there is a differ-

---

[1] Appendix, *Third Report of Royal Commission. Cf.* questions 16323,
16364, 16408-9.

ence, and the difference, speaking generally, is in favour of
the candidate who enters by the intermediate examination. . .

(*Chairman.*) That is not my point. My point is whether,
by selection from the second division you can get men who
are equal to those whom you get into the Service by the intermediate examination. Selection is very important if you have
a large area from which to select. I want to know whether
you can select from that large area of second division men
clerks of the same capacity as those you get by the intermediate
examination?—Certainly not in the area of second division
clerks actually serving at the Admiralty.[1]

It is unnecessary to quote more. The evidence given
shows that university education and experience are needed
in the civil service of Great Britain. It shows that the intermediate type of clerks is needed in some offices. It
shows that, while there ought to be more promotion from
the second division, more encouragement given to second
division men to pursue advanced studies, and more opportunities for intellectual work in the offices, the leading contentions of the second division clerks, to say nothing of
those of the assistant clerks, are not substantiated.

With due regard to the evidence, the present Royal
Commission can hardly come to other conclusions than
these:

(1) That there is not enough promotion from division II
to division I; that the rule requiring eight years' service in
the second division before promotion be abolished, or a
shorter term substituted; that more staff appointments be
set aside for division II; that more opportunity be given to
division II to do intellectual or original work instead of
mechanical work.

---

[1] Appendix, *Third Report of Royal Commission. Cf.* questions 16,480,
16,491.

(2) That the examinations for division I be modified so as to attract more men from the new universities.

(3) That the intermediate scheme be restricted to offices in which the difference in education between men so recruited and the second division represents a real asset and need, and that second division men be in some cases promoted and transferred to intermediate division offices.

(4) That the Treasury or department heads make an effort to recognize and reward second division men who employ their leisure to become bachelors of science, barristers, etc.[1]

(5) (Already mentioned above.)   That only such boy clerks be employed as can probably be absorbed into the assistant clerk class, and that these be required, as in the Post Office, to attend educational classes.

(6) That the pay of assistant clerks be raised to a living wage.

(7) Above all, that free education from primary schools through the universities in liberal arts or science be insured to every ambitious and deserving pupil; that the civil service examinations for such positions as boy clerkships and second division clerkships be arranged in conformity with primary and secondary education standards, so as to encourage and stimulate effort in the free schools.[2]

[1] "For the Estate Duty Office the Treasury have, we understand, sanctioned a scheme under which advancement to £200 per annum may be granted, after five years' service, to Officers of ability who have either been called to the Bar or taken a University degree in law." *The Civilian.*

[2] An important contribution of the present Royal Commission to civil service philosophy, suggested by Mr. Graham Wallas in cross examining a witness, was this: Macaulay and Trevelyan were satisfied to *follow* existing educational standards and choose the best men under the best existing conditions, while the present commission proposes to have the civil service *lead* national education, encourage new institutions, attract new types of men and thought, and educate those already in the service for higher duties.

It seems probable that action on these and other prospective recommendations of the Royal Commission will come, as usual, from the Treasury by Orders in Council, rather than from Parliament by statute. The Treasury and heads of departments will probably make as few changes as possible. An attempt will certainly be made to put most of the commission's recommendations into effect, but in a modified and cautious way. The government cannot revolutionize popular education in a day;[1] it must choose the best-fitted men where they are to be found. It is improbable that the first division examinations will be greatly modified, for it is not easy to attract many men from the new universities without lowering standards.

The writer's conclusions on this difficult question of democracy versus education in the civil service are these:

In a sense it is a cruel thing to set up class distinctions— even if they be only intellectual—in the service of a modern free state founded upon equality of opportunity. Because a man has been handicapped by obscure birth, indigence, and perhaps uncongenial early surroundings, because he has not conceived early enough the ambition to be well educated or has never had the time or the means for study and

---

[1] "And many of the suggestions made this afternoon would mean the expenditure of 5,000,000*l.*, 10,000,000*l.*, or 15,000,000*l.* a year very likely, or at any rate a very large amount of public money. Let me give you some examples of the questions that have been raised this afternoon: School accommodation, and the number of children in a class; the question of teachers' salaries; the question of the increase of the scholarship system; or of the accommodation in secondary schools; or the increase in industrial training. All those questions involve a very heavy expenditure.—They raise financial questions at every turn, of course."

(Mr. Wallas, of the commission, questioning a permanent secretary of the Board of Education. Appendix, *Second Report of Royal Commission*, p. 286.)

cultivated leisure, because, in brief, he lacks culture and a university degree, we place him in a subordinate position, employ him steadily upon mechanical or, at any rate, unimproving work, and then announce with a kind of mournful finality, that ·these people really cannot be promoted to higher tasks.

But where does our sympathy lead us? Can the state repair the defects of ·heredity or of early education? Can it endow the average individual with the intelligence, acuteness and cultivation which economic exigencies have denied him? Can the state make an assistant clerk over, because society has not given him a chance? What sort of an idea of competition is this, which decrees that the state, unlike private business, must prepare every one in its employ to be the head of a department? In the Irishman's army were none but generals. In the coming socialistic civil service there will be only heads of departments and prospective heads. When all educational and personal defects are remedied, there will be no need of distinctions of any kind.

The fact is that in the interests of every citizen the government must be run well. In the last analysis Pope's idea of government is right—whiche'er is best administered is best. There are all kinds of positions under a government, just as in private life. There are all kinds and classes of people available for government, as for private, work. There must be under secretaries and scavengers. Meanwhile, the state must recognize that there are differences of class and education and that the highest intelligence and the soundest education must be attracted into the civil service.

There is one thing which the state can and should do to vindicate its democracy—and, in a sense, this is forestalling and neutralizing social and educational inequalities. The government should see that its schools educate for all kinds of work, that ability and promise are lifted as far as possible above want and social handicap. But finally the government must choose the best men for positions varying greatly in qualifications, prospects, pay and dignity. There should be no social bar to promotion from the lowest to the highest place—but let us not fool ourselves. When we have made every possible provision for the encouragement of early promise, when we have prepared every child as far as possible for its suitable vocation, the subordinate employees of the government or of private enterprise who are fit to rise above the ranks will be few and far between. No doubt in the coming socialistic state all work will be of equal dignity, and no man will object to his appointed task. For the present we must recognize and be prepared to find men who are ambitious and dissatisfied, and for whom the state can do nothing; and we can extend only our sympathy to the stenographer or clerk of long standing who sees himself subordinated to recent university graduates, and feels that he has suffered the last indignity.

CHAPTER IX

ENGLISH EXPERIENCE AND THE UNITED STATES

"The fact is that Americans have ignored . . . the differences of capacity between man and man. They underrate the difficulties of government and overrate the capacity of the man of common sense."—Bryce, *American Commonwealth*.

THE early history of American civil service reform has been dramatically told in a dozen books and in hundreds of speeches. The reform movement, coming as it did from *outside* the administration and Congress, necessarily received its original impetus from books and gained in momentum through publicity and educated public opinion alone. The history of American reform is chequered and spasmodic.[1] The course of English reform is remarkably steady and uneventful. With the exception of the reactionary scepticism of the Playfair report, English reform has the

[1] See *Bibliography of Civil Service Reform,* published by the National Civil Service Reform Association, 1907; Congressional Report, 39 Congress, 2nd Session, Jan. 3, 1867. Hon. T. A. Jenckes; Carl Russell Fish, *The Civil Service and the Patronage,* Harvard Historical Studies, vol. xi, (New York, 1905); *Fifteenth Rep. of the U. S. Civil Service Commission;* E. B. K. Fultz, *The Federal Civil Service as a Career,* (New York, 1909); Parton's *Life of Jackson.*

For an excellent short account of the encroachment of civil service reform upon patronage in the United States, see Ostrogorski, *Democracy and the Organization of Political Parties* (New York, 1902), volume 2, pp. 484-499. The early efforts of Jenckes, Schurz, G. W. Curtis, and Eaton, and the derision they excited, are briefly and graphically portrayed. The important extensions of the classified civil service since President McKinley's death, followed, of course, the appearance of Mr. Ostrogorski's book.

appearance of a force moving irresistibly forward and driving patronage and incompetence before it. But reform in the United States has moved forward slowly and painfully; frequently it has stopped entirely, and at times it has actually been driven back. In the first decade of reform Congress simply withheld the appropriation for the tentative civil service advisory committee; and since the establishment of a permanent civil service commission, every President has had to resist the pressure of spoilsmen in Congress, and of politicians outside. Almost every year has seen riders to appropriation bills providing exemption from the classified civil service, promotion of temporary patronage appointees, transfers which violate the letter or spirit of the civil service law, illegal participation of civil servants in elections and enforced contributions to party funds, four-year tenure laws, dismissals for political reasons, appointments through senatorial " courtesy " and a dozen other forms of patronage and retrogression. Not a single administration at Washington since the Act of 1883 has an absolutely clean reform record; and in most cases this is no fault of the President and the cabinet.[1]

The conditions in the services of England and the United States at the beginning of reform were astonishingly similar. From the writings and speeches of Mr. Jenckes and Mr. Eaton, we can see that the problems of the unreformed departments at Washington in the sixties and seventies were those of the English public offices before 1853. There are whole passages descriptive of the personnel and demoralization of Washington departments, which might be attributed to writers in the English 1853 report without changing a

---

[1] President McKinley, however, has the unenviable record of surrendering to the spoilsmen thousands of positions in the classified service. This was done by executive order, not by act of Congress passed over the President's veto.

single word.[1] Mr. Sumner's speeches in Congress might
have been made by Mr. Gladstone; Mr. Chadwick's catalog
of incompetents might have been framed by Mr. Jenckes of
Rhode Island.[2] There were, of course, peculiar American

[1] Compare the remark of Robert Low, Viscount Sherbrooke: " Under
the former system there was never such a thing known as a man being
appointed because he was supposed to be fit for the place," with that
of the American, Parton, in his *Life of Jackson*: " In the year of
our Lord 1859, the fact of a man's holding office under the government is presumptive evidence that he is one of three characters—an
adventurer, an incompetent person, or a scoundrel."

[2] Compare with the descriptions by Chadwick and others in Chapter
I, pp. 4-5, this picture from the Jenckes report, of the United States
Customs House in 1868 (*anon.*).

" The revenue department of this government has been most shame-
fully maltreated, and by all political parties, as they have successively
come into power. Its various institutions, instead of subserving the
public interests as they should, have been converted into hospitals,
alms-houses, political fortresses, and places of refuge, (if not
refuse.) Instead of capable officers, honest, respectable and faithful
brawling politicians, broken-down hacks, and imbecile persons have
filled the places, through favoritism, nepotism, or corruption of some
kind. The government has lavished its funds, and for the purpose
of having its business faithfully transacted it has appropriated an
ample amount for that object; but intrigue and favoritism have almost neutralized its legitimate and intended effects in several ways.
Incompetent and inefficient men are foisted in; they constitute the
corps of loafers, whose time hangs idle on their hands, and who
are continually hovering about the industrious, and are serious obstacles to these. By means of personal influence, and plenty of
time to wield it, they generally secure the fattest salaries, especially
at a season when salaries are raised. Dishonest persons are another
corps, embezzlers, peculators, corrupt or venal; these insinuate themselves into all branches as furtively as Ulysses managed to elude the
searching hands of Polyphemus. Intemperate people also use the
public fund, not for their families, but to distress and tantalize them.
Partisans steeped in the elixir of ignorance disgrace the public books
with their scrawling chirography, their blundering arithmetic, and
their dislocated orthography, and their downright assassination of
grammar. . . . The government appropriates enough money to pay for
the *aggregate* services rendered to it, but the appropriation is so un-

vices—such as rotation, senatorial courtesy, and the
" spoils " system—but omitting these, the parallel between
the English and American unreformed services is perfect.

It was this parallel which particularly impressed Mr.
Eaton when he studied the English civil service and which
he succeeded in impressing upon his American readers.
The conclusions to be drawn from such an analogy were
obvious : Patronage demoralized the English and American
governments.   Civil service had purified the English government.   Therefore let us have civil service too and as
much like the English as possible.

Once the American civil service law was instituted on
English models, the analogy between the two countries unfortunately stopped.   We have been so busy fighting for a
full realization of the competitive principle and so busy preventing retrogressions, that the great problems of division,
of intellectual qualifications and examinations, of stimulating national education through civil service examinations
and attracting the best men into our government departments, have been quite neglected.   The English civil service,

equally and unjustly distributed that they who do the most work and
the best qualified get scanty salaries, while the . . . ill-qualified drones
realize large and altogether disproportionate compensation. . . . . .
Very few do the work, and are poorly paid; they work in and out of
hours, closely and incessantly."
    Similarly, it is interesting to compare the views of members of the
United States Congress opposed to the Pendleton Act with those of
opponents of the Trevelyan-Northcote scheme of 1853 (*Cf.* Chap. I.).
    " Mr. Horr said they [the proposed examinations] were all hum-
bug, and that he would prefer draw-poker or tossing coppers.
Equally numerous were the objections to the new system on the
ground that it was not an American product—was monarchial. Senator Brown expected that the officers of the government would become 'a praetorian guard,' and Senator Carpenter that they would
become a fixed aristocratic class." Fish, *The Civil Service and the
Patronage*, p. 220.

once fairly started on the straight path of reform, has had little need of mere reformers. In fact, we can no longer speak of civil service *reform* in England. This is the era of scientific development and experiment in the English .civil service. The artificial barriers and obstacles of patronage, graft, rotation, and sectional jealousies are not present to hinder a natural development and expansion.

It is to be hoped that the United States civil service will soon have passed from the " reform " stage, in which all honest men in and out of Congress and the cabinet must devote their time to the diseases of patronage and rotation, to the stage of healthy and normal development. Meanwhile, there are a number of cures to be effected and operations to be performed.

The Constitution of the United States provides (see Section 2, Art. 2) that the President " shall nominate, and by and with the Advice and Consent of the Senate, shall appoint Ambassadors, other public Ministers and Consuls, Judges of the Supreme Court, and all other Officers of the United States, whose Appointments are not herein otherwise provided for." The only discretion left to Congress in this matter is to permit by statute the appointment of inferior officers by the President alone, by the courts, or by the heads of departments. It is impossible to go at length into the origin and subsequent history of this clause, a disgraceful history, which includes constant altercations over senatorial " courtesy ", removals, and four-year tenure laws, and culminates in the impeachment of President Johnson. It must suffice to say that the clause originated in fear of presidential tyranny and official oligarchy, and that its history has shown that corruption of appointments has been largely the work of the Senate and of Congress as a whole.

Students of civil service in the United States agree that the Senate and House should waive their patronage; that all

positions, high and low, excepting those which have to do
with matters of party policy, should be classified under civil
service rules; and that the phrase " by and with the consent
of the Senate," should subject high political appointments
to senatorial scrutiny, to prevent jobbery not to encourage
it.   In order to attract good men into the civil service the
higher positions must be open to them.   At present every
change of administration involving a change of party sees
a wholesale removal of higher exempt officials and local
office-holders, resulting in chaos in the departments, political machinations in Congress, pernicious political activity
of office-holders at elections, and loss in money, time, efficiency, and prestige.   Almost all local offices and high departmental officials, excepting cabinet members and first
assistant secretaries, should be recruited from the permanent civil service, and enjoy permanent tenure on good behavior.   Almost all of the existing 10,000 presidential appointments should be in the classified service.

But extensions of the classified service are very difficult.
They inevitably give the party out of power the impression
that the President is guarding his appointees against possible dismissal in the future by giving them life jobs.   Thus
President Taft's order classifying some 36,000 fourth class
postmasters, the majority of them Republicans, enraged the
Democrats, who tried to persuade President Wilson on his
election to rescind the order and " turn the rascals out."
President Wilson fortunately refused, holding that Mr.
Taft's motives were honest and that a beginning had to be
made somewhere.

At present some 295,000 out of 391,000 federal employees are in the classified list.   Of the remaining 96,000
there are:

10,000 Presidential appointees.

3,500 Census employees.

13,000 Unclassified Post Office clerks.

20,000 Unskilled laborers.

21,000 Excepted from examination under Schedule A or subject to non-competitive examinations only.[1]

It will be seen that there is more open competition in the United States than in Great Britain, but the exemptions are less logical and competition in the United States is, as we shall see, rather illusory. If President Wilson realizes the plans of his university days and the promises of his party, the civil service classification will be extended to high departmental officials, to diplomatic agents, to the remaining Post officers, to Internal Revenue officers, Customs officers, United States marshals, and other exempted officials—but Congress is very tenacious of these contemptible remnants of a once glorious plunder.[2]

[1] *Proceedings of National Civil Service Reform Assn.*, Milwaukee, Dec. 5, 1912.

[2] Far from showing signs of further reform, the House has attempted to prevent the prospective income-tax collectors from being classified, and has recently succeeded, by means of a rider to an appropriation bill, in taking assistant revenue collectors and assistant marshals out of the classified list. President Wilson refused to veto this bill, but promised that the exempted positions would not be used as political spoils. While few will doubt the President's sincerity, every one must recognize that so far as concerns the authors and abettors of this rider in Congress, the claim that the exempted positions are confidential, fiduciary, etc., is a very thin disguise of their real purpose. In the Congressional debates we see them with the mask off:

"MR. JOHNSON (Democratic Representative from Kentucky). I am one who does not believe that when we have a Democratic President and a Democratic Congress that that completes and makes a Democratic administration. I do not believe we will have or can have a Democratic administration until every office is administered by Democrats. (Applause.) We find the departments in Washington, we find the departments in every part of the United States,

It may be said without exaggeration that there is no such
thing as real open competition in the United States. We
have only to consider these facts in connection with our
federal examinations in order to see how many obstacles

full of Republicans not in sympathy with the Democratic administration; and they are asked to administer the affairs of the Democratic
administration. (Applause on the Democratic side.) They are there
to make trouble for and to betray a Democratic administration.
(Applause on the Democratic side.) . . ."

"MR. KAHN (Republican Representative from California). For
sixteen years you on the Democratic side have been outside the en-
closure which surrounds the green corn. The boys at home have
been saying to you, 'For years and years we have supported you in
your candidacy. We have not had a job heretofore because you
were in the minority. Now that you are in the majority, we demand
of you that you give us the jobs.'"

"SEVERAL MEMBERS (on the Democratic side). That is right."

"MR. KAHN. Of course that is right from your standpoint. I am
glad you admit it; but the American people will not stand for this
attack upon the merit system. (Laughter on the Democratic side.)

    .   .   .   .   .

You gentlemen may laugh; but your laughter will turn to a sicken-
ing smile when the American people can be heard from upon this
subject. About one-third of the appointees in the marshals' offices
and in the collector of internal revenue offices have passed the civil
service examinations since the ægis of the civil service laws and
regulations was thrown over the employees of those offices.

You desire to break down the system and put your political henchmen into the offices. You have referred to the right of the superior
officer to surround himself in the confidential positions with men of
his selection. That is pure hypocrisy. The gentleman from Penn-
sylvania (Mr. Temple) pointed out the joker in this thing. The
last lines of the sentence read:

And the officer requiring such bond shall have power to revoke the
appointment of any subordinate officer or employee and to appoint his
successor at his discretion without regard to the act, amendments, or
regulations aforesaid.

Under that provision the superior officer can discharge his messenger; he can discharge his typewriter; he can discharge everybody
who is in the office, even to the unfortunate char-woman."

"SEVERAL MEMBERS (on the Democratic side). That is what
we want." (House of Representatives, October 10, 1913.)

separate the ablest of available competitors from the best available position:

(1) Apportionment, by which, if his state has received its full quota of appointments, the candidate has little or no prospect of appointment. There is no open competition under such circumstances. A man from New Mexico who has attained an average of 80 per cent in a competitive examination, may be preferred to a New Yorker who has an average of 85 per cent, because, forsooth, the fixed quota from New York cannot be exceeded until New Mexico has had the requisite share in government appointments. It is claimed that apportionment is a good thing, because it draws to Washington citizens from all over the country, creates understanding and sectional good feeling and a national atmosphere, and eventually sends missionaries of national patriotism home to the four corners of the nation. This argument, especially when applied to the rank and file of the civil service, is too ludicrous to merit an answer. No doubt every section of the country should be represented in the cabinet, but not necessarily in the permanent civil service. Let the sections compete.

(2) The practice of submitting to the appointing officer the names of three eligibles for each vacancy. This would be called limited competition in England.

(3) The low standards of examinations for all but technical and legal positions, which give the candidate no opportunity to display a sound education such as is given in our high schools. The government service need not appoint any one above the sub-clerical service who has not a public high-school education or its equivalent.

(4) The practice of preferring disabled veterans, soldiers and sailors, for all civil positions [1] and limiting the number of members of the same family to two.

[1] A striking example of this kind of false sentiment, in the case of

(5) The absence of any information on the part of the Civil Service Commission concerning the number of probable vacancies, and the existence of a waiting list. The Civil Service Commission should always have a more or less accurate idea of the number of places to be vacant.

(6) Bidding for salaries—the practice by which a candidate indicates the lowest salary he is willing to accept. If the candidate puts his bid at the legal minimum, he may be appointed and get much less than he deserves; if he bids higher, he may be postponed to others or may not receive any appointment at all. Entrance salaries and prospects of annual increments should be as uniform as possible throughout the various divisions of the service.[1]

When we consider these facts along with the poor pay and limited possibilities of promotion, since, excepting a few technical and legal positions, no man can hope to rise above $3,000, we can readily see why we have no true open competition and why the good men we attract by accident soon resign to get a fairer reward in private enterprise.[2]

an appointive officer, was that of General Black, until recently head of the United States Civil Service Commission. General Black is a veteran of the Civil War, and was appointed to the Commission out of sympathy and a desire to supplement his pension. He was never capable of discharging the duties of his office and was removed by President Wilson. In a congressional debate not long before his removal, it was said that General Black, the Civil Service Commissioner, was drawing a pension for complete mental and physical disability, and earned it.

[1] *Manual of Examinations*, United States Civil Service Commission, spring of 1913.

[2] The President's Commission on Economy and Efficiency, which has recently completed its labors, has recommended changes in organization, personnel, and conduct of business, including an annual budget, standardization, etc., which should greatly facilitate the work of the national departments and reduce waste of money and time and lack of coördination to a minimum. The work of this commission was much like that of the English Efficiency and Economy Commission of 1873.

While the pressing problems of patronage are being solved, it is to be hoped that President Wilson will begin to

A detailed consideration of this subject is not within the scope of this essay. There are certain recommendations of Mr. Taft's commission which are of striking interest:

(1) The commission recommended some kind of a permanent co-ordinating, harmonizing and supervising body—a Bureau of Central Administration—like the Efficiency Commission itself or the English Treasury.

(2) The commission flatly repudiated the system of apportionment of candidates for civil service positions.

(3) The commission recommended that all the higher appointments in the government, including at least one assistant secretary and all heads of bureaus to which appointments are made by and with the consent of the Senate, except those positions which have to do with the determination of policy, such as cabinet officers and first secretaries, be made by the President alone and placed in the competitive classified service. The commission recommended that competitive examination standards be fixed for these higher positions, and from this fact it may be gathered that not mere promotion from the clerk class, but some kind of a first division, university class was to be attracted into the clerical civil service. Similarly, the commission recommended that the local patronage offices in the Customs, Revenue, etc., mentioned above, be classified.

(4) The commission recommended a pension system—contributory pensions, not straight pensions as under the old English statute of 1859. The question of the comparative merits of the English and other pension schemes is very involved. The commission published a lengthy study of pensions in the English civil service and made this study, to a certain extent, the basis of their report. American students of the pension problem are almost unanimously agreed that the system of contributory pensions paid out of an interest-accumulating, separate fund, on an unsentimental business basis, is more logical, is cheaper, and removes the motives for keeping the incompetent and decrepit in the service. There is one very important consideration which these American advocates of contributory pensions do not weigh properly—that unless salaries are raised all round their plan is worthless. Employees will hardly welcome the plan of annual subtractions from a bare living wage, in order to get the deductions returned with interest when they are old or disgusted. The subject of pensions in the United States is closely bound up with that of fair salaries. See p. 174, *supra.*

improve the personnel and efficiency of the service by raising educational standards and salaries, and making a definite
appeal to men of the highest college and university training
and to those specially prepared, to choose the civil service as
a career. Technical and scientific positions are already attracting very able men to examinations which are annually
becoming more adequate and searching; but there is still a
feeling current that for untechnical departmental positions,[1]
academic qualifications and sound university education are
not requisite,[2] that anybody is good enough to be a clerk,

---

[1] An attempt is made to get college men for the Philippine Service
as assistants in the departments, officers of the Philippine Constabulary, etc. This has been a success, though there are not many
applicants.

[2] President Eliot of Harvard has urged a first division examination
on English models, followed, however, after two years by a practical
examination like those in the German services:
" To meet this situation we think it would be well to adopt, in part,
the plan which has worked so successfully in England of dividing the
service into a higher and lower grade and placing the higher administrative positions now unclassified in the United States service
in the upper grade. There would be but few positions in the upper
grade and these would be mostly confined to the departments in
Washington; for positions outside of Washington, now unclassified,
such as postmasters and collectors (with the possible exception of
those in the largest cities) could be satisfactorily filled by promotion.
But within the Washington departments are a number of high grade
positions such as chiefs of bureaus and the lower assistant secretaries
which demand a high degree of executive ability and frequently
special training.
For the filling of these positions in the upper grade we recommend
the holding of high grade educational examinations on a par with
university examinations, open alike to persons in the service in line
for promotion, not over 40 years of age, and to persons not connected with the service, not over 25 years of age. The examination
should be an open competition held in all parts of the United States.
Those standing highest in such examinations should be appointed to
service as apprentices in the department in positions as assistants to
chiefs of divisions, bureau chiefs, and assistant secretaries, and during
the two years following their appointment they should be subject

and that amongst so many clerks there are sure to be enough exceptional ones to fill the higher places. No one at Washington seems to have thought of the possible stimulating and standardizing effects of large competitions of college and university men upon national education, effects very obvious in England. There are many positions, not only at Washington but also in state and municipal governments, worthy the pursuit of our best educated young men, and if the government would but hold out opportunities of adequate pay and promotion, it could attract the very élite into our civil services.

The United States Patent Office is an excellent example, both of the advisability of attracting highly educated men into the service, and of the folly of driving them out by low pay and poor prospects.

Owing to the better salaries offered by commercial concerns, the Patent Office has sometimes had difficulty in getting competent men to take the civil service examination. It has

to frequent transfer so that they may become thoroughly familiar with department methods in different branches. After a two years' apprenticeship they should be subject to a further examination dealing with departmental methods of administration and as a result of this examination should be promoted as vacancies occur to positions of chiefs of division and higher positions, or else dropped from the service.

If these examinations for entrance to the upper service are held annually they will continually provide for the infusion of new blood at the needed points, and will serve as a constant incentive to men who entered the service at the lower grades to seek a broader education with the chance of aspiring to the most responsible and highest paid non-political positions in the United States government."

Respectfully submitted,

CHARLES W. ELIOT.

(*Promotions in the Civil Service,* Report of Special Committee of the National Civil Service Reform Association, published by the National Civil Service Reform League, New York, 1911, pp. 16, 17.)

been necessary then to make temporary appointments, selecting such material as could be found and made use of. About
the time that these men were trained, the temporary appointments have come to an end and the men had to be dropped.
The Patent Office would have little chance at all to obtain
good examiners were it not successful in picking up young
men immediately after their graduation from college. These
are usually men of fine ability, but without practical experience of any kind, who, while hesitating which unknown road
to take, are attracted by the definite proposals of the Patent
Office. Able to pass the difficult examinations set for them
by the Civil Service Commission and not yet tempted by offers
of more lucrative work, they enter the service. Perceiving
that there is little hope of rapid promotion or ultimate reward commensurate with their worth, they resign in three or
four years after having acquired the experience which is the
one thing they have thus far lacked. Many of those who
enter the examining corps of the Patent Office are young men
of splendid attainments and represent the best product of our
American universities. Since the increase of the entrance
salary in 1908 less difficulty has been experienced in securing
the necessary number of eligibles, but the number of assistants who resign after three or four years of service has
steadily continued because of the slowness of promotions. The
following quotation from the annual report of the Commissioner of Patents for the year 1907 is interesting in this connection :

" The examiners are all graduates of colleges, mostly polytechnic colleges, and 90 per cent have been graduated in general and patent law, and with office experience are invaluable
to the service; but after about three years' experience in this
office and when they are fully experienced and valuable in the
work thereof they are also fully equipped to go out, and do
go out, to accept positions that pay all the way from $2,000 a
year up. The office has become merely a post-graduate school
for the technical and legal education of young college men who
enter the service. The General Electric Co. has in its patent

department 12 or more men who were formerly examiners in this office, and other corporations have taken hundreds from this office, and this company also, like many others, takes men from the graduating classes of polytechnic colleges at higher salaries than are provided on entrance to this office, so that we are now competing with outside institutions for men to do the technical work of the office.   One hundred and thirty-five examiners out of a corps of 300 have resigned in a period of less than five years." [1]

Many problems of our state and city civil service cannot be treated here.   As a matter of fact there are still a number of states and a majority of cities without any or without adequate civil service laws.[2]   In some cases civil service laws have been declared unconstitutional; and in others they have been rendered inoperative by refusal of appropriations.   The same patronage and exemption problems exist in states and cities as in the national government, and there are far too many officials elected by the people who ought to be appointed by the executive or classified in the civil service.   In the next pages it is possible only to indicate that higher educational standards and experiments are as essential in states and cities as in the national government, and that foreign experience is equally instructive in these fields of American government.

In the United States, as in England, we are creating new departments of government activity—part of the social-altruistic trend of the times toward paternalism and state socialism.   These new departments must have leaders and a

---

[1] From *Report of the Investigation of the United States Patent Office*, 1912, p. 116.

[2] The English local civil services are comparatively undeveloped. The influence of the central civil service of the Kingdom on local public offices has been astonishingly small.   See Wallas, *Human Nature in Politics*, pp. 256, 257.

personnel with new and peculiar duties, and to a certain extent with peculiar qualifications. We have built the Panama Canal and staffed it temporarily with conspicuous success. We shall need a permanent service of commercial experts and clerks to deal with the enormous problems of world trade and shipping to which the Canal has given rise. In state governments we are planning great insurance departments against accident, disease, old age, unemployment, minimum wage, etc. In these new departments we need new men and we have the possibility of making new and important experiments in civil service recruitment. In England the labor exchanges and the new Insurance Commission for National Health adopted new methods of recruiting their staffs. Similarly, we may well make our initial choices from three sources, from the existing civil service, the experienced expert outside the service, and from the educated youth just graduated from schools and universities. We might well demand of all superior officers a college education, including economics and politics.

Supposing that a great state workmen's compensation act is passed setting up a compulsory or voluntary state insurance system by employers against accidents or illness of employees. The staff of such a department would undoubtedly consist of four general groups: (1) stenographers, bookkeepers, and minor office assistants; (2) clerks of good education for routine work; (3) a higher class of inspectors and clerks to do the more difficult field, directing, and intellectual work; (4) executives and technical experts. The third class might well be recruited by an examination of university standing like the Indian civil service examination, excepting that economic subjects should be compulsory. Graduate students in political science and economics would be available, and the recommendations of professors as to the real promise and probable usefulness of a candi-

date might be demanded. The stimulus to university education would be enormous.[1] There can be no doubt that
many young B. A.'s and graduate students would prefer
such state service to an academic or business career. They
are young, cultivated, enthusiastic. They can be quickly
taught the work of an office. They have neither the arro-
gance and conceit of the young Prussian official, nor the
aloofness of the English university-bred civilian.

Certainly it is worth while to find out whether, after all,
any prolonged practical training for administrative positions is essential or even desirable. Shall we profit by the
experience of England in this respect, or choose our models
in Germany, where technical or practical knowledge goes
hand in hand with a general education almost unattainable
in the United States? Perhaps we may be able to combine
the best points of English and German methods without a
stupid eclectic compromise. In our new city departments—
which grow up with municipal home rule, municipal owner-
ship and general city growth—we must have higher educa-

[1] The success of western state universities in making themselves
the very center of the administrative and political life of the state is
being watched in other parts of the United States with growing ad-
miration. Legislators and executives go to the seminars of the university for suggestions, and professors and students use the government departments as their laboratories. Theory and practice go hand
in hand, and government and university coöperate cordially in the
service of the state. Such a system cannot but produce an admirable *corps d'élite* in the civil service, which will represent the state
universities and the new citizenship. But whether this can be imi-
tated elsewhere, for instance in states like New York where business
is vastly more complex, where there are racial, economic and socio-
logical problems unknown in smaller communities of an equable,
homogeneous, German caste—that is a question which must almost
certainly be answered in the negative. The "Wisconsin idea" is
admirable; but it is no panacea for the misgovernment prevalent elsewhere.

tional standards.[1] At present it is found that cramming schools can supply quickly and cheaply to any glib pupil the amount of " practical knowledge "—be it of stenography or factory laws—necessary to get on the eligible list.[2]

[1] For higher positions in municipal governments, something like a combination of English and German methods appears in the new American Bureau of Municipal Research and Training School for Public Service. The field work of the New York Bureau of Municipal Research presents an ideal way of giving practical instruction to *selected* candidates. Though at present a privately endowed institution, such a school might be financed by the city and state and its *fellows* be chosen from amongst university and graduate school students by open competition. Probably this is the system of the future in American cities; but it applies only to the upper positions in the civil service.

There are several dangers which these private bureaus of municipal research must successfully contend with before they can take their place as a salutary arm of our municipal government. Members of such boards and their pupils are necessarily busybodies. They are forever criticizing the work of city officials and telling them the right way to go about it. It requires much tact to avoid the united dislike and opposition of city employees, and much self-restraint to avoid pressing doctrinaire theories of organization, methods, and accounts, which are foreign to the practice of departments, uncongenial to the rank and file or illogical to executive officers. The investigators of the bureau of municipal research are in constant danger of being told to go and mind their own business.

For a discussion of the qualifications requisite in heads of departments in American municipalities, and of the comparative values of various methods of selection, tenure and pay, see Munro, *Government of American Cities* (New York, 1912), p. 237 *et seq.* Professor Munro has a good chapter on civil service in cities, in which he touches on the methods of constituting civil service commissions of examining, promoting and removing, and on the objections to civil service reform and pensions, (p. 264 *et seq.*).

[2] In the United States we have an incredible number of civil service schools and teachers, manuals of instruction, and advisory newspapers, which cram candidates for almost any civil service position, clerical, scientific, technical, or physical. They will teach a man in three weeks how to pass the examination for food inspector, prepare a fire chief for promotion, or stretch a police candidate who is just

Even now, the success of the bureau of municipal research as a training school marks unmistakably the beginning of a class I system in our services like the English class I—a division as inevitable as it is salutary. Such a system is far more democratic than the one we have in most places now. Where there are few places and many aspirants, there must be discrimination of some kind. We *must* discriminate at the start on the basis of education. No doubt there should be every provision for promotion of outstanding ability from the ranks; but such promotions would inevitably be rare, and only a democratic perversion could make them the rule rather than the exception.

There is not a profession in the United States today which has not suffered from lack of proper academic education on the part of its practitioners. There is not a profession which is not steadily raising its demands in this

---

below the required height. These schools have a percentage of successes which is extraordinary, if we do not reflect upon the quality of examinations which are calculated to put a premium on just such hasty cramming. Which is better, to invite a mediocre and often ill-educated man or woman into the service because he or she has glib cram book information about the duties and laws of an office, or to put a premium on general sound education and let some of the technical information wait until a period of apprenticeship is over? No doubt there will always be cramming schools for civil service as well as for universities—as long as there are standardized and stereotyped examinations—but the state should go behind the crammed information to the sound school education of years. Can we speak of selection and merit when numbers of civil service schools can promise to get every pupil on any eligible list—and come very near to justifying the boast? If we require technical or practical knowledge, let us see that they are not overemphasized and that they are combined with the soundest general education our schools have given. It is to be hoped that our future vocational public schools will offer that combination of technical and general knowledge which the lower positions in the civil service require. The relation between our schools, elementary, high schools, and colleges, and the government services, needs careful study.

respect. Almost every professional university course is a graduate course. The United States is filling up; professions are overcrowded, and their practice grows daily more complex and discriminating. Our pseudo-legal ideas of freedom are more and more constrained by the exercise of the police power. The government touches us everywhere; and we are extending the functions of the government every day. Unsound or haphazard education has always been dangerous; it is fatal now, and especially in the conduct of the government itself. Where the professions and private business demand so much, can the government, which is daily arrogating new functions to itself and encroaching more on the fields of every private calling, demand less?

Even those who see the need of higher standards are constantly raising the bugaboo of bureaucracy. Generally these critics have in their mind a vague and disturbing idea of a bureaucrat—as a stout, fierce man in a uniform, who pries into your private business, insults you, and threatens to report you to a fiercer man in a finer uniform who will put you to death. We need hardly deal at length with this American tourist conception of Prussian officialism. What Gladstone said in England is true here—under a democratic government responsible to the people, the extreme Prussian bureaucrat is impossible. But even the Prussian bureaucrat is preferable to many an American state or city official.[1] Neither of them is the servant of the people. The difference lies in the fact that the Prussian feels he is responsible only to the Emperor, to whom he gives the best that is

[1] In many American cities and states the civil service is already admirably independent and efficient, *e. g.*, in the City of Chicago and in the State of Wisconsin. In most cases, even though there is a comprehensive civil service law, the educational requirements or standards of examination are too low.

in him of service and loyalty, while the boss-ridden American official is responsible only to his patron, to whom he gives not honest service but profit, and whom he will desert if he gets a chance.

In conclusion it may be said that we are only just beginning to experiment on civil service recruitment. We have only just reached the period in which we can set up a standard of " efficiency and economy," to use the already familiar descriptive phrase, without compromising with patronage and graft. We shall have to wage a final battle with false democracy—an old ally of patronage and inefficiency—before we are through. We shall have to discover the principles upon which our civil service can be most highly developed, and we shall have to consider how far civil service recruitment may be made to stimulate public education and reward early promise. We must test everything and, with due and respectful regard to foreign experience, adopt the system that suits us best. We must decide how far open competiton can be extended with success; where limited competition is better; and where competition in any form is undesirable. We must determine on the basis of experiment, not of doctrinaire theories, how far we must demand specialized, practical training and field work, and how far we may trust the intelligent and alert college graduate of merely academic training to acquire specific knowledge of his life business in the civil service itself. In municipal government we shall need field work and training such as the bureaus of municipal research are giving now; in national government offices this is probably often unnecessary and sometimes undesirable. We must decide without political pressure and false democratic theories how promotions in the civil service are to be made, and how much encouragement we may honestly offer to those who expect to rise from the ranks without the almost

essential early education of the university.man.   The great
questions of salary, pensions, and transfers must receive
careful attention.

In Europe, titles and orders, and (in monarchies) the
exaggerated respect paid to civil servants as the visible sym-
bols of royal power, attract the brains of these countries
into government work in spite of low salaries.   If vanity
and other pardonable human weaknesses can be capitalized
at all, a C.B., a knighthood, a *Herr Oberregierungsrath,*
or a *Geheimer* must be capitalized so as to double the existing salaries of the title holder.   We have, perhaps unfortunately, no such gewgaws here, and though we may hope
that the privilege of serving the government is one to stimulate the enthusiasm and pride of every young citizen, we
must pay our officials fair salaries or else we shall not be
able to compete with private enterprise.   A list of resignations from our national civil service at Washington in a
single year, representing the departure of the best men in
government offices to more lucrative private business positions, will convince any honest Congressman of the need
of a revision of our scale of salaries.   In 1907 there were
15,289, and in 1908, 11,153 resignations from the United
States civil service.[1]   We must compete with the large corporations for administrative talent.

When we have settled upon these practical principles of civil
service, we must revise them every decade or so to keep up
with the times.   A fixed code of civil service regulations is
as dangerous as an unchanging code of law.   We must
weigh the cases and experiences of a decade and revise intelligently.   The cumulative evidence of ten years might
well be submitted to periodical commissions of investiga-

---

[1] *Promotions in the Civil Service,* a pamphlet published by the
National Civil Service Reform Association, 1911.

tion, in city, county, state, and national governments, as it has been in England, as the basis for legislative action. And meanwhile we must be alert to see that patronage does not creep back into the services. We may trust to the bureaus of municipal research, to the civil service reform associations, and to newspapers to watch every act of Congress, state legislature and aldermen affecting the civil service. The heads of the hydra of graft and patronage grow on again.

Another danger, already felt in England and always threatening in France, is that of organized unions of public employees to coerce the executive and influence the legislature for higher salaries, free promotions, etc.[1] We must

[1] As an example of this danger, the author quotes from an editorial in the current issue of the *Civil Service Chronicle* of New York (Sept. 20, 1913). The editor threatens to hand over the votes of 100,000 civil service employees to Tammany Hall, in case Mr. Mitchel, the Fusion candidate, will not promise to raise salaries and oppose reductions in the city forces. As Collector of the Port of New York, Mr. Mitchel had incurred the enmity of many United States civil service employees on account of reductions in numbers in the interests of economy and efficiency.

"We have estimated that there are 100,000 civil employes in New York City who can vote on election day, which is, equal to saying that they can influence 400,000 votes, for each employe is capable of influencing three persons—a father, son, brother or friend—to help him in a fight to better his living conditions.

That the Chronicle's warnings are not passing unnoticed may be seen from the announcement in the New York *Times* that the Fusion leaders are alarmed lest Collector Mitchel's proposed cut of 424 Customs Inspectors to 200 array the civil service employes against him. Even a political manager so disdainful of employes as Fire Commissioner Johnson made as one of his strong points against Collector Mitchel last week that the City employes would not vote for him.

The *Chronicle* wishes it to be understood that it is not opposing Collector Mitchel, but it is simply warning him against cutting the force of Customs Inspectors from 424 to 200, or attempting to throw all the burden of economy on employes. But on this and on all other matters the *Chronicle* will reserve decision until Mr. Mitchel has had

keep politics out of the civil service at any cost. We may trust to growing intelligence on the part of legislatures, to increasing *esprit de corps* and loyalty in the service itself, to fair consideration of grievances on the part of executives, and, in the last analysis, to the remorseless exercise of the executive power of suppression and dismissal to solve this question.

We are on the eve of great changes in our government at Washington. The full significance of President Wilson's election to the presidency and of his success in office, has not yet been appreciated. The writings of President Wilson's student days show not only a clear understanding of the defects of our congressional government and civil service, but also a keen realization of the executive leadership necessary to remedy them. The ideas of a thesis [1] and the

a fair opportunity of declaring himself. Up to date the *Chronicle* is neither for nor against any candidate.

Some of the LEANERS among the employes are almost frightened at the thought suggested by the *Chronicle* that the employes can control the coming election. They have so long believed that employes have no rights and have so long been servile that it seems like blasphemy to suggest that they should rise and go to the polls in a body and vote for whomsoever they believe will be most likely to grant a few of the things coming to them.

But it was not so very long ago that there was a combination of civil employes in New York that accomplished practical results in an election. It happened in 1901, when the Police, the Firemen and the Letter Carriers combined to defeat Sol. Blumenthal, Chairman of the Cities Committee of the Assembly, and Senator Webster, Chairman of the Cities Committee of the Senate. These gentlemen in a high-handed manner had refused to give consideration to a request for salary increases for the Police and Firemen, and as the Letter Carriers wanted the support of the Police and Firemen in a Congressional fight they were interested in, the three forces just naturally combined."

[1] See Woodrow Wilson, *Congressional Government*, originally submitted for the degree of Ph. D. at Johns Hopkins in 1884.

In President Wilson's professorial days he already predicted the

comparative studies of the seminar are guiding the nation to-day.

It is interesting to note the preface which President Wilson wrote when his *Congressional Government* was reprinted in 1900:

New prizes in public service may attract a new order of talent. The nation may get a better civil service, because of the sheer necessity we shall be under of organizing a service capable of carrying the novel burdens we have shouldered.

It may be, too, that the new leadership of the Executive, inasmuch as it is likely to last, will have a very far-reaching effect upon our whole method of government. It may give the heads of the executive departments a new influence upon the action of Congress. It may bring about, as a consequence, an integration which will substitute statesmanship for government by mass meeting.

possibility of the scholar in politics. He pointed with pride to the great influence of Professor Gneist on Prussian administrative evolution (see Woodrow Wilson, *The State*, Boston, 1895, p. 278), and looked forward confidently to the day when a more enlightened United States would invite the aid of students of government.

APPENDIX A [1]

Order in Council of 10th Day of January, 1910, Repealing Earlier Orders, and Consolidating the Rules Applicable to Admission to the Home Civil Service and to the Conditions of Service Therein

Whereas by several Orders in Council, dated respectively . . . . provision has been made for testing according to fixed rules the qualifications of persons who may seek or be proposed for appointment, either permanently or temporarily, to situations or employment in any of His Majesty's Civil Establishments, and for regulating the conduct of His Majesty's said Civil Establishments and the conditions of service therein.

And whereas it is expedient that so much of the aforesaid Orders as is now in force should be consolidated, with certain amendments, into one Order in Council.

1. Now therefore His Majesty, by and with the advice of His Privy Council, doth order and it is hereby ordered, that, as from the date of this Order, so much of the aforesaid Orders as is now in force shall be repealed, and that the provisions following shall have effect in substitution for them:—

Provided that such repeal or substitution shall not affect the validity of anything done under or by virtue of such orders or any of them.

Provided also that nothing in this Order shall affect any right, privilege, or exemption enjoyed by any person in His Majesty's Civil Establishments under Regulations in force at the date of the passing of this Order.

[1] Note particularly Clause 7.

Part I

2. Such persons as His Majesty in Council shall have approved shall be His Majesty's Civil Service Commissioners (herinafter called the Commissioners) for testing the qualifications of the persons proposed to be appointed to any situation or employment in His Majesty's Civil Establishments, and for testing, in conformity with regulations to be from time to time issued by the Army Council, the literary qualifications of candidates for admission by means of competitive examinations to the Royal Military College at Sandhurst, and to the Royal Military Academy at Woolwich, and shall hold their offices during the pleasure of His Majesty; and shall have power, subject to the approval of the Lords Commissioners of His Majesty's Treasury (hereinafter called the Treasury) to appoint from time to time such assistant examiners and others as may be required to assist them in the performance of the duties herein assigned to them.

Provided that any Commissioner appointed for the purpose aforesaid may, subject to the approval of the Treasury previously obtained, by writing under his hand authorize the Secretary for the time being to the Civil Service Commission to act as Commissioner at any time during the absence of any of the Commissioners or during any vacancy among the Commissioners or for such period during such absence or vacancy as may be fixed by such authorization.

The Secretary, when acting in pursuance of such authorization, shall have all powers, duties and authorities assigned by this or any future Order in Council to the Commissioners for the time being appointed for the purposes aforesaid.

3. Subject to the provisions of Clause 7 of this Order and to the exceptions specified in the Schedule marked B, appended hereto, the qualifications of all such persons as may seek or be proposed for appointment, either permanently or temporarily, to any situation or employment in any of His Majesty's Civil Establishments shall, before they are so appointed, be tested by or under the directions of the said Commissioners; and no person (save as excepted in the said Schedule B) shall be ap-

pointed to any such Establishment until a Certificate of his qualification shall have been issued by the Civil Service Commissioners declaring that he has satisfied them—

1st. That he is within the limits of age prescribed for the situation or employment to which he desires to be admitted;

2nd. That he is free from any physical defect or disease which would be likely to interfere with the proper discharge of his duties;

3rd. That his character is such as to qualify him for such situation or employment; and

4th. That he possesses the requisite knowledge and ability to enter on the discharge of his duties.

4. The rules applicable to each Establishment (hereinafter called Department), under each of the above heads, shall be settled, subject to the approval of the Treasury, by the Commissioners and the Head of the Department.

5. Save as hereinafter excepted, all appointments which it may be necessary to make to any of the situations in the Departments included in Schedule A appended hereto, or any other situations included or to be included in that Schedule, shall be made by means of competitive examinations, according to regulations framed or to be from time to time framed by the Commissioners, and approved by the Treasury, open to all persons (of the requisite age, health, character, and other qualifications prescribed in the said regulations) who may be desirous of attending the same, subject to the payment of such fees as may be prescribed under this Order, or may have already been prescribed under the Orders of 4th June, 1870, and of 22nd March, 1879, now repealed. Such examinations shall be held at such periods, and for such situations or groups of situations, as the Commissioners, with the approval of the Treasury, shall have from time to time determined, and shall have reference, as the Commissioners, after consultation with the Head of the Department concerned and with the approval of the Treasury, may deem expedient, either to the vacancies

existing at the time of the examination, or to the number of vacancies which may be estimated as likely to occur within any period not exceeding six months after the commencement of the examination, or to such vacancies occurring within any period not exceeding six months from the date of the announcement of the result of the examination as the Head of the Department may desire to have so filled.

6. After the candidate has passed his examination and his certificate of qualification has been issued by the Commissioners, he shall enter on a period of probation of one year, or such extended period not exceeding two years in all, as may be prescribed by the Head of his Department. During this time his conduct and capacity shall be subjected to such tests as may be determined by the Head of the Department, and he shall not be finally appointed to the Public Service unless and until his probation shall have furnished to the Head of his Department satisfactory proof of his fitness.

7. In case the Head of a Department to which a situation belongs and the Treasury shall consider that the qualifications in respect of knowledge and ability deemed requisite for such situation are wholly or in part professional, or otherwise peculiar, and not ordinarily to be acquired in the Civil Service, and the Head of the Department shall propose to appoint thereto a person who has acquired such qualifications in other pursuits, or in case the Head of the Department and the Treasury shall consider that it would be for the public interest that the prescribed examination and the rules in regard to age should be wholly or partially dispensed with, the Commissioners may, if they think fit, dispense with such examination wholly or partially, and with such rules in regard to age, and may grant their certificate of qualification upon evidence satisfactory to them that the said person is fully qualified in respect of age, health, character, and knowledge and ability.

8. When a person has been selected for appointment to an office in any Department, and the state of business in that Department makes it necessary that it should enter upon his duties before the issue in his favour of a certificate by the

Commissioners, the Treasury may, if they think proper, direct that his salary shall be payable from the date on which he commences the discharge of his duties, provided that they are satisfied that the delay in the issue of the certificate is owing wholly to causes beyond his control. If such person is on a scale of salary, the first incremental period of such scale shall be reckoned from the date on which his salary became payable, provided that a certificate shall in the meanwhile have been. issued by the Commissioners.

9. Fees shall be paid of such amount, in such manner, and at such times, by persons attending examinations held by the Commissioners, or certificated by them under Clause 7 of this Order, as they, with the approval of the Treasury, have prescribed, or shall from time to time prescribe, by notice published by them in the *London Gazette*.

The Commissioners may, with the like approval, exempt from the payment of fees such classes of persons as they may think fit to exempt. Every such exemption shall be published in the *London Gazette*.

The Commissioners, with the like approval, may, by notice in the *London Gazette,* cancel any preceding notice therein, or any part thereof, and may, by such or by any further notice, vary the amount of the fees to be paid by persons attending examinations held by them, or the manner, or the time, of paying such fees, or the classes of persons required to pay them, or exempted from paying them.

10. All appointments and promotions with respect to which certificates have been issued by the Commissioners, and all assignments and transfers of Second Division Clerks, shall be published by the Commissioners in the *London Gazette*.

11. The situations included in the schedule marked B, hereto appended, shall be wholly excepted from the operation of this Part of this Order.

Provided that the Head of any Department, with the approval of the Treasury, may from time to time, by notice in the *London Gazette,* add situations to either of the said Schedules, marked A and B respectively, or withdraw situations therefrom.

Part II

RULES APPLICABLE TO ALL PERMANENT OFFICERS IN HIS MAJESTY'S CIVIL ESTABLISHMENTS

12. It shall be competent for the Treasury to direct, should they see cause, that inquiry be made at intervals of not less than five years into the pay and numbers of officers employed by any Department of State.

13. Attendance Books shall be kept in every Department for the purpose of recording the times of arrival and departure of persons employed therein.

14. Officers are required to attend not less than seven hours a day, but they shall be allowed a half-holiday on alternate Saturdays, provided that the Head of their Department is satisfied that the progress of public business will not be prejudiced thereby.

15. It shall be competent for the Head of any Department to call upon any officer of such Department to retire at any time after reaching the age of sixty on such pension as by the length of his service he is qualified to receive.

Retirement shall be compulsory for every officer on attaining sixty-five years of age. But in special cases the Treasury may, at the instance of the Head of a Department, extend an officer's employment for a further period not exceeding five years, on being satisfied that such officer's retirement at 65 would be detrimental to the interest of the Public Service.

16. Any officer seeking a seat in the House of Commons shall resign his office so soon as he issues his address to the electors, or in any other manner publicly announces himself as a candidate.

17. No officer shall be allowed to accept any part in the management of any society, or any trading, commercial, industrial, or financial firm or company which would require the attendance of such officer at any time between the hours of 10 a. m. and 6 p. m.

18. An annual increment of salary shall not be allowed to any officer at the date at which it would in ordinary course

become due without a certificate from his immediate superior, countersigned by the Head of the Department, or such person as he may designate for the purpose, to the effect that the service of such officer during the year preceding the date of such certificate has been approved.

Provided that if, at the date when the increment would in ordinary course become due, the certificate cannot be given, the Head of the Department may specify a period from the expiration of which, if the officer's service in the meanwhile has been approved, the increment may be allowed, and may from time extend the period so fixed. If the officer's service after the grant of the deferred increment shall continue satisfactory, the Head of the Department may, if and when he thinks fit, increase the salary to an amount not exceeding that at which it would have stood if no increment had been withheld or deferred. Every such increase shall be reported to the **Comptroller and Auditor-General.**

19. Sick leave may be granted to any officer by the Head of his Department subject to the following conditions, viz:—

(1) After two days' continuous absence, a certificate by a duly qualified medical practitioner shall be furnished stating the cause of such absence.

(2) If the number of days during which any officer is absent in any year without such medical certificate shall exceed seven in the aggregate, the number of days of absence in excess of seven shall be deducted from the amount of ordinary annual holidays which may be allowed under this Order.

(3) Continuous sick leave on full pay shall not be granted for any period longer than six months, but at the expiration of such six months the Head of the Department may at his discretion grant further leave on half-pay for any period not exceeding six months. After twelve months' continuous sick leave, no officer shall receive any salary, except with the consent of the Treasury; who may, in special circumstances, allow payment of salary to

an officer during any further period of sick leave at a rate not exceeding the amount of pension (if any) for which, at the expiration of twelve months' sick leave, the officer would have been qualified.

(4) When the sick leave granted to any officer shall have amounted in the aggregate to twelve months during any period of four years or less, and it is desired to grant to him any further sick leave during such period, the case shall be reported to the Treasury, who shall decide what payment (if any) shall be made to him in respect of salary during such further sick leave.

Part III

RULES APPLICABLE TO PERMANENT OFFICERS IN HIS MAJESTY'S CIVIL SERVICE DRAWING SALARIES OR PLACED ON SCALES IN EXCESS OF THOSE OF THE SECOND DIVISION

20. Promotion of officers to whom Part III. of this Order applies from one class to another shall be strictly according to merit, and shall take place subject to the following conditions:

(1) That there is a vacancy in the higher class which, under the arrangements sanctioned for the time being by the Treasury, it is competent for the Head of the Department to fill;

(2) That the work of the Department requires such vacancy to be filled;

(3) That the officer proposed for promotion has been reported by the Head of his Department or Branch as fit to discharge the duties of the higher office.

21. The ordinary annual holidays allowed to officers to whom Part III. of this Order applies shall not exceed thirty-six week-days during each of their first ten years of service and forty-eight week-days thereafter, exclusive in all cases of Christmas Day, Good Friday, the King's Birthday, and (subject to the requirements of the Public Service) Bank Holidays: Provided that nothing in this clause shall affect the rights

of existing officers who, under the regulations in force before the 15th day of August, 1890, in the respective Departments in which they were then serving, are entitled to holidays in excess of those herein prescribed.[1]

Part IV.—Chapter I

RULES APPLICABLE TO THE SECOND DIVISION OF HIS MAJESTY'S CIVIL SERVICE

22. The Second Division of the Civil Service, as hitherto constituted shall continue and shall consist of Clerks engaged to serve in any Department of the Civil Service to which they may from time to time be appointed or transferred.

23. No Department of the Civil Service shall be permanently increased or regulated afresh without provision being made that such of its duties as are of a suitable character shall be performed by Clerks of the Second Division or other officers of a rank below that Division.

24. No vacancies shall be filled nor any new appointments made in any Department, except by appointing Clerks of the Second Division, or other officers of a rank below that Division, until the Treasury have been satisfied that the number of officers serving in such Department with salaries higher than those of the Second Division will not be excessive.

Chapter II

RULES APPLICABLE ONLY TO CLERKS OF THE SECOND DIVISION WHO HAVE NOT BEEN PLACED ON THE SCALE OF SALARY PRESCRIBED BY CLAUSE 28 OF THIS ORDER

25. The salaries of Clerks of the Second Division to whom this Chapter applies shall commence at seventy pounds per annum, and shall rise by annual increments, as follows, viz. :—

> From seventy pounds to one hundred pounds by annual increments of five pounds.
> From one hundred pounds to one hundred and ninety pounds by annual increments of seven pounds ten shillings.

[1] Note how few rules are fixed for the first division.

From one hundred and ninety pounds to two hundred
and fifty pounds by annual increments of ten pounds.

The Higher Grade of the Second Division, with salaries
commencing at two hundred and fifty pounds per annum, and
rising by annual increments of ten pounds to three hundred
and fifty pounds, shall continue only for Clerks to whom this
Chapter applies.

26. When the salary of any Clerk to whom this Chapter applies reaches one hundred pounds, a special report, to be officially recorded in writing, on his competence, character, and
diligence, shall be required from the Head of the room and
from the Head of the Branch in which the Clerk is serving or
has served; and until this report is received and countersigned
by the Head of the Department as satisfactory the Clerk shall
not receive any further advance in salary.

When the salary of any Clerk to whom this Chapter applies
reaches one hundred and ninety pounds, he shall not receive
any further increment unless he obtains a report, to be officially
recorded in writing, from his immediate superiors, confirmed
by the Head of the Department, that he is thoroughly competent to perform efficiently work of a superior character.

27. Promotion to the Higher Grade mentioned in Clause 25
of this Order shall be made according to merit, and not according to seniority.

A promotion to the said Higher Grade shall be made whenever any Clerk who remains on the scale of salary prescribed
by Clause 25 shall reach a salary of two hundred and fifty
pounds if there be a Clerk qualified for and deserving of such
promotion; but the Head of a Department may at any time
recommend, and the Treasury may sanction, as a very exceptional case, the promotion to the Higher Grade of a specially
meritorious Clerk remaining on the scale of salary prescribed
by Clause 25 who is in receipt of a salary less than two hundred
and fifty pounds. When a promotion has been made to the
Higher Grade of a Clerk other than the Clerk who reached the
salary of two hundred and fifty pounds, the latter may, never-

theless, at the discretion of the Head of his Department, receive promotion to the Higher Grade, at or after the date
when the Clerk who was actually promoted would in ordinary
course have reached a salary of two hundred and fifty pounds.

CHAPTER III

RULES APPLICABLE TO ALL SECOND DIVISION CLERKS OTHER THAN
THOSE REFERRED TO IN THE PRECEDING CHAPTER

28. The scale of salary of Second Division Clerks (except
as provided in Chapter II. of this Part of this Order) shall
commence at seventy pounds per annum, and shall rise by annual increments as follows, viz.:—

> From seventy to one hundred and thirty pounds, by an-
> nual increments of seven pounds ten shillings.
> From one hundred and thirty pounds to two hundred
> pounds, by annual increments of ten pounds.
> From two hundred pounds to three hundred pounds, by
> annual increments of ten pounds.

29. When the salary of any Clerk of the Second Division
shall reach the sum of one hundred and thirty pounds a report
in writing on the competence, character and diligence of such
Clerk shall be required from the immediate superior under
whom the Clerk is serving, and until this report has been
countersigned as satisfactory by the Head of the Department,
or such officer as he may designate for the purpose, the Clerk
shall not receive any further increment of salary.

30. No increment of salary beyond two hundred pounds per
annum shall be allowed to a Clerk of the Second Division,
without a report in writing from his immediate superior, countersigned by the Head of the Department, or such officer as he
may designate for the purpose, to the effect that such Clerk is
competent to perform efficiently the highest duties ordinarily
assigned to Clerks of the Second Division in the Department
in which he is serving.

31. If, on the first day of April of any year, the salary of
any Clerk certificated before the first day of April, 1908, but

placed on the scale prescribed by Clause 28 of this Order, shall amount to a sum intermediate between one hundred and twenty-two pounds ten shillings and one hundred and thirty pounds, the annual increment of salary accruing next thereafter shall be calculated at the sum of—

(*a*) The portion of an increment at the rate of seven pounds ten shillings per annum proportionate to the period between such first day of April and the date next thereafter upon which (but for his having been placed on the said scale) an increment would have accrued, and

(*b*) the portion of an increment at the rate of ten pounds per annum proportionate to the period between the last-mentioned date and the first day of April next following.

Chapter IV

RULES APPLICABLE TO THE WHOLE OF THE SECOND DIVISION

32. The ordinary annual holidays allowed to Second Division Clerks shall not exceed fourteen week-days during each of their first five years of service, twenty-one week-days during each of their next ten years of service, and twenty-four week-days thereafter, exclusive in all cases of Christmas Day, Good Friday, the King's Birthday, and (subject to the requirements of the Public Service) Bank holidays.

Provided that nothing in this clause shall affect the rights of existing Clerks who, under the regulations in force before the 21st day of March, 1890, in the respective Departments in which they were then serving, are entitled to holidays in excess of those herein prescribed.

33. Notwithstanding anything contained in Clause 25 and Clause 28 of this Order, the Treasury may, upon the recommendation of the Head of a Department, advance by such amount, not exceeding four annual increments, as they may deem expedient, the salary of any Clerk who, having served for not less than six years in the Second Division, is reported to be exceptionally meritorious.

34. Any Clerk who is or who has been a Second Division Clerk may be appointed, without a further certificate of qualification, to any clerkship in the Department in which he is serving, provided that:—

  (a) Such clerkship is not one which is ordinarily filled by open competition under the scheme known as " Class I.," or under special regulations;
  (b) The maximum salary of such clerkship does not exceed five hundred pounds per annum; and
  (c) Such clerkship does not lead in the ordinary course of promotion to a clerkship of which that maximum salary exceeds five hundred pounds per annum.

35. Any Clerk of the Second Division appointed to a Minor Staff clerkship the maximum salary of which does not exceed three hundred and fifty pounds per annum shall be, in all respects other than that of salary, subject to the regulations governing the Second Division; and, if the maximum of the Minor Staff clerkship is less than three hundred and fifty pounds, may, at such time after he has attained the said maximum as the Treasury may decide, be placed upon the scale of the Second Division at the point represented by such maximum, and may proceed by the usual annual increments to a maximum of three hundred and fifty pounds if appointed to the Minor Staff clerkship before 21st December, 1907, or of three hundred pounds if appointed to such clerkship after that date.

36. A Clerk shall not be promoted from the Second Division to any post carrying a maximum salary exceeding £500 a year, or leading in the ordinary course of promotion to posts of which the maximum salary exceeds £500 a year, without a special certificate from the Commissioners, to be granted exceptionally, after not less than eight years' service, upon a special recommendation from the Head of the Department, and with the approval of the Treasury; and every such promotion shall be published in the *London Gazette,* with a note of such recommendation, certificate, and approval, and shall have effect from the date of such publication.

37. (i.) Redundant Second Division Clerks may be transferred from one Department to another without reference to their age or the amount of salary of which they are in receipt.

(ii.) Except in the case of redundancy no Clerk of the Second Division shall be so transferred without the consent of the Commissioners.

(iii.) The consent of the Commissioners and the approval of the Treasury shall be required to the making redundant of any Second Division Clerk who has been appointed to that Division on the ground that his retention in a particular Department was necessary.

CHAPTER V

EXAMINATION OF CANDIDATES FOR THE SECOND DIVISION AND ASSIGNMENT OF SECOND DIVISION CLERKS

38. The Commissioners shall at fixed intervals, or whenever they may, with the approval of the Treasury, decide it to be necessary, hold competitive examinations for clerkships of the Second Division in such subjects and under such regulations as they, with the approval of the Treasury, may from time to time prescribe.

39. Lists of the successful competitors shall be made out, in the order of merit, up to the number required, if so many are found by the Commissioners to be qualified for appointment to the Second Division. In ascertaining the order of merit, such allowance may be made as the Commissioners with the approval of the Treasury may from time to time prescribe in respect of previous service as Registered Boy Clerk.

40. From lists made out as aforesaid, the Commissioners, on the application of Departments, may assign Clerks for permanent or temporary service. Assignment shall, as a general rule, be made by the Commissioners according to the order of the names on the list, an older list taking precedence over a more recent list. Provided that:—

(i) They may assign to any Department any unassigned successful competitor who has shown special qualifications in any particular subject included in the

scheme of examination if special application for a
Clerk so qualified be made by that Department;

(ii) If a successful competitor has at the date of the commencement of the competition served as a Boy
Clerk or Assistant Clerk ("Abstractor") for not
less than six full months in a Department, he may,
on the application of the Head of that Department, be specially assigned thereto.

41. Under conditions to be settled by the Commissioners,
with the approval of the Treasury, successful competitors will
be allowed, subject to the requirements of the Public Service,
to select the Departments in which they may prefer to serve,
but any successful competitor refusing to serve in the Department to which he is assigned may be removed from the list.

42. On a successful competitor being assigned to a Department his name shall be removed from the list. If the assignment has been for temporary service, the Clerk's name shall
be restored to the list on the termination of such service, if
approved; but the Commissioner may assign any Clerk, who
is serving in a Department, to a permanent Clerkship therein.

43. A Second Division Clerk shall be regarded as accepted
by a Department to which he has been assigned for permanent
service, when he has completed twelve months' continuous service in that Department, unless the Commissioners are informed by the Head of his Department that he has not afforded satisfactory proof of his fitness in accordance with the
provisions of Clause 6 of this Order.

A Second Division Clerk shall not, except for grave misconduct, be rejected on probation till he has served for at least
three months in the Department to which he has been assigned.

If a Second Division Clerk is rejected on probation by the
Department to which he has been assigned, the Head of the
Department shall report to the Commissioners the reasons for
his rejection; and the Commissioners shall decide whether the
rejected Clerk shall be finally discharged, or shall be re-assigned for service in another Department.

In the event of a rejected Second Division Clerk being re-assigned as aforesaid, the Commissioners shall decide whether his previous service should be reckoned, with or without conditions, towards increment of salary. If they decide that his service should not be so reckoned, the fact and the conditions, if any, shall be notified by the Commissioners to the Comptroller and Auditor-General.

Part V

RULES APPLICABLE TO SITUATIONS OR EMPLOYMENTS BELOW THE SECOND DIVISION

44. Below the Second Division persons may be employed for copying, routine work under direct supervision, or other work inferior to that of Clerks of the Second Division, in accordance with regulations framed from time to time by the Commissioners with the approval of the Treasury and at rates of pay from time to time prescribed by the Treasury.

45. An established Civil Servant of a rank below the Second Division may be appointed to that Division on the ground of special merit with a certificate from the Commissioners under Clause 7 of this Order. But such certificate shall only be granted exceptionally after not less than six years' established service (towards which not less than one year's and not more than two years' approved service as Registered Boy Clerk may be allowed to reckon), upon a recommendation from the Head of the Department and with the approval of the Treasury. Whenever such an appointment is made, the Treasury may allow the person appointed to enter the scale of the Division at such salary as they shall think fit, not being higher than that which he was receiving at the date of his said appointment; and he shall be entitled to the same amount of annual holiday as if his previous established service had been in the Second Division.

46. A Clerk of the class known as " Assistant Clerks " or " Abstractors " may, with the consent of the Commissioners, be transferred from one Department to a similar situation in another, without a further certificate of qualification.

Schedule A

All situations in the undermentioned Departments except such situations as have already been withdrawn from the Schedule A. appended to the Order in Council of the 4th June, 1870, or have already been added to the Schedule B. appended to the Order.

Admiralty.

Agriculture and Fisheries, Board of.

Charity Commission.

Chief Secretary's Office, Ireland.

Civil Service Commission.

Colonial Office.

Customs and Excise, Board of.

Deeds, Registry of, Ireland.

Ecclesiastical Commission.

Education, Board of.

Exchequer and Audit Department.

Home Office and Subordinate Departments.

India Office.

Inland Revenue, Board of.

Local Government Board, England.

Local Government Board, Scotland.

Mint.

National Debt Office.

Paymaster-General's Office.

Police Office, Metropolitan, Dublin.

Public Works Office, Ireland.

Record Office, England.

Register House Departments, Edinburgh.

Registrar-General's Office, England.

Registrar-General's Office, Ireland.

Scotland, Office of Secretary for.

Stationery Office.

Trade, Board of, and Subordinate Departments.

Treasury and Subordinate Departments.

Valuation and Boundary Survey, Ireland.

War Office.

Woods, Office of.

Works, Office of.

Throughout His Majesty's Civil Establishments:—

Clerkships (Class I.).

Clerkships of the Second Division.

Assistant Clerkships of the Abstractor Class.

Schedule B

Situations altogether excepted from the operation of Part I. of this Order.

1. All situations to which the holder is appointed directly by the Crown.

2. All situations included in any Order or Warrant made by the Treasury under Section 4 of the Superannuation Act, 1859.

3. All situations which are filled, in the customary course of promotion, by persons previously serving in the same department.

4. All situations which have already been added to the Schedule B: attached to the Order in Council of the 4th June, 1870, and have not since been withdrawn therefrom.

APPENDIX B

CASES DEALT WITH BY THE CIVIL SERVICE COMMISSION, 1910–1911

Table showing the number of cases dealt with in the year ended December 31, 1910, and the manner in which they were decided

	Total of Cases..
Number of cases dealt with. Classified as	
General Total.	49,620
Candidates Nominated Singly.	9,092
Candidates Nominated to Compete.	12,947
Candidates at Open Competitions.	27,581
Number of Persons.	
Absent, declined, or withdrew.	4,996
Ineligible in respect of Age.	57
Ineligible in respect of Physical Qualifications.	101
Ineligible in respect of Character.	11
Excluded by Departments for other reasons or for reasons not mentioned.	140
Rejected on Literary Examination.	438
Unsuccessful in Competition.	24,723
For whom Certificates were not required.	2,369
For whom Certificates were granted: After Open Competition.	2,613
For whom Certificates were granted: After Nomination to Compete.	1,137
For whom Certificates were granted: After Nomination Singly.	5,692
For whom Certificates were granted: Under Clause VII of the Order in Council.	706
(For whom Certificates were granted, total)	10,148
Yet to appear or still under consideration.	6,637

Cases Decided = 42,983.

APPENDIX C

Class I [1] Clerkships, Indian Civil Service and Eastern Cadetships

SALARY OF CLASS I CLERKS

Results of the Examinations, Subjects and Marks, and Specimens of Papers Set in 1910

The same examinations are used to test nominees for clerkships in the Foreign Office, attachés in the diplomatic service, and student interpreters in China, Japan, and Siam; but a total of 4,000 instead of 6,000 points is set as a limit. It is claimed, with reason, that Foreign Office and diplomatic officials cannot safely be chosen by open competition.

For the first division posts the maximum scale of salary is:—

           Third Class...........£200.........£20......... £500
           Second Class......... 600......... 25......... 800
           First Class........... 850......... 50.........1,000

This scale, however, is only a maximum, and within that maximum the present varying scales of the Upper Establishments (many of which are at lower rates) will be maintained, at all events for the present.

Clerks of Class I. are employed in the following departments:—Admiralty (Head Office); Chief Secretary's Office, Ireland; Civil Service Commission; Colonial Office; Constabulary, Ireland (Inspector-General's Office); Customs and Excise Department; Home Office; India Office (Correspondence, Political, Accountant-General's, Store, and Audit Departments); Inland Revenue; Local Government Board, England

---

[1] Class I = division I. The latter would seem to be the better term, since there are all kinds of first classes in the civil service.

and Ireland; Lunacy Commission; Patent Office; Post Office (Secretary's Office and Surveyors' Department) ; Privy Council Office; Record Offices, England and Ireland; Scottish Office; Trade, Board of; Treasury; War Office; Works, Office of.

The concurrent open competitive examinations held in August, 1910, for Class I. Clerkships in the Home Civil Service, for the India Civil Service, and for Eastern Cadetships were attended by a total of 209 candidates.

The candidates were separated into the following groups according to the services for which they competed:—

For Class I, India Civil Service, and Eastern Cadetships..	163
Class I and India Civil Service........................	14
Class I and Eastern Cadetships	1
India Civil Service and Eastern Cadetships.............	5
Class I only	23
India Civil Service only	2
Eastern Cadetships only	1
	209

When the results were declared there were 60 vacancies existing for the Civil Service of India and 14 for the Home Civil Service. As, however, the regulations for the latter service are framed with a view to supplying the requirements of the public service during the six months following the declaration of the result of the examination, the total of those successful was ultimately raised to 28 by the occurrence of subsequent vacancies. The number of Eastern Cadetships filled was 25.[1]

Candidates for the Home Service are allowed to choose, according to their place on the list, among the vacancies (a) for which they are duly qualified; or they may elect to wait for the chance of a vacancy (b). When vacancies (b) occur, they are offered in rotation to the qualified Candidates then on the

---

[1] *Cf.* Fifty-fifth Report and other recent publications of the Civil Service Commissioners, *passim*.

list, who are free to decline them without forfeiting their claim to subsequent vacancies.

The limits of age for these positions are 22 and 24.

Candidates must have attained the age of 22 and must not have attained the age of 24, on the first day of August in the year in which the Examination is held. Fee £6.

The following are the subjects of examination:

		Marks
1.	English Composition	500
2.	Sanskrit Language and Literature	800
3.	Arabic Language and Literature	800
	Greek, not less than two sub-divisions, of which one must be Translation:—	
4.	Translation	400
5.	Prose Composition	200
6.	Verse Composition	200
7.	Literature, &c.	300
	Latin, not less than two sub-divisions, of which one must be Translation:—	
8.	Translation	400
9.	Prose Composition	200
10.	Verse Composition	200
11.	Literature, &c.	300
12.	English Language and Literature	600
13.	Italian, Translation, Composition and Conversation..	400
14.	Italian, History of the Language and Literature	200
15.	French, Translation, Composition and Conversation..	400
16.	French, History of the Language and Literature....	200
17.	German, Translation, Composition and Conversation	400
18.	German, History of the Language and Literature....	200
	The History of these Languages and their Literatures can only be taken by Candidates who also offer themselves for the rest of the examination in those Languages.	
19.	Lower Mathematics	1,200
20.	Higher Mathematics	1,200
	Natural Science, *i. e.*, any number not exceeding *four* of the following or *three* if both Lower and Higher Mathematics be also taken:—	

21.	Chemistry	600
22.	Physics	600
23.	Geology	600
24.	Botany	600
25.	Zoology	600
26.	Animal Physiology	600
27.	Geography	600
28.	Greek History (Ancient, including Constitution)	500
29.	Roman History (Ancient, including Constitution)	500
	English History, either or both sections may be taken :—	
30.	I. to A. D. 1485	400
31.	II. A. D. 1485 to 1848	400
32.	General Modern History	500
33.	Logic and Psychology	600
34.	Moral and Metaphysical Philosophy	600
35.	Political Economy and Economic History	600
36.	Political Science	500
37.	Roman Law	500
38.	English Law	500

From the marks assigned to candidates in each subject such deduction will be made as the Civil Service Commissioners may deem necessary in order to secure that no credit be allowed for merely superficial knowledge.

Consistently with the limitations specified above, candidates are at liberty to name any of the foregoing subjects, provided that the maximum number of marks that can be obtained from the subjects chosen is limited to 6,000. If this maximum is exceeded by a candidate's selection he will be required to indicate one of his subjects, the marks for which should, in his case, be reduced so as to bring his maximum marks within the prescribed limit. The marks so reduced will be subject to a correspondingly reduced deduction.

Moreover, if a candidate's handwriting is not easily legible a further deduction will, on that account, be made from the total marks otherwise accruing to him.

EXAMINATION PAPERS [1]

SUBJECTS FOR ENGLISH COMPOSITION

Time allowed, 3 hours

Write an essay on *one* of the following subjects:—
" Socialism strikes at capital, Liberalism at monopoly."
Or,
" The aim of the 19th Century was to liberate; the aim of the 20th Century will be to control."
Or,
" Literature and art are flowers that border the road of national decline."
Or,
Classic and Romantic Ideals.

GEOGRAPHY. PAPER 2

Time allowed, 3 hours

Question 1 and any three of the others to be answered. Question 1 carries double marks. The remaining questions carry equal marks. Illustrate your answers by sketch maps and diagrams wherever possible

1. Write an essay on any one of the following subjects:—
     (a) The influence of Marco Polo on European knowledge of the East.
     (b) The attempts to determine the figure of the Earth.
     (c) The lakes and lake-basins of Eastern Africa.

---

[1] It will be seen how much of a political complexion is given to these papers. All but the mathematics and political science papers require or presuppose some knowledge of political thought, and the candidates who specialize in mathematics and natural sciences almost all take political science and political economy to fill up their 6,000 points. Even the prose passages set for translation into foreign languages may be said to be borrowed from political literature. Thus some training in *staatswissenschaft* is almost essential to success in this examination.

(d) The settlement of British Indian emigrants within the British Empire.

(e) The economic and political significance of the coalfields of the Pacific drainage area.

2. Describe the general structure and the physical and political divisions of Baluchistan with special reference to the routes of approach to India.

3. Discuss the probable characteristics of the earliest Mediterranean peoples, and state what is known as to their migrations and the present distribution of the type.

4. Give a geographical review of the economic conditions and potentialities of *either* Argentina *or* Mexico.

5. Discuss the relations between position and trade in the case of the chief ports of Australia.

6. Give an account of the physical history and characteristics of the Saint Lawrence and trace the bearings of the facts you mention on its value as a waterway.

7. Discuss the physical basis of the political divisions of the Chinese Empire.

GREEK COMPOSITION

Time allowed, 3 hours

I

For Greek Prose:—

Mr. Cowley answered somewhat sharply: " I am sorry, Sir, to hear you speak thus. I had hoped that the vehemence of spirit which was caused by those violent times had now abated. Yet, sure, Mr. Milton, whatever you may think of the character of King Charles, you will not still justify his murder?"

" Sir," said Mr. Milton, " I must have been of a hard and strange nature, if the vehemence which was imputed to me in my younger days had not been diminished by the afflictions wherewith it has pleased Almighty God to chasten my age. I will not now defend all that I may heretofore have written. But this I say, that I perceive not wherefore a king should be exempted from all punishment. Is it just that where most is given, least should be required? Or politic that where there is the greatest power to injure, there should be no danger to restrain? But, you will say, there is no such law. Such a law there is. There is the law of self-preservation written by God himself on our hearts. There is the primal compact and bond of society, not graven in stone, or sealed with wax, nor put down on parchment, nor set forth in any express form of words by men of old when they came together; but implied in the very act that they so came together, presupposed in all subsequent law, not to be repealed by any authority, nor invalidated by being omitted in any code; inasmuch as from thence are all codes and all authority."—*Macaulay.*

III

[Alternative for Verse Composition]

One subject only to be attempted

For a Greek Oration:—

A panegyric on the reign of Queen Victoria.

Or,

The Two-power standard of naval supremacy.

Latin Composition

III

[Alternative for Latin Verse Composition]

One subject only to be attempted

For a Latin Essay:—

" To be master of the sea is an abridgment of a monarchy."
—*Bacon.*

Or,

" Who ever knew Truth put to the worse in a free and open encounter ? "—*Milton.*

Translate into French:—

IV

Roads

From the very earliest days, in all ages, in all countries, the road has been the handmaid of prosperity. Without it men cannot communicate, law and order cannot be upheld, commerce cannot exist. It carries with it the principle of interchange of ideas, and of the products of ideas. Look backward over the pages of history. Rome was a giant builder of roads. They were part of her process of civilisation, of her scheme of Empire. Together they grew, together they decayed. Then the progress of the great world was stayed. It shrunk into fiercely conflicting communities, and men were content with haphazard tracks. Along these moved kings and their armies, on horseback and on foot, from one place of strength to another, from walled city to castle, from castle to abbey.

The people moved but little. At certain spots, dictated sometimes by natural advantages, sometimes by love or fear of their fellow-mortals, they herded into villages and towns. In process of time there came to England trade, at first only seaborne, afterwards penetrating inwards from the coast, picking its way by devious routes up and down the land. By degrees our network of tracks grew, criss cross, from house to house, from hamlet to hamlet, from town to town. These tracks, originally intended more for pack horses than for wheel traffic, became our roads, nine-tenths of them crooked, formless, and without plan. In time we had a Macadam, who reformed their surfaces, but, though Telford did his best, we never had a Napoleon to decree their direction. Their virtue was that they spread out the population equally over the surface of these islands. In this respect they were good for the land and good for the people.

V

It will soon be forty years since Ruskin in his first Oxford lecture, nominally on fine art, made his magnificent appeal to his young hearers to go out as colonists into the waste places of the earth, and there to take England with them as a spiritual

Power, informing them with high purpose to serve her even at the ends of the world. That appeal is perhaps now by most men at home forgotten, and was indeed little heeded even at the time, yet it was not made in vain, and probably gave the first impulse to more than one of those who have since been known as Empire-builders. Ruskin was an observer of rare accuracy, and though he was aware of strong currents tending to sap the foundations of character in the generation to which he was speaking, he yet asserted that the race was still strong and good, free from taints that had affected some others. He did not believe that there was widespread degeneracy. But he urged with all his might upon the young men who listened to him that they should choose their purpose in life and pursue it steadfastly. Perhaps that call too has met with wider response than is sometimes realised, for there are many men to-day who have lived in its spirit, and have raised the level of public and private life by unostentatious yet effectual service.

Translate into Italian:—

V

It is no easy matter to picture to ourselves the blazing trail of splendour which in such a pageant must have drawn along the London streets,—those streets which now we know so black and smoke-grimed, themselves then radiant with masses of colour, gold, and crimson, and violet. Yet there it was, and there the sun could shine upon it, and tens of thousands of eyes were gazing on the scene out of the crowded lattices. Glorious as the spectacle was, perhaps, however, it passed unheeded. Those eyes were watching all for another object, which now drew near. In an open space behind the constable there was seen approaching a white chariot, drawn by two palfreys, in white damask, which swept the ground, a golden canopy borne above it making music with silver bells: and in the chariot sat the observed of all observers, the beautiful occasion of all this glittering homage; fortune's plaything of the hour, the Queen of England—queen at last—borne along upon the waves of this sea of glory, breathing the perfumed incense of greatness which she had risked her fair name, her delicacy, her honour, her self-respect, to win; and she had won it.

There she sat, dressed in white tissue robes, her fair hair flowing loose over her shoulders and her temples circled with a light coronet of gold and diamonds—most beautiful—loveliest—most favoured, perhaps, as she seemed at that hour, of all England's daughters. Alas! within the hollow round of that coronet—

> Kept death his court, and there the antick sat,
> Scoffing her state and grinning at her pomp.
>   —*Froude.*

Political Economy. Paper i

Time allowed, 3 hours

Six questions, and no more than six questions to be answered. Candidates must answer one at least of the first three questions. All questions carry equal marks.

1. To what causes do you attribute the gradual extinction of the yeoman farming-class in the latter part of the eighteenth and the early years of the nineteenth century?

2. Illustrate the close relation between economic and political movements and conditions in the seventeenth century.

3. "Some of the social problems which confront the statesmen of to-day were the subjects of legislation in the time of Elizabeth." Examine this statement.

4. Give a short account of the chief points with regard to which Ricardo criticised Adam Smith. Compare their methods in dealing with economic problems.

5. "High wages are the best economy."
   Discuss this statement, and give some account of the evidence adduced in its support.

6. Examine the economic policy of the Labour Party in England, and compare it with that of the Social Democratic Party in Germany.

7. Consider and illustrate the effect of different systems of land tenure and cultivation upon agricultural production and efficiency.

8. Interest has been described in Socialist literature as a species of rent. Comment on this. Is there any resemblance, and, if so, what resemblance, between rent of land and interest on capital.

9. Examine the importance of *Elasticity of Demand* with reference to (*a*) economic theory, (*b*) taxation.

10. Distinguish between the various forms of wage payments, viz., time wages, task wages, piece wages. State the industrial conditions which render these respectively applicable.

POLITICAL ECONOMY. PAPER 2

Time allowed, 3 hours

Answer question 1 and any FIVE *of the remainder. Questions 2-10 carry equal marks*

1. Either—Consider the chief *statistical* difficulties in determining the quantity of metallic money in a country. Give some account of the attempts that have been made to estimate the metallic circulation in (1) The United Kingdom, (2) India.

   Or—Compare the more important methods that have been employed for the purpose of measuring the relative standard of comfort of the working classes (1) in different countries, (2) at different periods in the same country.

2. " There is nothing in the laws of value which remains for the present or any future writer to clear up; the theory of the subject is complete."

   Indicate the leading features of the theory of value thus accepted by J. S. Mill; and notice the several distinct lines on which it has been criticised by later economists.

3. Sketch broadly the organisation of the modern "Produce" market. How would you estimate the effect of dealings in " Futures " on the price fluctuations of the commodity dealt in?

4. " Money is a creation of the State."

Critically examine this dictum, with special reference to (*a*) The selection of the money material, (*b*) its bearing on the " cost " and the " quantity " theories of the value of money.

5. The essential characteristics of a good currency system are (1) stability, (2) elasticity. Explain clearly what is meant by each of these qualities, and consider how far they are secured under the actual currency systems of any *two* of the following countries:—(*a*) Great Britain, (*b*) France, (*c*) Germany, (*d*) The United States.

6. Discuss carefully (*a*) the causes, (*b*) the consequences of an export of capital. To what extent is the growth of dealings in international securities connected with the international movement of capital?

7. Compare the different views that have been taken respecting the advantages of foreign trade. In particular examine the following statements:—

(1) " The only direct advantage of foreign commerce consists in the imports."

(2) " In gauging the advantages which a country secures from international trade, we should look primarily to the range and the variations of money incomes."

8. Trace fully the incidence and effects of *one* of the following taxes:—

(*a*) An export duty on raw cotton leaving the United States.

(*b*) An import duty on petroleum entering the United Kingdom.

(*c*) An *ad valorem* stamp duty on the transfer of securities.

9. Contrast the chief characteristics of *central* and *local* taxation.

Describe the various modes in which the two systems may be correlated, and estimate the advantages of each mode.

10. Under what conditions is borrowing on the part of the State admissible?

Explain the following terms employed in connection with debt operations:—Conversion; Floating Debt; Sinking Fund; Terminable Annuity.

POLITICAL SCIENCE. PAPER I

Time allowed, 3 hours

Answer any SIX *questions. All the questions carry equal marks.*

1. Either—Sketch and criticise any Ideal Commonwealth that has been suggested by philosophers.

Or—State and comment upon the actual origin of Commonwealths as conceived (*a*) by Hobbes, (*b*) by Herbert Spencer.

2. State and explain the origins (*a*) of customs, and (*b*) of laws; and give, together with your reasons, the true relation between customs and laws.

3. Discuss, with due reference to authorities, the reality and meaning of Natural Law. Also indicate briefly its relation, if any, to the Moral Law, the Civil Law, and International Law.

4. Discuss the right of a majority of the electorate to make fundamental changes (*a*) in the Civil Law, (*b*) in the Constitution of the Government of a given State.

5. " The course of Civilisation is properly to be regarded as one, though many particular civilisations have perished."

" The precedence given in the Judicature Act of 1873 to the principles of Equity over the principles of the Common Law, marks the final triumph of Roman jurisprudence over the customs of the nations by whom the Roman Empire was overthrown."

Explain and comment on each of these statements.

6. Modern society, it has been said, rests mainly upon property and contract. Explain, and point out the limitations, if any, in each case.

7. Give in outline the method and fundamental principles employed in political speculation by any *two* of the following:—T. H. Green; Henry Sidgwick; Rousseau; Burke.

8. Distinguish Private and Public Law, giving the chief departments of each; and explain fully why the former tends to be nearly the same in all civilised communities.

9. Define the following conceptions, and point out their relations (if any) to each other:—Sociology, Social Evolution, History of Civilisation, Philosophy of History, Philosophy of Right.

10. How far does a society resemble an organism, statically viewed? How far does it pass through similar stages of growth and decay, dynamically viewed? In what important respects does the analogy fail in each case?

11. Explain briefly how the geographical situation of England has influenced her (*a*) political, (*b*) economic history.

12. Discuss fully the statement, that it is of importance to Great Britain that the rights of belligerents, rather than the rights of neutrals, should be wide.

POLITICAL SCIENCE. PAPER 2

Time allowed, 3 hours

Answer question 1, and any five *of the remaining questions. Questions 2 to 12 carry equal marks; question 1 carries higher marks.*

1. Explain, and briefly comment upon, any four of the following quotations:—

(3) Aristotle, in his political philosophy, made ample provision for the claims of intellect, but none for the rights of man.

(4) A multitude of men are made one person when they are by one person represented.

(5) Quel que soit le vrai principe de la propriété, ce que l'on doit admirer dans Locke, c'est avoir établi que ce principe est antérieur à la loi civile.

(6) À l'instant que le gouvernement usurpe la souveraineté, le pacte social est rompu; et tous les simples citoyens, rentrés de droit dans leur liberté naturelle, sont forcés mais non pas obligés d'obéir.

(7) The speculations of the eighteenth century concerning mankind in a state of nature are not unfairly summed up in the doctrine that " in the primitive society property was nothing, and obligation everything" . . . if the proposition were reversed, it would be nearer the reality.

(8) In this partnership [society] all men have equal rights, but not to equal things.

(9) Starting from anti-Jacobin premises, Bentham's logic led him to Jacobin conclusions.

(10) The difference between civil and political rights is essential—a person's claim to govern himself is a totally different thing from his claim to govern others.

2. Trace the part played by the lawyer in political theory, in ancient or in modern times.

3. Compare the different kinds of answers that have been given in ancient or modern theories of democracy to the question of the place to be assigned to the specialist expert in the determinations and execution of social policy.

4. " It is utterly impossible to deduce the science of government from the principles of human nature."

" The study of human nature by the psychologists has advanced enormously since the discovery of human evolution, but it has advanced without affecting or being affected by the study of politics."

Consider these statements in their bearing upon the relation between political science and psychology.

5. Examine the conception of " a right to work ", whether from the point of view of theory or of practice.

6. Consider, and illustrate with reference to any proposed legislation, the extent to which comparative study of politics is of practical value.

7. Consider some of the modern problems raised by the right of association.

8. Sketch the history and examine the significance of the permanent Civil Service in English constitutional development. In what respect does the English system contrast favourably or unfavourably with that of the Civil Service in other countries?

9. Describe the structure and functions of local government in England, with special reference to the proposal to transfer the various functions of the English Poor Law from boards of guardians elected *ad hoc* to county or county borough councils.

10. " The modern development of representative institutions has done little but illustrate the general inability of democratic institutions to express the general will." Discuss this dictum whether as a statement of fact or as the statement of a problem.

11. " The end of [ethics *or*] politics is not the greatest happiness of the greatest number. Your happiness is of no use to the community, except in so far as it tends to make you a more efficient citizen." Examine this statement in reference to its political and legislative bearings.

12. Estimate critically the political philosophy of *either* Hegel *or* Comte.

APPENDIX D

Intermediate Division

SALARY

Results of the Examinations of 1910. Subjects and Marks, and Specimens of Papers Set in 1911

The usual scale of pay is £100—£10—£200, £200—£15—£350, with provision for promotion to staff offices, for extra pay, and for allowances when serving abroad, *e. g.*, in the Admiralty Dockyards and Naval Yards.

The revised scheme which was introduced in 1906 has now been adopted for the examination of candidates for the following Departments, viz.:—Admiralty, Junior Appointments in the Supply and Accounting Departments; Crown Agents for the Colonies, Class III. Clerkships; Ecclesiastical Commission, Junior Clerkships; Exchequer and Audit Department, Examinerships; Inland Revenue Department, Assistant Surveyorships of Taxes and Second Class Clerkships in the Estate Duty Offices, London, Edinburgh, and Dublin; Metropolitan Police, Second Class Clerkships in the Commissioner's Office and Second Class Clerkships in the Receiver's Office; War Office, Junior Appointments in the Royal Ordnance Factories.

Two competitions were held in 1910 for this group of situations. In July, out of 380 effective competitors, 30 received appointments. The examination held in December was attended by 310 candidates. When the results were declared (early in the present year), there were 20 vacancies existing; ultimately the total of those successful was raised to 25.[1]

---

[1] *Cf. Fifty-fifth Report* and other recent publications of the *Civil Service Commissioners, passim.*

In 1911, 334 qualified and 25 were appointed.

1. The limits of age for these situations are 18 and 19½, the half-year being reckoned by calendar months. If an examination commences in one of the first seven months of any year Candidates must be of the prescribed age on the first of May of that year. If an examination commences in one of the last five months of any year, Candidates must be of the prescribed age on the 1st of November of that year.

2. The following are the subjects of examination:

CLASS I.

	Marks
Mathematics I.	2,000
English	2,000

CLASS II.—(LOWER STANDARD.)

Mathematics II.	2,000
French	2,000
German	2,000
Physics	4,000
Latin	2,000
Greek	2,000
History (English)	2,000
Chemistry	2,000
Physics	2,000

CLASS III.—(HIGHER STANDARD.)

Mathematics III.	4,000
French	4,000
German	4,000
Latin	4,000
Greek	4,000
History (English and European)	4,000
Chemistry	4,000

Both the subjects in Class I. must be taken up. No Candidate will be eligible who fails to pass a qualifying examination in Arithmetic and English.

From Classes II. and III. Candidates may select subjects, one of which must be a language, carrying marks up to a maximum of 10,000, making with the subjects in Class I., 14,000 in

all. The same subject may not be selected both in Class II.
and in Class III.

   *   *   *   *   *   *

4. A fee of £3 will be required from each Candidate attending an Examination.

Examination Papers

English History. Class III

Period 2.—a. d. 1485 to 1901

Answer the question in Section A, three *questions in Section
B, and* three *questions in Section C. All the questions
carry equal marks.*

Section A

1. (*a*) Draw a map of the Low Countries at the outset of
the Spanish Succession War, and mark on it the places
where English troops were engaged during the war.

   (*b*) Describe the difficulties encountered by Marlborough,
while general, other than those of actual fighting.

Section B

2. In what ways did the rule of Henry VII benefit commerce
and the middle classes in England?

3. How far was the type of rule applied by Henry VIII adhered to, and how far departed from, under Elizabeth?

4. Is there evidence in James I's reign that a struggle for sovereignty in the constitution was then proceeding?

5. Show how considerations of religion influenced politics
within England between 1644 and 1653.

6. Compare the foreign policy of England under Cromwell
with that under Elizabeth.

7. When, and to what extent, in Charles II's reign did foreign
relations influence home politics.

Section C

8. Burke said of the Revolution that it was a revolution "prevented, not made." Is this true of the Revolution judged
by its results before the close of William III's reign?

9. Does Walpole rank as a great British statesman, or merely as a successful finance-minister?

10. Trace and explain the relations of Britain with Austria and Prussia between 1740 and 1757.

11. How did (*a*) George III, (*b*) Burke and (*c*) Charles James Fox view the royal prerogative?

12. Write an account of the National Debt, including its administration, since 1783.

13. Write (*a*) an estimate of the foreign policy of Canning, and (*b*) an account of the beginnings of the movement for " Imperial Federation."

EUROPEAN HISTORY. CLASS III

PERIOD 3.—A. D. 1519 TO 1901

Answer the question in Section A, THREE *questions out of Section B, and* THREE *questions out of Section C. All the questions carry equal marks.*

Section A

1. (*a*) How was the development of Prussia in the eighteenth century, down to Frederick II's death, affected by her geographical conditions?

   (*b*) By means of a sketch-map show what her functions were (*a*) in 1715, and (*b*) at the close of 1772.

Section B

2. Compare Lutheranism and Calvinism in their attitude to the civil power, and give illustrations.

3. Compare the international position and power of Spain at the following times:—1572; 1598; 1618.

4. Describe and comment upon the attitude of Richelieu toward the Huguenots.

5. Expound and criticise the economic policy of Colbert, and briefly compare it with that of Sully.

6. Show (*a*) the part taken by William of Orange in international affairs before he was invited to England, and (*b*) the Continental situation, as affecting his interests, at the time of his acceptance of the invitation.

7. To what extent was the development of Russia under Peter the Great promoted by the condition of neighbouring States?

8. Examine the influence of the theory of the Divine Right of Kings during the seventeenth century in Continental Europe.

Section C

9. How was the European situation affected by the death of Louis XIV?

10. What were the circumstances that led to the formation of the Family Compact? How far was the Compact effective during the eighteenth century?

11. Consider the importance of the reign of Catherine II as affecting (*a*) Russia, and (*b*) other European States.

12. On what grounds, and to what extent, may Napoleon be deemed a statesman?

13. Show how the arrangements made by the Congress of Vienna were responsible for subsequent disturbances.

14. What was the significance of (*a*) the part taken by Sardinians in the Crimean War, and (*b*) the formation of the North German Confederation?

15. Write notes on *four* of the following:—Rousseau's *Contrat Social*; " Sovereignty resides essentially in the nation "; " the Hundred Days "; the *Ausgleich*; the Dual Control in Egypt.

FRENCH ESSAY. CLASS III

Time allowed, 1 hour

Write in French between 200 and 300 words on *one* of the following subjects:—

1. Rural depopulation in Britain.

2. The qualities necessary in the perfect statesman.

3. " A foot-ball match and a bull-fight are equally noble, equally brutal."

English Essay. Class I

Time allowed, 2 hours

Select *one* of the following subjects:

1. The transformation made in our daily life by applied science during the past century. Is it entirely wholesome.

2. " He that wrestles with us strengthens our nerves and sharpens our skill. Our antagonist is our helper."— *Edmund Burke.*

   Write an essay on the truth of this.

3. " The fickle herd." Discuss the changeability of public opinion.

APPENDIX E

SECOND DIVISION CLERKSHIPS [1]

Results of the Examinations of 1910. Subjects and Marks, and Specimens of Papers Set in 1911

Second Division Clerks are now employed in the great majority of the Departments of the Civil Service.

An open competition for Second Division Clerkships was held in September, 1,716 candidates competing for 100 appointments. [2]

The entire number of assignments of Second Division Clerks for service since the date (12th February, 1876) of the Order in Council which created the Division was, at the end of last year, 14,120, including 1,108 exceptionally appointed, chiefly from the class of Temporary Copyists and from Abstractors.

One hundred and eleven Second Division Clerks were transferred from one Department to another in 1910. Ninety-eight of these Clerks had been declared redundant in the Savings Bank Department of the Post Office. The entire number of such transfers since the Order in Council of February, 1876, is 1,011.

There were no cases in 1910 of the rejection of a Second Division Clerk on probation.

Under the Order in Council Second Division Clerks are allowed to name the Departments in which they would prefer

---

[1] For salary, see Appendix A.

[2] 100 further appointments were made following the 31st December, 1910, from the results of that examination.

As a result of the Sept., 1911 competition, there were 100 initial appointments out of 2016 candidates.

to serve, and it was found to be possible last year to give effect to these preferences in a large majority of cases.[1]

On the 18th of September, 1911, and following days, an Open Competitive Examination will be held in London, Edinburgh, Dublin, Bedford, Birmingham, Bristol, Cardiff, Leeds, Liverpool, Manchester, Newcastle-on-Tyne, Nottingham, Plymouth, Southampton, Aberdeen, Dundee, Glasgow, Belfast, Cork, and Limerick, under the subjoined Regulations, at which Examinations not fewer than 100 candidates will be selected for Clerkships in the Second Division of the Civil Service, provided they satisfy the Civil Service Commissioners that they are duly qualified.

*   *   *   *   *   *

Civil Service Commission,
    4th July, 1911.

1. The limits of age are 17 and 20. If an examination begins in one of the first six months of any year, candidates must be of the prescribed age on the first day of March in that year. If an examination begins in one of the last six months of any year, candidates must be of the prescribed age on the first day of September in that year.

2. The subjects of examination will be as follows:—

   1. Handwriting and Orthography, including Copying Manuscripts—600.
   2. Arithmetic—600.
   3. English Composition—600.
   4. Précis, including Indexing and Digest of Returns—400.
   5. Book-keeping and Shorthand Writing—400.
   6. Geography and English History—400.
   7. Latin (translation from the language, and composition)—400.
   8. French (translation from the language, and composition)—400.

[1] *Cf. Fifty-fifth Report* and other recent publications of the *Civil Service Commissioners, passim.*

9. German (translation from the language, and composition)—400.

N.B.—*Only two of these three languages may be taken up.*

10. Elementary Mathematics—400.

11. Inorganic Chemistry, with Elements of Physics—400.

N.B.—*Not more than* four *of the subjects numbered 4 to 11 may be offered.*

Thus the highest possible total is 3400.[1]

*   *   *   *   *   *

3. Service marks * * * may be allowed to candidates attending examination who are serving or have served as Registered Boy Clerks or Boy Copyists * * *.

*   *   *   *   *   *

5. A fee of £2 will be required from every candidate attending an Examination.

Examination Papers

Geography

Time allowed, 2 hours

SECTION II.—DARK BROWN BOOK

Answer any three *questions in this section in the Dark Brown Book provided*

1. From what countries does Great Britain import tea, coffee and rice? Describe the geographical conditions favourable to the growth of each of these in the countries from which they come.

2. Give examples (one of each type) of regions (*a*) with summer rainfall, (*b*) with winter rainfall, (*c*) with rainfall at all seasons of the year. In each case give what explanations you can.

---

[1] In 1911, changes were made in this scheme, and hereafter Elementary Mathematics and a foreign language are practically compulsory, while book-keeping and stenography are optional. It is hoped by these changes to attract the best Secondary School boys without recourse to cramming schools.

3. Describe the ocean currents of the North Atlantic Basin, and illustrate your description by a sketch-map.
4. Discuss the distribution of the fishing centres of the United Kingdom.

SECTION II.—PURPLE BOOK

Answer any three *of the remaining questions in the Purple Book provided*

5. Describe and explain the characteristic vegetation of *either* the countries bordering upon the Mediterranean *or* that part of North America between the 100th meridian of west longitude and the Rocky Mountains.
6. Discuss the more important geographical causes which lead to the foundation and growth of towns. Illustrate your answer by reference to towns in Great Britain and North America.
7. Describe and compare various methods by which altitude can be indicated upon a map. Draw maps of a mountainous island to illustrate each of the methods you describe.
8. On the map of the North of Ireland supplied to you indicate and name the principal upland regions, and the Bann, the Foyle and the Lagan. Mark, without boundaries, the situation of the counties of Donegal, Down and Tyrone, and show the position of Drogheda, Dundalk, Newry and Sligo. Insert the railway route from Belfast to Londonderry.

HISTORY

Time allowed, 2 hours

Section I.—Answer three *questions in this Section in the Light Blue Book provided*

1. Show how the Danelaw came into existence, how it varied in extent, and why it is important in the history of England.

2. Compare the Parliament of 1295 (*a*) with Simon de Montfort's Parliament in respect of composition, and (*b*) with Parliament at the close of Edward III's reign in respect of powers.

3. Give evidence of the growth of the material prosperity of England in the fourteenth century.

4. Was Richard Neville, Earl of Warwick, moved in his career rather by political than by personal considerations?

5. How far was the policy of Wolsey continued, and how far departed from, after his death, by Henry VIII and Thomas Cromwell?

6. Compare the England of 1603 with the England of 1558 in respect of (*a*) national unity and (*b*) international prestige.

Section II.—Answer three *questions in this Section in the Scarlet Book provided*

Candidates must answer at least one of the questions marked with an asterisk

*7. State the geographical position of *seven* of the following, and the connection of each of the seven with the history of England:—Arras; Cintra; Delhi; Kenilworth; Lagos; Namur; Ravenspur; Stamford Bridge; Wallingford.

8. In what respects did the reign of James I depart from the political traditions of Elizabeth's reign; and with what immediate consequences?

9. Show the connection of (*a*) Scotland and (*b*) Ireland with the political situation in England during 1638-42.

10. Compare the Restoration and the Revolution in their bearings on the relative powers of King and Parliament.

11. How far does Walpole's policy seem to you to be justified or to be condemned by events between his fall and the close of the reign of George II?

*12. Describe the struggle with the American colonies in 1777 and in 1780-81, and illustrate your answer with two sketch-maps.

13. Whom do you consider to be, among British statesmen, (*a*) the greatest War Minister of the 18th and 19th centuries, (*b*) the greatest political thinker of the 18th century, and (*c*) the greatest Finance Minister of the 19th century?

Concisely give your reasons for your selection in each case.

APPENDIX F

boy clerkships' examination of january, 1911

English Composition (Paper 1).—Time allowed, 1 hour

Choose one of the following subjects:—

1. Electricity is modern Life.

2. If you had a fortnight's holiday to spend without sleeping away from home, how would you spend it?

3. Write a letter to a friend describing the advantages and disadvantages of being a Boy Scout. Do not sign your letter with your own name.

English Composition (Paper 2).—Time allowed, 1 hour

1. In the following extracts correct all errors, giving your reasons for each correction you make:—(*a*) It pays one sometimes to change our mode of living. (*b*) I didn't used to get up before six o'clock. (*c*) I received your welcome letter this morning, and is very glad you are going to pay my wife and I a visit.

2. Rewrite the following passages (without commenting on them), so as to bring out clearly the meaning of the writers:—(*a*) The Victoria Cross has been gained by many soldiers who have risked their own lives in order to simply get one of their own. (*b*) Mr. Brown has left off clothing of every description and wishes to purchase same. Distance no object, keeping our own conveyance. (*c*) Still a greater danger is attached to a policemans life, in the performance of that duty known as they arresting of Lunatics as they are always in receipt of

318   [318

some deadly weapon, so the policeman, is then, their pray, and
receives severe punishment from there hands.

3. Express in your own words the substance of the following verses:—

THE SAILOR'S CONSOLATION

One night came on a hurricane,
   The sea was mountains rolling,
When Barney Buntline slewed his quid,[1]
   And said to Billy Bowline:
"A strong nor'-wester's blowing, Bill,
   Hark! don't ye hear it roar now?
Lord help 'em, how I pities them
   Unhappy folks on shore now.

"Foolhardy chaps as live in towns,
   What danger they are all in,
And now lie quaking in their beds,
   For fear the roof should fall in!
Poor creatures, how they envies us,
   And wishes, I've a notion,
For our good luck in such a storm,
   To be upon the ocean!

"And as for them that's out all day,
   On business from their houses,
And late at night returning home,
   To cheer their babes and spouses;
While you and I, Bill, on the deck
   Are comfortably lying,
My eyes! What tiles and chimney-pots
   About their heads are flying!

"Both you and I have oft-times heard
   How men are killed and undone,
By over-turns from carriages,
   By thieves and fire in London.
We knows what risks these landsmen run,
   From noblemen to tailors;
Then, Bill, let us thank Providence
   That you and I are sailors."

[1] Shifted his chew of tobacco.

Geography.—Time allowed, 2 hours

[All questions carry equal marks. Work shown up in the wrong book will not receive full credit. Sketch-maps should be drawn to illustrate the answers where possible.]

SECTION I.—PURPLE BOOK

Answer any three questions in this Section

1. Draw an outline map of S. America, marking the Equator and one meridian of longitude. Name, without inserting boundaries, Peru, Brazil, British Guiana, the Selvas. Insert and name the Andes, the rivers Amazon and Orinoco, and the towns Para, Rio de Janeiro, Valparaiso, Buenos Aires and Bahia.

2. (*a*) The Ancient Greek mariners used to make an annual voyage to India from the mouth of the Red Sea. At what time of the year would they make their outward and homeward voyages respectively so as to obtain favourable winds? (*b*) What are the two important wind systems of the North Atlantic Ocean? How would a sailing ship shape her course so as to make use of these winds on a voyage from Spain to the West Indies and back?

3. In what parts of the world are the following occupations carried on on a large scale: (*a*) cattle-ranching, (*b*) wheat-growing, (*c*) fur-collecting. In what ways are these occupations determined by local geographical conditions?

4. Describe as fully as you can the vegetation and scenery of the Alps of Switzerland. Mention any important occupations of the Swiss people, and show how far they are determined by geographical conditions.

GIRL CLERKSHIPS' EXAMINATION OF OCTOBER, 1910

GEOGRAPHY.—SECTION II.—DARK BROWN BOOK

Answer any three of the following questions

5. Give an account of the economic products, communications, and chief ports of China Proper.

6. Write notes on the position and importance of the following towns:—Philadelphia, New Orleans, Chicago, Denver, Birmingham (U. S. A.).

7. Describe briefly the regions passed through on a journey from Montreal to New Westminster by the Canadian Pacific Railway, and mention the characteristic industries and occupations of the inhabitants of each region.

8. According to a recent estimate the surface of the United Kingdom may be divided as follows:—

	Cultivated Land.	Permanent Pasture.	Upland Pasture, Woodland and Unproductive Land.
	Per cent.	Per cent.	Per cent.
England.....	33.3	42.3	24.4
Wales.......	16.8	41.6	41.6
Scotland.....	17.6	7.4	75.0
Ireland......	17.5	56.2	26.3

Show how far these figures may be explained by the differences in the climate, relief, and soils of the four countries.

APPENDIX G

Specimens of First Grade General Clerical Examinations for the United States Civil Service [1]

Compare with preceding English examinations. Every second class clerk, and even the boy clerks in England, would scorn such examinations as tests of education. Note that the American geography and government questions ask for facts which have been memorized; while the English geography and history questions require considerable knowledge and thought.

Sec. 39. First-grade Subjects.—1. Spelling: Twenty words of more than average difficulty. 2. Arithmetic: Fundamental rules, fractions, percentage, interest, discount, analysis, and statement of simple accounts. 3. Penmanship: Rated on legibility, rapidity, neatness, and general appearance. 4. Report writing: Test in writing in letter form a report not more than 200 words in length, summarizing and arranging in logical order a series of facts included in a given statement of 400 or 500 words. 5. Copying and correcting manuscript: Test in making a smooth, corrected copy of a draft of manuscript which includes erasures, misspelled words, errors in syntax, etc. 6. Geography and civil government of the United States.

The following questions and tests, which have been used, indicate the general character of these subjects:

Spelling.—Spelling is dictated by the examiner. The words are written by the competitor in the blank spaces indicated on the first sheet of the examination. All words should be commenced with capital letters. The examiner pronounces each

---

[1] *Manual of Examination,* United States Civil Service Commission, Washington, 1912.

word and gives its definition as printed below. The competitor is required to write only the word and not its definition.

Cylinder: A long, round body. *Promissory:* Containing a promise; as, a promissory note. *Essential:* Necessary or indispensable. *Discernible:* Apparent or visible. *Opportunity:* A fit or convenient time. *Deceitful:* False or tricky. *Deference:* Respect or regard. *Insertion:* The act of placing in; as, the insertion of an advertisement. *Facilitate:* To make easy; as, to facilitate business. *Schenectady:* A city of the United States. *Adjacent:* Lying near or bordering on. *Souvenir:* A token of remembrance. *Conceding:* Yielding or giving up; as, conceding a point. *Lineage:* Line of descent or ancestry; as. of royal lineage. *Deleterious:* Harmful or injurious; as, deleterious to health. *Horizontal:* On a level. *Patrimony:* An estate inherited from one's father. *Certificate:* A written testimony; as, a marriage certificate. *Reservoir:* A place of storage; as, a water reservoir. *Privilege:* A right; as, the privilege of voting.

Arithmetic.—In solving problems the processes should be not merely indicated, but all the figures necessary in solving each problem should be given in full. The answer to each problem should be indicated by writing " Ans." after it.

1. This question comprises a test in adding numbers crosswise and lengthwise. There are usually three columns of about twelve numbers each to be added. 2. Divide 47 by $7\frac{3}{5}$, multiply the quotient by $3\frac{4}{5}$, and to the product add 0.0907 of 214.6. 3. A father invested a sufficient sum of money in Massachusetts 5's at $97\frac{1}{4}$, brokerage $\frac{1}{4}$ per cent, to give his son an annual income of $1,200. What was the sum invested? 4. The appropriation for the Civil Service Commission for the fiscal year ended June 30, 1897, was $98,340. During that year 50,000 persons were examined. If 34 per cent of this number failed to pass, and $17\frac{1}{2}$ per cent of those who passed were appointed, what was the average cost to the Government of each appointment? 5. On April 1, 1904, Amos Ward owed Graves & Coon $68.90 on account. April 4, he

sold them 68 barrels potatoes at $2.75 per barrel. April 6, he gave them a draft upon San Francisco for $1,860, which they accepted at ¼ per cent discount. April 9, they sold Ward 894 bushels corn at 38½ cents per bushel. April 16, they bought of him 2,960 feet lumber at $1.25 per hundred feet. April 19, they sold him 34½ dozen chairs at 90 cents each. April 21, Ward bought of them 1,260 eggs at 14 cents per dozen. April 28, he gave them a note for $1,820 due in 60 days. April 29, he bought of them 2,980 pounds hay at $15 a ton. Make an itemized statements of the above account as it should appear taken from the books of Ward; make a proper heading; close the account, and bring down the balance as it should have appeared May 1, 1904.

Geography and civil government of the United States.—
N. B.—Competitors are cautioned not to exceed the number of points called for in the question, as the full value of a point will be charged for each incorrect point in the answer.

1. Name States (or Territories, if any) as follows: Two which border Florida on the north; two which border Colorado on the north; two which border New York on the east; two which border Wisconsin on the west; one which borders Oregon on the north; one which borders New Hampshire on the east. 2. Name the largest two rivers which border on Kentucky; the largest two lakes which border on Michigan; the largest two sounds on the coast of North Carolina; the two bodies of water which the Niagara River connects; a river which borders on Nevada; the river on which Omaha is situated. 3. In what State (or Territory, if any) is each of the following-named prominent cities located: Asheville, Trinidad, Amsterdam, Findlay, Lynchburg, Sedalia, Walla Walla, Keene, Macon, Superior. 4. (*a*) How are justices of the Supreme Court appointed? (*b*) How many amendments have been added to the Constitution of the United States? 5. (*a*) Name two ways in which a bill may become a law without the President's signature. (*b*) Name the following officials: Speaker of the National House of Representatives; Chief Justice of the United States; Secretary of State.